Rumrunners

Rumrunners

*Liquor Smugglers
on America's Coasts, 1920–1933*

J. Anne Funderburg

McFarland & Company, Inc., Publishers
Jefferson, North Carolina

ISBN 978-1-4766-6757-7 (softcover : acid free paper) ∞
ISBN 978-1-4766-2670-3 (ebook)

LIBRARY OF CONGRESS CATALOGUING DATA ARE AVAILABLE

BRITISH LIBRARY CATALOGUING DATA ARE AVAILABLE

On the cover: Burlocks filled with bottles of liquor are visible
on the deck of a contact boat, *Whispering Winds.* The Coast
Guard confiscated this boat and added it to the Dry Navy
(National Archives and Records Administration)

Printed in the United States of America

*McFarland & Company, Inc., Publishers
Box 611, Jefferson, North Carolina 28640
www.mcfarlandpub.com*

Table of Contents

Preface

The present work is the first accurate, comprehensive history of liquor smuggling on the high seas during the Volstead Era (1920–1933). Previous histories of the war between the rumrunners and the Dry Navy have relied heavily on anecdotes and personal recollections. This book is based on legal records, scholarly sources, newspaper archives, and the U.S. Coast Guard files at the National Archives and Records Administration.

In general, previous histories of rumrunning have focused on one geographic area. This book examines liquor smuggling along the entire coastline of the United States, spotlighting the busiest centers: New York, New Jersey, Florida, and California. The author chronicles America's most daring rumrunners, including two fascinating but little known women, Gertrude Lythgoe and Edith Stevens.

Unlike previous histories, *Rumrunners* presents a balanced view of the conflict, looking at the losses and victories on both sides. The author covers both rumrunners and the Coast Guardsmen ordered to enforce Volstead. She looks at corruption in the Coast Guard but also gives accounts of honest Guardsmen who risked their lives to capture liquor smugglers.

The author analyzes both the domestic and international legal issues involved in confiscating ships and liquor cargos. She also discusses the foreign policy repercussions of Volstead enforcement, particularly the disputes spawned by the Coast Guard's seizure of Canadian ships with British registry.

1

Rum Row
Mother Ships and Mosquito Boats

A romantic aura surrounded rumrunners during Prohibition's early years. They were renegades, swashbucklers, adventurers. They sailed the high seas, outwitting hijackers, dodging the Coast Guard, and delivering the good stuff from exotic ports of call. They were daring, rugged individualists defying a law hated by millions of Americans. When the rum smuggler brought his liquor cargo ashore, he struck a blow for personal liberty and the right to choose gin instead of ginger ale. Drinkers admired him. Prohibitionists despised him.

The rumrunner took serious risks on every voyage. Any rumrunning trip could end violently with a hijacking, a shipwreck, or a shootout with the Coast Guard. Rumrunners "live close to danger and are not unfamiliar with the image of death," a newsman wrote. Rumrunners chose to dare death because they loved the thrills and the money. "Rumrunning is a game that may be a profitable game beyond any dream of fisherman or merchant skipper. They have elected to take a chance."[1]

The booze buccaneer was "the true heir, not only of the old-time Indian fighters and train robbers, but also of the tough and barnacled deep-water sailors, now no more," wrote H.L. Mencken. He likened the rumrunners to the Minutemen who fought for freedom in the American Revolution. "Liberty, driven from the land by the Methodist White Terror, has been given a refuge by the hardy boys of the Rum Fleet. In their bleak and lonely exile, they cherish her and keep her alive."[2]

Mencken, who loathed Prohibition, demonized the Methodist Church because it had played a pivotal role in the U.S. temperance movement. Early Methodist leaders, including John Wesley and Francis Asbury, had preached the importance of moderation in drinking. Puritan divines Cotton and Increase Mather and Congregational minister Lyman Beecher were among the first public figures to warn Americans about alcohol abuse. Quaker and Presbyterian leaders also endorsed sobriety as a virtue for individuals and for society as a whole. Nevertheless, Americans were slow to grasp the concept of substance abuse because they viewed alcohol as a blessing. In fact, alcoholic beverages were commonly called "God's good creatures."

The American colonists used fermentation and distillation to preserve fruits, grains, and vegetables because alcoholic beverages had a long shelf life. Unlike fresh foods, potent potables didn't rot. The colonists used alcohol as medicine and relied on it to treat virtually every illness that plagued mankind. Whether sick or healthy, adults drank alcohol, often in the form of beer or hard cider, from breakfast to bedtime. In many families, even young children routinely drank beverages with low alcohol content.

In the early nineteenth century, the perception of alcohol as a blessing faded as drinking habits changed. Distilled spirits displaced America's traditional fermented beverages with low alcohol content, such as apple cider. Ardent spirits, especially rum and corn whiskey, became immensely popular because they were cheap and potent. Americans drank to excess more often, and drunkenness had a negative impact on society. Heavy drinking often played a role in crime, violence, and domestic abuse.

To combat alcohol abuse, religious and civic leaders started temperance groups to encourage moderation and sobriety. For the most part, the dry leaders didn't demand total abstinence from alcohol, but they called for responsible drinking to reduce drunkenness and the evils associated with it. The temperance societies formed national organizations and persuaded millions of Americans to join the dry crusade.

Before the Civil War several state governments enacted laws that prohibited the manufacture and sale of alcoholic beverages. These laws had little impact because bootleggers and illegal saloons sold liquor in the dry jurisdictions. During the Civil War the temperance movement lost its momentum as the nation dealt with crucial problems that threatened the Union. After the war, Americans focused on rebuilding the nation, and the temperance activists slowly regrouped.

In the 1870s church women formed the Woman's Christian Temperance Union (WCTU) to rid America of drunkenness and the ills that accompanied it. Women didn't have the right to vote, which limited their impact on elections and legislation. Hence, the ladies' crusade emphasized moral suasion, anti-alcohol education, and wholesome activities for young people. In 1893 male activists founded the Anti-Saloon League (ASL) and set out to harness the political power of the dry bloc. The ASL focused on mobilizing dry voters to elect officials who would enact prohibitory laws at all levels, from local to federal.

The ASL and WCTU led an informal alliance of anti-alcohol groups, often called the Cold Water Coalition. Dry activists usually had more than one reason for joining the crusade; the most common motivations were religion, progressive reform, and/or nativism. Many devout Christians believed that drunkenness was the gateway sin on the road to hell. They wanted to save souls by keeping everybody sober and focused on the Gospel. Progressive reformers viewed alcohol as a basic cause of violence, crime, broken homes, prostitution, poverty, and other social ills. They believed that abolishing the saloon and passing strict liquor laws would greatly improve the quality of life for individual families and for the community as a whole.

Religious and progressive reformers had altruistic motives, but nativism had ugly undercurrents of racism and xenophobia. The nativists embraced a nostalgic, romanticized view of U.S. history. They believed in the supremacy of pure, "old-stock" Americans. They questioned the patriotism of newcomers and worried that immigrants were bringing foreign ideas and strange customs to the United States. They demanded rigorous programs of Americanization to teach American values to the "foreign element."

Nativists believed that certain racial and ethnic minorities had a dangerous propensity for drunkenness. When these people drank, they were likely to become violent and/or commit crimes. A legal ban on alcohol would protect society from the moral depravity of these flawed minorities. Hence, white supremacists, including the Ku Klux Klan, staunchly supported Prohibition.

Under ASL tutelage, the Cold Water Coalition greatly expanded its political power through bloc voting and high-pressure lobbying. The coalition endorsed politicians who voted dry, even if those men drank in private. Dry strategists ignored party affiliations and supported anti-alcohol candidates whether they were Democrats or Republicans. This tactic paid off, preventing a division along party lines on crucial alcohol votes in Congress and the statehouses.

In 1917 Congress started the ratification process to add a new amendment, the Eighteenth, to the U.S. Constitution. To make Prohibition the law of the land, three-fourths of the nation's states had to ratify the proposed amendment. On January 16, 1919, the dry bloc triumphed when the votes for ratification reached the magic number. Prohibition would go into effect one year later at 12:01 a.m. January 17, 1920. To implement the Eighteenth Amendment, Congress passed the National Prohibition Act (AKA the Volstead Law) which spelled out the details of the ban and set up the apparatus for enforcement.

The year's delay in implementing Prohibition gave the country time to make a smooth transition from wet to dry. Distilleries, breweries, saloons, and merchants needed time to dispose of their liquor inventories. Most breweries and distilleries prepared to close their doors, but that wasn't the only option. A brewery could apply for a government permit to become a cereal beverage plant making "near beer" that had little or no alcohol content. With the proper license, a distillery could become a bonded warehouse and sell distilled spirits for legal uses in medicine and industry. Nevertheless, the dry law would eliminate most legal jobs in the liquor industry, so hordes of workers had to find new employment.

Speculators had their own way of preparing for Prohibition. They bought vast quantities of distilled spirits and shipped the booze overseas. They expected to reap windfall profits by smuggling the spirits back to the United States after the dry law went into effect. They never doubted that drinkers would pay premium prices for alcoholic beverages, whether legal or illegal. They may not have envisioned Rum Row, but they knew that smugglers would sneak liquor into the United States because the profits would be enormous.

In Volstead's early days a small-time smuggler could make big money in the rum-running racket. Anyone who owned a boat and could muster up the nerve to smuggle liquor could earn a comfortable living or even get rich. An enterprising smuggler with a seaworthy vessel generated an income that dwarfed the average worker's wages. Arrests and violence were rare. Experienced seamen threw caution overboard, choosing a life of crime as the route to Easy Street.

The heyday of the amateur liquor smuggler proved to be quite short. Almost overnight rumrunning changed from a low-risk game to a brutal, cutthroat racket ruled by heavily-armed mobsters. Urban mobs formed rum rings to acquire the capital, the ships, and the manpower needed for smuggling on a large scale. The independent, lone-wolf rumrunner couldn't compete. He quit the game or joined a rum ring.

A Coast Guard patrol boat closes in on a shore runner carrying a cargo of liquor (courtesy Boston Public Library, Leslie Jones Collection).

Rumrunning 101

When the Arid Era began, the media used the terms "bootlegger" and "rumrunner" interchangeably. Over time, the press began to differentiate between the two: a bootlegger was a liquor trafficker who plied his trade on land; a rumrunner smuggled liquor on the waterways. The media popularized "rummer," "booze buccaneer," and "Prohibition pirate" as alternate terms for "rumrunner." Rummers felt superior to bootleggers because smuggling on the high seas required more skill and nerve than bootlegging. "It is considered a distinction in some circles to be ranked a rumrunner; a bootlegger merely sells the stuff," wrote an observer.[3]

In Volstead lingo, oceangoing vessels that carried large cargos of booze were known as mother ships, liquor freighters, or rum schooners. Rumrunning vessels were also called black ships because they ran without lights at night. They were usually painted drab colors that blended into the darkness of the night sky and the deep water. Black, gray, and dark green were popular colors. To eliminate telltale lights from a black ship's interior, the portholes were painted over or covered with canvas.[4]

Speedy motorboats picked up liquor from the mother ships and delivered it to shore. These small vessels were dubbed contact boats, daughter boats, shore runners, rum luggers, feeder boats, pullers, or mosquito boats. They were also called fireboats because they carried firewater. Collectively, they were the Banana Fleet because of their oblong shape, the Mosquito Fleet because they flitted around, or the Sunset Fleet because they left shore as the sun sank below the horizon. They were also tagged the Whiskito Fleet, a combination of mosquito and whiskey.

The U.S. Coast Guard (CG) enforced Volstead on the waterways, with assistance from the customs service, the border patrol, and the local port authorities. Collectively, the CG and other law enforcement vessels made up the Dry Fleet or the Dry Navy. Rumrunners derisively called the Volstead enforcers Hooligan's Navy, and Coast Guardsmen were informally known as Coasties.

Washington created the Prohibition Unit (later the Prohibition Bureau) to take charge of enforcing Volstead. This federal agency worked primarily on land but cooperated with the Coast Guard on major seaborne offensives. As a rule, the federal Prohibition agents worked along the waterfront while the Guardsmen sailed on patrol boats, pursuing rummers on the water. Collectively, the Prohibition Unit and the federal agents were called "the Prohis."

Rum rings were organized crime syndicates run by mob bosses who viewed Volstead as a despicable law passed by a bunch of fanatic, ignorant do-gooders. They saw themselves as public benefactors because they supplied a product enjoyed by millions of Americans. Rum rings delivered vast quantities of illegal booze via the roadways, waterways, and railways. The syndicates' large-scale liquor smuggling required substantial capital, and the "investors" expected handsome returns on their investments.

The major rumrunning rings owned mother ships and fleets of contact boats. To maximize profits and avoid arrest, the ring's operations had to be smoothly coordinated. In a typical operation, the skipper of the mother ship decided when and where he would drop anchor. Via cable or wireless, he notified the syndicate boss onshore. Crews working for the syndicate sailed their contact boats to the rendezvous point to meet the mother ship. Meanwhile, men in trucks sped along beachfront roads to the landing spot so the liquor could be quickly transferred from the boats to trucks.

The men dispatched to unload the contact boats were called swampers or the shore crew. Before Prohibition, the word "swamper" was widely used to denote a common laborer or a general handyman. In the retail liquor trade, it referred to an employee who did menial chores in a saloon. Since unloading a cargo of booze required no special skills, "swamper" seemed to fit the job description.

"No detail pertaining to unloading is overlooked," wrote a Prohibition administrator. "The trucks arrive simultaneously with the landing of the boat…. Every truck driver has definite orders, and the moment he gets the number of cases assigned to him, he immediately starts for his prearranged destination. In an unbelievably short time the boat is unloaded and shoves off; the trucks are speeding in a dozen different directions to deliver their illicit cargoes." The administrator compared the operation to the teamwork of a winning football team. But a fumble meant more than lost yardage. "Discipline is most rigid and anyone who disobeys is beaten up or meets a more tragic fate."[5]

Distilleries packaged bottles of liquor in wood crates to prevent breakage. But the heavy crates caused problems for rummers because they were hard to handle and added weight to the boat. Moreover, they floated. If the Coast Guard chased a rummer and he tossed his cargo overboard, the Coasties could easily grab a few crates to use as evidence in court. The remaining crates might float to shore and be picked up by beachcombers before the rumrunner could retrieve them.[6]

For easy handling, rumrunners jettisoned the heavy, cumbersome crates and stacked the whiskey bottles in a triangle inside a burlap sack. To protect the bottles, the packers added a cushioning material, usually straw or sawdust. To keep everything tightly packed, the top of the sack was securely tied or sewn closed. Rummers called the sack of bottles a "burlock" or a "ham."

The typical burlock held six fifths, although some rumrunners preferred ten or 12 fifths per sack. (A fifth held one-fifth of a gallon.) When a burlock held pints or half-pints, it contained up to 24 bottles. Burlocks could be tightly stacked in the hold or on deck, with virtually no wasted space. The bottles in a well-packed burlock could survive both rough seas and careless handling.

East Coast rumrunners typically used burlocks, but some West Coast rummers preferred cardboard cases. The standard cardboard case held 12 quart bottles cushioned with excelsior (curled wood shavings). To prevent a case from floating if the rummer jettisoned it, the packer added lead weights and drilled holes in the cardboard. When thrown overboard, the case quickly sank.[7]

Not all mother ships transported their liquor in bottles. At the shipyards in Liver-

Burlocks filled with bottles of liquor are visible on the deck of a contact boat, *Whispering Winds*. The Coast Guard confiscated this boat and added it to the Dry Navy (National Archives and Records Administration).

pool, Nova Scotia, a rum ring customized a banana boat with storage tanks for whiskey. The rumrunners bought scotch malt whiskey in barrels in Scotland. When the barrels arrived in Nova Scotia, the whiskey was poured into the banana boat's tanks. The rum-runners sailed their cargo to a beach town in New Jersey, where they built what appeared to be a gas station. Via flexible hose, they connected the tanker to the gas station's underground tanks, and the whiskey gurgled through the hose to safe storage.[8]

"The Rum Line"

When Volstead began, the United States' territorial waters ended three miles from the U.S. shore. During the Arid Era, this invisible three-mile boundary was called "the rum line." U.S. law enforcement had broad powers to chase and capture liquor smugglers within the rum line. Beyond the rum line lay international waters, where the United States' power to enforce Volstead was greatly restricted. To avoid capture, liquor smugglers stayed in international waters as much as possible.

Beyond the rum line, mother ships with booze cargos rode at anchor in a loose formation known as Rum Row or Liquor Lane. Rum Row was fluid, changing its size and shape in response to a variety of factors. Weather, sailing conditions, or pressure from law enforcement could cause the ships on Rum Row to sail far out to sea or shift to a new location along the coast.

Although people spoke of Rum Row as if there were only one, Liquor Lanes popped up to serve different regions. The largest Rum Row, a virtual city of seagoing vessels, operated near Ambrose Lightship, which marked the main shipping channel for New York harbor. When New York and New Jersey residents first spotted the armada of strange ships, they were puzzled. America had recently fought the Great War, and alarmists feared that a foreign power was set to invade the Northeast. Newspapers hired boats, sent reporters out to investigate, and informed the public that the ships carried firewater, not firepower.

The mother ships came and went, changing the configuration of Rum Row at Ambrose Lightship. At times, the line of mother ships stretched from the eastern end of Long Island, New York, to Cape May in southern New Jersey. In warm weather, as many as one hundred liquor freighters rode at anchor in this sector. In 1922 Prohibition Commissioner Roy Haynes said, "They are laden with liquors of all kinds, and the small craft are steaming up to them bringing prospective buyers who sample the liquors and dicker over the prices.... Off the New Jersey coast alone there are probably sixty foreign ships and hundreds of small craft right at this very moment."[9]

In the beginning, the Rum Fleet was a motley collection of watercraft old and new, big and small. The rumrunners sailed fishing schooners, steam trawlers, freighters, tug-boats, scows, sea skiffs, tramp steamers, yachts, windjammers, and more. The gutsy rum-mers sold to all comers; some even displayed large banners advertising their liquid cargo. Boat traffic was heavy as bootleggers, speakeasy owners, and individuals sailed out to Rum Row to stock up. Thrifty buyers could travel from one smuggling ship to another, shopping for the best price.

Shoppers weren't the only visitors to Rum Row. "Amenity boats" brought prostitutes out to service the crewmen. A frequent visitor to Rum Row was the *Beacon of Hope*, a schooner commanded by Skipper Salvation, a white-bearded Bible thumper. Elderly volunteers, who made up Salvation's crew, sang gospel songs accompanied by an accordionist. Tolerant Rum Row captains allowed Skipper Salvation to come aboard to hand out religious tracts. However, hostile rumrunners outnumbered the friendly ones. After repeatedly being cursed at and doused with water, Skipper Salvation opted to spread the gospel on dry land in the Bowery.[10]

The Rum Row around Ambrose Lightship wasn't the nation's only Liquor Lane. In fair weather, a Rum Row formed off the New England shore, from Massachusetts to Rhode Island. When winter brought harsh conditions, the liquor freighters sailed away. In 1922 "no fewer than five hundred vessels of all sorts and descriptions" smuggled whiskey from Canada's Maritime Provinces to the New England seaboard. Other rumrunners brought booze from Europe, St. Pierre, or the Bahamas.[11]

A Liquor Lane thrived along the Gulf Coast, supplying the Deep South with hooch from Cuba, Mexico, and elsewhere. Mother ships hovered beyond the rum line and sold to contact boats that raced out from Mobile, Tampa Bay, and other coastal areas. Liquor freighters formed a short Rum Row near the Chandeleur Islands, a chain of uninhabited barrier isles off the coast of Louisiana. Shore runners carried the liquor inland via Lake Borgne or Lake Pontchartrain. In the mid–1920s the Coast Guard beefed up its Gulf fleet, prompting the Chandeleur Rum Row to move westward to the Atchafalaya Bay. Mosquito boats navigated the Atchafalaya's dangerous swamps, delivering booze to bootleg gangs.

Florida had countless rumrunners but no Rum Row. The area's proximity to foreign islands allowed the mosquito boats to dash back and forth, so they didn't need to anchor offshore.

On the West Coast mother ships assembled on Rum Row to supply booze to California cities, with the lion's share going to San Francisco. During the early 1920s the vessels hovered near the Farallon Islands and the Golden Gate. Initially, the Coast Guard made little effort to enforce Volstead on the West Coast, due to a shortage of patrol boats. After the CG enlarged the Pacific fleet in the mid–Twenties, the mother ships moved far offshore to avoid capture. In Prohibition's latter years, ships formed a Liquor Lane near Ensenada, Mexico, in Baja California.

California's mother ships sold mostly to contact boats, but private yachts also ventured out to buy booze. Hollywood stars created a stir when they showed up on Rum Row. Comedic genius Buster Keaton sailed out in his yacht, *Kamin*, to buy liquor on at least one occasion. Actor John Barrymore, a notoriously heavy drinker, often took his yacht, *Infanta*, to Rum Row.[12]

Foreign Flags

A rumrunning ship flying a foreign flag enjoyed a certain level of protection from U.S. law enforcement. Naturally, Prohibition pirates wanted to fly a foreign flag. Many rumrunning ships had legitimate foreign registrations, but others were owned by U.S. citizens. An American rumrunner could sell, or pretend to sell, his ship to a citizen of another country and then register it under the new owner's name.

At least 332 large foreign-owned vessels smuggled liquor into the United States in 1924, according to the Department of Justice. The vast majority of these rumrunners flew the British flag. Despite the large number of foreign-owned rum freighters, Volstead enforcers captured only two mother ships with foreign registry in FY1924. In 1925 the number of mother ships with foreign registry rose to 385. British registry was still the most popular, but Norway, France, and several other countries were also represented. Most of the smugglers picked up their liquor cargos in Canada or the Caribbean, although a few brought their contraband from Europe or Asia.[13]

Dry leaders argued that the three-mile limit made it easy for contact boats to escape capture by racing across the rum line into international waters. Extending U.S. territorial waters would improve Volstead enforcement because the Coast Guard would have the authority to chase and overtake rumrunners farther from shore. Court decisions in rum-running cases had the effect of moving the limit farther out, but this unilateral change created diplomatic tension with other countries. To avoid international disputes, Washington wanted to formally renegotiate the limit with other naval powers.

In May 1924, the King of England signed a treaty with the U.S. extending the limit. Britain agreed to allow U.S. authorities to board private vessels flying the British flag within one hour's sailing time of the U.S. coast. American officials could examine the vessel's papers and interrogate anyone onboard. If the craft appeared to be carrying contraband, U.S. officials could search it. If they had "reasonable cause" to believe it was violating Volstead, officials could haul it into port and subject it to U.S. law.[14]

President Calvin Coolidge issued an official proclamation to implement the new treaty with Britain, moving the rum line to "an hour's steaming distance" from shore, which was on average 12 miles. Since faster ships steamed farther than the average in an hour, they had to remain farther from land. When two or more rum vessels were involved in an incident, the speed of the fastest one determined the limit of the Dry Navy's power.[15] Washington negotiated similar treaties with other European governments.

2

Island Oases
St. Pierre and the Bahamas

The Volstead law had many unintended consequences. Most were unfortunate, if not truly tragic. However, the U.S. dry law had at least one unforeseen benefit: rumrunning enriched the islands that became hubs for the illegal liquor traffic. Alcohol exports boomed in the Bahamas and in St. Pierre et Miquelon. The liquor exporters could obey the laws of their own country while selling to rumrunners, and the island governments had no compelling reason to stop the export of booze to the United States. When Washington pressured other governments to help enforce Volstead, foreign officials resisted or offered half-hearted, grudging cooperation. "The Americans passed Prohibition, let the Americans enforce it" was the ruling principle.

The Great Drought brought almost instant wealth to the Bahamas, an island chain colonized by Great Britain. Bahamians weren't breaking the law when they imported liquor and resold it for export, if they paid the tariffs on it. Because the islands had a long history of dealing with freebooters and blockade runners, the locals neither feared nor condemned the Prohibition pirates.

"The Colony's financial situation has been transformed!" crowed the Bahamian governor a few months into Volstead. Legal clearings of liquor for export rose from less than 38,000 gallons in 1917 to more than 1.34 million gallons in 1922. The Bahamian government collected tariffs on the liquor and used the revenue to pave roads, dredge the harbor, dig artesian wells, pay off the colony's debt to Great Britain, and accumulate a sizable budget surplus.[1]

The islands' tourist industry boomed, thanks to the free-spending visitors in the liquor trade. The cash registers rang in the bars and cafes. Hotels and boardinghouses hung out no-vacancy signs. To supply the demand for upscale lodging, the Bahamian government financed a new luxury hotel to be built by an American company.

The Americans might be felons at home, but they were job creators in Nassau. Virtually any man who wanted work could find it on the docks or a rum schooner. The Bahamian women joined the workforce, too, rolling barrels of whiskey through the narrow streets to the wharves. "Everyone in Nassau is in the whiskey business—even priests and police bandsmen," said a British captain. A minister and a constable were among the locals who joined the rumrunning fraternity.[2]

Before Prohibition, Nassau's liquor merchants specialized in importing and exporting

U.S. sailors leave Prohibition at home and enjoy drinks with a group of men on a Caribbean island (Naval History and Heritage Command).

genuine, aged Scotch and Irish whiskies. They sold quality products at reasonable prices. But this became the exception, not the rule, during Volstead. The lure of easy money attracted greedy men who weren't content with a normal profit margin. They opened "cutting houses" to dilute whiskey and rebottle it before selling it to the rumrunners. (Since the typical liquor trafficker also watered down his booze before selling it, the American consumer usually bought a very pale imitation of the real thing.)

Nassau became the islands' financial center, an offshore Wall Street. Nassau's Bay Street, the main thoroughfare along the waterfront, teemed with foot traffic. American mobsters hustled about, making deals for booze and boats. Nassau "was filled with slit-eyed, hunch-shouldered strangers, with the bluster of Manhattan in their voices and a wary turbulence of manner," wrote an observer. "The faces that passed your shoulder in ten minutes on Bay Street would have given a New York cop nightmares for a week."[3]

While the islanders welcomed the influx of money, some community leaders worried that the rumrunners were corrupting the locals. "Prohibition in the United States is spelling the moral ruination of many of the natives in Nassau," said a Bahamian official. "This was a law-abiding community before the rumrunners infested it. I wish the United States would keep its scum at home."[4]

At night the rumrunners liked to party around bonfires on the beach. The typical evening climaxed with the native fire dance, a religious ceremony that had morphed into "the most indecent and disgusting orgy debased human minds could conceive." To entice the natives to dance, the rummers doled out whiskey and shillings. To the beat of a tom-tom, the drunken natives performed a frenetic, sexually suggestive dance. The rumrunners drank, bantered, and cheered the dancers on. The revelry lasted "until the dancers, exhausted by their fiendish exertions or overcome by drunken stupor, fell senseless on the ground."[5]

The liquor traffic gave the islanders an unexpected bonus—a free supply of a scarce resource. Liquor bottles were packaged in wood crates, which the rummers discarded when they repacked the fifths in burlocks. The empty wood crates were precious because Grand Bahama Island had few trees. The discards could be recycled as shingles, flooring, or furniture. The cast-off wood was especially handy to patch holes in roofs damaged by tropical storms. On Sunday at St. Mary's Anglican Church, the worshippers could cast their eyes heavenward and meditate on the logos for Old Monarch Scotch, Mumm's Extra Dry, and Johnnie Walker.[6]

Bimini, a cluster of tiny islands within the Bahamas, functioned as an alcohol supermarket for both rumrunners and tourists. Boats and airplanes brought tourists to the tropical resort to enjoy a drinking man's holiday, only 50 miles from Miami, Florida. On Bimini's Rum Row, booze was stored on barges, typically 30 by 50 feet with space for thousands of wood crates. At each end of the barge, a cabin served as sleeping and eating quarters for the crew. Mosquito boats scuttled back and forth, carrying booze from the barges to Florida.[7]

The federal government inadvertently provided free navigational aid to rumrunners sailing from Bimini to the Sunshine State. The U.S. Department of Commerce paid for a chain of aerial beacons that stretched along the entire length of the Florida Peninsula. The powerful flashing lights, intended to guide aircraft, were clearly visible from Bimini. To find his way home, a Florida-bound rumrunner could take a bearing on two of the lights to establish his position and set his course.[8]

Bruce Stanley Bethel, a disabled British soldier, ran a major wholesale liquor operation. He opened a liquor store in Nassau and then moved to Bimini because it was closer to Florida. He stocked a corrugated metal warehouse with liquor, set up a makeshift bar, and invited the booze buccaneers to hang out. The rummers congregated at Bethel's place, sampling the stock and swapping yarns. His business thrived and expanded.[9]

Bethel built large brick warehouses and also used a concrete ship, *Sapona*, for floating storage. *Sapona* was a cargo steamer built as a Liberty Ship in World War I, but it never went into military service. After the war the government sold it to a Miami Beach developer, who resold it to Bethel. During a hurricane *Sapona* ran aground on a reef. The stern broke apart. Wind and water swept its huge liquor cargo overboard. Islanders picked up cases of liquor that washed ashore on Bimini, Cat Cay, and Gun Cay. Bethel abandoned the badly-damaged *Sapona* because salvaging it would be too expensive. (During World War II, the U.S. military used the rusty vessel for target practice. Later the wreck became a popular site for snorkeling and shallow-water diving.)

Tropical storms sometimes disrupted the Bahamian liquor traffic for days or even weeks. In 1926 violent weather decimated Bimini's Rum Row three times in only four months. During one hurricane, winds with a velocity of 120 mph blew across the islands. The rumrunner *Mahtoc* tried to ride out the storm but was blown ashore and wrecked on Gun Cay. Although the crew salvaged what liquor it could, most was lost.[10]

So much liquor flowed from the Bahamas into the United States that Washington asked London for help with Volstead enforcement. The two governments agreed to coordinate their efforts to prevent the false registration of rumrunning ships. In addition, London gave Washington permission to establish a regional intelligence service with undercover agents who would keep tabs on the rumrunners and trace illegal liquor shipments.

As early as 1921, Washington stationed undercover agents in the Bahamas to monitor the rumrunning traffic. When a mother ship or Bimini boat left a Bahamian port, a secret agent alerted Prohibition officials in Miami. They telegraphed federal agents along the East Coast, giving the vessel's name and destination. Despite the heads-up, this rarely led to the capture of a rumrunner, simply because the Dry Navy had a shortage of resources for deployment.[11] After the expansion of the Coast Guard in the mid–Twenties, this type of intelligence produced better results.

Despite Washington's efforts to stop rumrunning, the Bahamian liquor traffic flourished. According to official trade records in 1928, the Bahama Islands were importing enough booze for each resident—man, woman, and child—to consume 36 fifths of hard liquor every month![12] Most of this hooch traveled on to the United States, where it gurgled down American gullets.

The French Connection

Roughly two thousand miles from the Bahamas, the archipelago of St. Pierre et Miquelon became the northern hub for rumrunning on the East Coast. The tiny, rocky isles were French possessions in the Atlantic Ocean, about 30 nautical miles from Newfoundland. Seafaring clans lived on the sparsely-populated islands, which once had been a penal colony. To protect the "last scraps of the empire that was New France," the French navy manned a base on the islands and stationed a destroyer off the coast. In the early 1920s, the Parisian company Morue Francaise dominated the island economy because it owned the commercial fishing fleet, the postal service, the bank, and several stores.[13]

Travelers marveled at the islands' isolation, compact size, and somber landscape, including Execution Rock, the site where condemned prisoners met their death. One visitor called the isles "little dots of gorse and granite." Another noted that "the white gloom" of fog blanketed everything. "Roundabout icebergs sail majestically in the lonely seas, and sportive whales fill the air with spray. Most of all, there is the sad, cold fog," he wrote.[14]

Visitors found Old World charm in the village of St. Pierre. "The narrow streets that wound about the harbor, the overhanging clapboard houses, the neat little churches—all were a bit of old France set down in the Atlantic." A town crier strolled along the streets, ringing a bell and shouting the news on street corners.[15]

According to island lore, Bill McCoy was the first American to exploit St. Pierre's potential for rumrunning. While McCoy was sailing a liquor-laden schooner off the coast of Nova Scotia, a serious mechanical problem developed and he needed to put into port. At that time, Nova Scotia had a prohibition law and rumrunning ships weren't welcome in the harbor. (More than a few Nova Scotia boat owners leased their vessels to American rum rings, but the ships had to avoid their home port when they carried liquor.)[16]

McCoy took a launch from his disabled schooner to shore and checked into a Halifax hotel. By chance, in the hotel lobby he struck up a conversation with a Frenchman who was a ship's agent and merchant in St. Pierre. The Frenchman suggested that McCoy take the crippled schooner to St. Pierre for repairs. This chance meeting led to a profitable partnership for American rumrunners and St. Pierre's populace.[17]

In 1921 "ever-increasing numbers of very busy American businessmen" visited St. Pierre. "It is said that the parties of well-dressed, black-cigar smoking gentlemen go to the isles for the purpose of purchasing and arranging delivery of whiskey and the like to Canadian and United States bootleg rings," a newspaper explained.[18]

The drama of rumrunning unfolded on St. Pierre's "ancient quay trodden by discoverers, by conquerors and conquered, by felons and seafaring men of the centuries," a visitor wrote. "The modern freebooters hold the stage. Every day the argosy sails away or comes to port. Warehouses are filled and unfilled, wealth pours through the banks, a thousand wheels are turned…. It is something to see a rum schooner going down the bay of St. Pierre, hull deep in the water, sails bellying to the breeze. Every whistle in port blows her good luck and a safe return."[19]

When a liquor shipment arrived in St. Pierre, the buyer had to warehouse it until a ship was available. The influx of booze filled the island's commercial storage facilities, so merchants rented sheds and basements for the overflow. St. Pierre's biggest building was a fish processing plant that suddenly had no raw product because the fishermen took up rumrunning. The plant had a dock on the waterfront, so it was easily converted into a liquor warehouse.[20]

St. Pierre upgraded its infrastructure for the rumrunning business. The islanders built new concrete wharves and chutes that made it easy to move cargo from a truck onto a ship. A "ponderous dredge" was used to widen and deepen the channel. Two great breakwaters were built to protect the entrance of the inner harbor from northerly winter storms. The telegraph company moved to a prominent location on the main square, and a powerful radio station was built on a hill.[21]

St. Pierre's rum fleet included fast, seaworthy speedboats that served as mother ships but carried less cargo than a typical liquor freighter. Representing "a new pattern in marine architecture," the speedboats cost $75,000 to $150,000. They were 75 to 150 feet long with broad beams, deep hulls, and up to ten feet under their decks. They carried roughly three thousand cases of whiskey and usually had at least ten crewmen aboard. They stayed at sea for ten to 14 days, rendezvousing with contact boats that took the cargo ashore.[22]

The St. Pierre seamen who worked for the rumrunners were paid "handsome bounties." The locals gossiped about "certain sailors who used to be impecunious, but have become free spenders and flashy dressers." Some nouveau riche islanders even bought cars. An automobile dealership opened and prospered, even though St. Pierre's longest stretch of road was only four miles long.[23]

St. Pierre's residents, like the Bahamians, coveted the rumrunners' discarded wood crates because timber was scarce. "There are exactly four trees gracing the landscapes of St. Pierre and Miquelon," wrote a visitor, with only slight exaggeration. Homeowners collected the empty cases and burned them as firewood during the dark, frigid winters. The empties that weren't burned made good building materials. The manager of an import-export firm built the Cutty Sark Villa using crates from that brand of scotch.[24]

Even St. Pierre's religious community benefited from rumrunning largess. A trio of liquor traffickers paid a courtesy visit to the island's Catholic bishop. The prelate described the plans for a new parochial school and mentioned that more funding was needed to complete the project. The following morning a messenger called on the bishop to deliver a check for $10,000.[25]

Visiting rumrunners had money to spend, so St. Pierre's bars did a land office business. Predictably, rowdy drunks sometimes started brawls. The American rummers liked to carry guns, which occasionally led to bloodshed. In one case, an American sailor had a grudge against the engineer on a Norwegian ship, which was in port unloading cargo. The American found the Norwegian engineer in a bar, confronted him, and shot him point-blank in the chest.

Before lawmen arrived on the scene, the American ran to the harbor and boarded his ship, the *Cote Nord*. The wounded Norwegian was taken to the hospital, but doctors couldn't save him. While the victim lay dying, the *Cote Nord* crew helped the American hide from police. Although the gendarmes searched the ship repeatedly over the next two days, they couldn't find the gunman. Convinced that he wasn't on the ship, authorities allowed *Cote Nord* to leave the port. (The American's shipmates had thwarted the police by rolling the shooter up in a sail and hoisting him part way up the mast.)

The American gunman escaped from the island but not St. Pierre's criminal court system. He was prosecuted *in absentia*, convicted of murder, and sentenced to life in prison at hard labor. If he ever again stepped on French soil, he would be arrested and imprisoned.[26]

Clearance for Heaven or Hell

Canadian distillers formed export syndicates that took over virtually all of St. Pierre's liquor trade. The syndicates operated out of offices in Montreal, and American rum rings paid cash for cargos that would be picked up in St. Pierre. The major Canadian syndicates were the Northern Export Company, Consolidated Exporters, Consolidated Traders, the Great West Wine Company, and United Traders.[27]

The American rumrunners liked to do business in St. Pierre because the port authorities showed little, if any, curiosity about their cargo or destination. "The master of a vessel may ask for clearance papers to heaven or hell and receive them without being required to answer any embarrassing questions." Naturally, rummers liked the secrecy this afforded.[28]

St. Pierre's laxity made it even more popular with rumrunners after Canada changed its liquor export regulations in 1930. Until that time, Ottawa had argued that its customs officials were paid to enforce Canadian laws and liquor exports were legal; therefore, a ship with a liquor cargo could receive clearance papers for U.S. ports. But Washington pressed the issue, and Ottawa finally agreed to amend its Export Act. Under the new rules, Canadian customs refused clearance and official documentation to all large vessels with liquor cargos designated for the United States. Canadian ships carrying liquor could clear for St. Pierre with no hassle, making the French island an ideal transshipment point for booze headed to the United States.

Before Canada amended the Export Act, roughly $4 million worth of Canadian liquor went to St. Pierre et Miquelon each year. Under the new policy, Canadian exporters shipped more than $8.8 million worth of whiskey to the French outpost in FY1931. This equaled almost 38 gallons per month for every adult and child on the islands! But this wasn't all. In addition to the Canadian liquor, St. Pierre et Miquelon imported alcoholic beverages from France, Scotland, and other countries.[29] The tiny islands truly were an alcohol superstore.

3

The Coast Guard
A New Mission

The federal government created the United States Coast Guard in 1915 by combining two maritime forces, the Revenue Cutter Service (established 1790) and the Life-Saving Service (established 1878). Prior to World War I, the services had mandates to combat smuggling and respond to emergencies at sea. During the war, the Coast Guard joined the armed forces under the operational control of the Navy Department.

When Prohibition began, the federal government handed the Coast Guard a new mandate: enforce the Volstead law on the high seas and inland waterways. Initially, the service couldn't fulfil this mission because it simply didn't have the manpower or vessels to stop the rampant liquor smuggling. A high-ranking officer explained the enormity of the task. "In the maritime sense, we have more than thirteen thousand miles of coastline," he said. "Really we have more than fifty thousand miles of actual shoreline, taking into account the indentations that are havens for bootleggers."[1]

To use its limited resources as effectively as possible, the Coast Guard focused on the Rum Row at Ambrose Lightship, due to its pivotal role in the liquor traffic. Each night the Whiskito Fleet raced out to buy booze from the mother ships. The captains of legal ships complained that the density of vessels made navigation hazardous, especially after sunset. The rumrunners refused to budge, but they understood the need for safety. They lit up their armada after dark, turning on bright riding lights visible for a mile or more.

The Whiskito Fleet suffered its first "casualty" on January 11, 1923. A Coast Guard vessel captured *Margaret B*, a contact boat carrying $100,000 worth of whiskey. That same night, the cutter *Surveyor* "plowed into the swarming flotilla of little craft ... sending them scattering like a brood of frightened ducklings." But *Surveyor* failed to capture any of them; the fastest contact boats raced to shore while the others sailed to safety beyond the rum line. Twenty-two shore runners evaded capture and landed 35,000 cases of whiskey at Highlands, New Jersey. (Prohibition officials admitted that boats had taken liquor ashore at Highlands, but they believed the quantity was quite small. One official called 35,000 cases "a pipe dream.")[2]

In March 1923, 15 liquor freighters lay at anchor off Highlands, New Jersey. To patrol the area, the Coast Guard and Customs had only two cutters, *Porpoise* and *Lexington*; neither could match the speed of the shore runners. The contact boats dashed

19

out to Rum Row, picked up booze, and sped past the cutters on their return trip to shore.[3]

Rum Row's mother ships were arranged in a crescent shape with the tips pointing toward the Jersey shore in April 1923. The liquor freighters included *Istar*, a British vessel called the flagship of the Rum Fleet. *Istar* had no grace or elegance, but it carried a big payload of whiskey from Scotland. With a crew of about 50 men, it could stay on Rum Row for months without going into port. The flagship held $2 million worth of liquor and made $350,000 profit on each trip to Rum Row, according to a government source.[4]

The Dry Navy couldn't destroy Rum Row, so Washington decided to fight the rum-runners onshore. The Prohibition Unit ramped up its offensive around Ambrose Light-ship in May 1923. Federal agents from Philadelphia, brought in to help the local Prohis, made several highly-publicized arrests when contact boats brought liquor ashore. After the arrests, the liquor freighters shifted away from the lightship. Some mother ships moved eastward, positioning themselves below Long Island near Fire Island or Jones Inlet.[5]

The mother ships anchored below Long Island formed a triangle stretching for a distance of about 20 miles. The Coast Guard assigned the cutter *Manhattan* to patrol this area, but one vessel simply wasn't enough. The rumrunners' triangle was so large that contact boats would speed out to a mother ship at one corner while the slow-moving *Manhattan* was at another corner. The mosquito boats would load their liquor cargo before the cutter arrived. If *Manhattan* tried to give chase, the speedboats would easily outrun it.[6]

When the mother ships moved away from Ambrose Lightship, *Istar* and three others sailed south to the Virginia Capes. The rumrunning grapevine spread the word of their new location. Speedboats dashed out to the liquor freighters and picked up booze for delivery to Norfolk, Baltimore, and Washington, D.C. The market in Wash-ington was especially strong because the city was gearing up for the National Shriners' Convention.

The Coast Guard sent *Apache*, a heavily-armed cutter, to search for *Istar*. For several days, the cutter patrolled Chesapeake Bay from Cape Charles to Cape Henry but failed to find *Istar* or the other mother ships. Meanwhile, contact boats safely landed thousands of cases from the flagship in Baltimore.[7]

The Coast Guards continued to search for liquor freighters until they located *Istar* and *Cartona* anchored outside the rum line east of the Virginia Capes. The CG cutter *Manning* kept a solitary watch while men at the navy yard hurriedly mounted guns on another patrol boat, *Mascoutin*. With its new firepower, *Mascoutin* joined *Manning* to picket the mother ships, in order to prevent the shore runners from picking up liquor.[8]

Only days after leaving Rum Row at Ambrose Lightship, a number of the mother ships returned to their old location. In a short time, at least 20 liquor freighters were positioned along the Jersey coast, and another half-dozen were anchored in a crescent formation close to the lightship. For the rumrunners, it was business as usual. Never-theless, Prohibition officials seemed confident that they had crushed Rum Row and turned their attention to other matters.[9]

As the winter holidays neared in 1923, 15 mother ships rocked at anchor along the

Ambrose Lightship marked the entrance to the congested Ambrose Channel in New York harbor (National Archives and Records Administration).

Jersey coast near Ambrose Lightship. They were spread out in a long line, so it took a Coast Guard cutter two hours to sail the entire length. This allowed contact boats to do business with freighters at one end of the line while the CG cutter was at the other. The Mosquito Fleet kept busy because drinkers wanted refreshments for their holiday parties. Business flagged only when bad weather kept the small boats in port.[10]

More mother ships arrived until 22 of them were positioned in two sectors off the New York coast. One flotilla stuck close to Ambrose Lightship, while the other anchored off Jones Inlet, south of Long Island. When the CG patrol boat headed for the east end of Rum Row, the west was unguarded. "The rumrunners hailed the departure of the ship as the signal for a dash for the liquor fleet," an observer wrote. "From nearly every cove and inlet the speedboats suddenly emerged. It seemed as if they all started out to the liquor fleet at the same time. They easily might have been mistaken for entrants in a motorboat race." When the contact boat reached the mother ship, the rummers knew the routine.[11]

After the holidays, icy gales and sub-zero temperatures greatly reduced the size of Rum Row. Most mother ships sailed away to find safer, warmer seas. Only "a half-dozen ice-weighted, sorry-looking vessels" remained on Rum Row in January 1924. "They look like frost-mantled ghosts out there," a CG captain said. The winds sent sea water "high into the rigging to freeze," so the ships were "burdened from the top lights to plimsoll line with ice." Many nights, the bad weather kept the contact boats from going out to Rum Row.[12]

When the weather improved, more liquor freighters anchored near the lightship. Rum Row had liquor cargos worth $11 million in March 1924. Twenty-eight mother ships, including the notorious *Istar*, were positioned near Jones Inlet, Fire Island, Montauk Point, and Sandy Hook. Rum Row had a festive air. Launches ferried passengers and musicians to parties on the mother ships. Federal agents intercepted radio messages inviting women to come out to Rum Row. They also found paper invitations sent the old-fashioned way: in bottles bobbing on the waves. The sound of voices, laughter, and jazz music wafted over the water. The federal agents noted that "there was evidence of much drinking."[13]

Full Force Ahead

Because of a shortage of men and vessels, the Coast Guard did little to stop rum-running. In 1924 the Volstead enforcers intercepted only five percent of the liquor sent ashore from Rum Row. Naturally, dry leaders decried this sad state of affairs. They wanted law enforcement to stop all the illegal liquor traffic on the waterways. The National Congress of Mothers and other civic groups urged the President to use the U.S. Navy to fight the Prohibition pirates.[14]

"The thing to do, and the only thing to do, is to detail U.S. destroyers to round up these ships, bring them into port, confiscate the ships and their cargos, and jail every man found on them!" declared an influential dry leader. A top Prohibition official also endorsed a militant approach. "This smuggling cannot be eliminated with gondolas or canoes. It will require fast and swift, eagle-winged boats," he said. "The boats must be armed combatant boats. They must represent speed and force.... There is only one thing that will stop smuggling and that is a gun of sizable size. One thing better than that is two guns."[15]

Although dry activists clamored for the U.S. Navy to lead the battle against the Rum Fleet, the top brass resisted this idea. The armed services had a military mission; naval personnel and vessels were not intended for domestic crime fighting. Secretary of the Navy Edwin Denby declared that the powers granted to the Navy did not include criminal law enforcement in the civilian sector.[16]

President Calvin Coolidge entertained the idea of ordering the Navy to enforce Volstead, but the attorney general argued that there was no Constitutional authority for using the U.S. Navy for civilian law enforcement. An exception might be made in an extraordinary national emergency, but no such crisis existed. Coolidge finessed the issue by asking Congress for funds to recondition Navy vessels that would be transferred to the Coast Guard to enforce Prohibition. He also asked for money to build new cabin cruisers and small motorboats suitable for fighting the rumrunners.[17]

In 1924 Congress appropriated the funds to beef up the Coast Guard with new and reconditioned vessels. CG officials made plans to build three hundred new vessels and recruit nearly five thousand more Guardsmen. A modest portion of the new funding would be spent on biplanes, radio technology, and shore facilities.[18]

Coast Guard brass inspected the Navy's idle destroyers and chose six to be over-hauled. Subsequently, a team of officers selected an additional 20 destroyers for conversion to rum chasers. All of these vessels, which were driven by steam turbines, had seen service in World War I. They were in various stages of disrepair and needed work before they could compete with the Rum Fleet. As the repairs were completed, they would be phased into service.[19]

By spring 1925 most of the reconditioned destroyers had joined the Dry Fleet. A mine sweeper and a seagoing tug were also transferred from the Navy to the Coast Guard. The Navy's castoffs were costly to operate and couldn't keep up with the fast, maneuverable contact boats that raced from ship to shore. However, on the positive side, the destroyers were oceangoing vessels so they could follow the mother ships far out to sea. A few experienced officers and chiefs took command of the destroyers, but most of the sailors were new recruits who needed time to learn the ropes.[20]

The Coast Guard expansion included a fleet of new 75-foot patrol boats, called "six-bitters." The CG sent an engineering officer to Nova Scotia to study the rum boats under construction there. His reports and similar studies were used in designing the new vessels that would battle the rumrunners. Because most of the six-bitters would sail on the Atlantic Ocean, about three-fourths of them were built on the East Coast. Contractors on the Great Lakes and the West Coast built the remainder. More than two hundred six-bitters were commissioned in 1925.[21]

A six-bitter, which could stay out on patrol for up to one week, carried a crew of eight men commanded by a boatswain. Durability and ease of maintenance were high priorities for the six-bitter fleet. Standard equipment included a machinegun and a one-pound cannon mounted on the foredeck. Powered by twin six-cylinder gasoline engines, the six-bitter had a maximum speed of about 16 knots.[22] (A knot is a unit of speed equal to one nautical mile or roughly 1.15 statute miles per hour.)

As part of the build-up, the CG added more than one hundred new 38-foot picket boats with a top speed of 24 knots. Each picket boat had a machinegun on the foredeck. With three crewmen onboard, these new vessels were ideal for patrolling rivers and inlets. The CG also acquired a group of diesel-powered patrol boats up to 125 feet in length. To serve as mobile headquarters for Volstead enforcement, the CG added six floating bases.[23]

The service purchased a seaplane to use for rescue missions as well as for surveillance of Rum Row. The seaplane proved to be so useful that the CG bought more aircraft. Over the course of Prohibition, the CG added air patrol detachments at Gloucester, Massachusetts; Buffalo, New York; Fort Lauderdale, Florida; San Antonio, Texas; and San Diego, California.[24]

The build-up turned the Coast Guard into a strong force with real crime-fighting muscle in the late Twenties. The CG's new vessels were heavily-armed, and the Guardsmen were trained to take lives as well as save them. A top officer declared, "We are going to make smuggling precarious not only in the sense of capture but, when need be, in the sense of life itself. Coast Guardsmen are instructed to use violence only when necessary.... But they are instructed to use force to the full when necessary, even to the taking of life."[25]

Under the Coast Guard's new get-tough policy, rumrunners found it harder to sell their cargo in international waters. Although the Guards needed permission to board a foreign ship outside the rum line, the CG could "chaperone" a vessel anywhere. Therefore, the CG patrol boats could take a position near a mother ship to prevent it from doing business in international waters. At night the Guards aimed searchlights at the liquor freighter, in order to expose any approaching boats. The skippers of daughter boats prudently stayed away from the mother ship. After several nights of inactivity, the liquor freighter would sail away, looking for a better place to do business. The CG rum chaser would tail the ship for hundreds of miles, keeping a searchlight on the vessel, making sure it didn't try to enter a U.S. port.[26]

A second major expansion of the CG fleet came in the early 1930s. To battle the thriving liquor traffic on the Great Lakes, the service added lightweight, V-bottom speedboats capable of 30 knots or more. To police Long Island Sound, the CG acquired 78-foot patrol boats with speeds around 24 knots. Twenty-one new picket boats joined the Dry Navy in 1930–31. The CG fleet had more than three hundred large vessels at its peak during the Great Drought.[27]

"Starvation and Surveillance"

After Congress appropriated funds to expand the Coast Guard, the build-up progressed at a rapid pace. By May 1925, the CG was ready to launch an all-out offensive against Rum Row on both sides of Ambrose Lightship. The CG brass planned a "starvation and surveillance blockade" to keep the mother ships from selling liquor to the Whiskito Fleet. In addition to stopping the ship-to-shore flow of liquor, the blockade would prevent contact boats from delivering food and fresh water to the crews on the liquor freighters, thereby hastening their departure from Rum Row. Government officials hoped to "sweep the rum armada from the Atlantic seaboard" in less than a month.[28]

The government flotilla, based at Staten Island, had 54 vessels assigned to blockade duty. CG brass onshore directed the vessels' movements using radio and wireless telegraphy. The cutters carried six-inch guns, anti-aircraft guns, one-pounders, and machineguns. The picket boats were armed with one-pounders and machineguns. When intercepting a rumrunning vessel, the Guards' standing orders were to fire warning shots across the bow and then "shoot to kill" if the crew didn't surrender.[29]

The CG blockade stretched from Barnegat, New Jersey, past Ambrose Lightship to a point south of Fire Island, New York. The government boats lined up opposite 68 mother ships that rode at anchor beyond the rum line. When a contact boat attempted to ferry liquor from a mother ship to shore, the CG rum chasers stood ready to intercept it, arrest the crewmen, and confiscate the booze.[30]

In the blockade's opening skirmish, a Coast Guard vessel clashed with a high-powered, speedy contact boat. After taking a load of liquor from the mother ship, the motorboat crew raced toward land. The CG gunner fired his machinegun and hit two men on the motorboat. Blood splattered across the cockpit as a bullet punctured the helmsman's arm. The rummers, including the wounded ones, jumped into the water. Fighting a swift current, they struggled to swim to shore.[31]

With no one at the wheel, the speeding boat careened out of control. It spun around

Top Prohibition officials check the "war zone map" for the battle against rumrunners on the East Coast (Library of Congress).

and hit a submerged jetty, which acted like a ramp, sending the vessel airborne. The motorboat soared through the air and landed in the yard behind a hotel in Sea Bright, New Jersey. The Guardsmen hurried ashore to confiscate the booze. Despite the swift current, the rumrunners made it to shore. Prohibition agents found one of the wounded rummers in a local hospital, but the others escaped.[32]

Word of the opening battle spread quickly among the rumrunners on the East Coast. The Guardsmen were challenging Rum Row more aggressively than ever before. Wise skippers kept their contact boats at the dock. Liquor Lane shrank because mother ships moved farther out to sea or sailed away to find a stretch of unprotected coastline. However, the liquor freighters riding at anchor nearest New York Harbor didn't budge. Those five schooners and four steamers stayed at their customary stations. A number of liquor freighters also remained along the New Jersey coast, awaiting "instructions from their land allies."[33]

With the mother ships scattering, jubilant Prohibition officials rushed to declare victory. "So far as the big importation of liquor is concerned, it is a thing of the past," boasted a top official. He spoke too soon. Over the next few days, Rum Row grew with the arrival of five new liquor freighters, including big steamers from France and Germany.

Since these large vessels carried ample food and water, they wouldn't need new supplies for a month or more. They could play the waiting game, biding their time until contact boats could slip through the blockade.[34]

The rumrunners who stayed at Ambrose Lightship had limited contact with the outside world. The blockade interfered with normal communications between the rummers and their accomplices on land, so they resorted to sending messages via carrier pigeon. When the Guards saw the heavy pigeon traffic, they realized what was happening and caught the birds whenever possible. On one occasion the Guards intercepted a message that enabled them to capture a contact boat.[35]

Informed observers forecast a protracted war along the New York–New Jersey coast. Assistant Treasury Secretary Lincoln Andrews called the Rum Row blockade "a test" and "not in any sense a big drive." He said, "We want to see how the rumrunners will defend themselves against this treatment. Then we will take the offensive against whatever move they make, and so on, until … we can operate against them in a really successful way. When that time comes, then you will see real naval liquor warfare."[36]

Critics predicted that the blockade would fail over the long term. "The increased activity of the Coast Guard in concentrating its ships off Rum Row is futile and a waste of money," warned a retired sea captain. "The so-called successful bottling up of Rum Row is nothing less than a farce." He said, "In the old Revolutionary days the entire British navy was sent to these coasts to stop smuggling. The immediate result of this action was the making of real sailors out of the American smugglers. History repeats itself. The vigilance of the Coast Guard will make skillful seamen out of the rumrunners."[37]

After four days of the blockade, a CG officer declared, "There is nothing coming ashore and any attempt to approach or leave the rum boats would bring trouble." Despite the danger, a few shore runners sailed out to Rum Row. One breached the blockade and landed a cargo of champagne at Easthampton, Long Island. Off the New Jersey coast, a CG cutter chased a gasoline yacht carrying cases of scotch. The CG crew fired many rounds of ammunition at the yacht as it headed north and then suddenly turned south. Racing toward Cape May, the rumrunners tossed cases of whiskey overboard. The lighter load enabled the yacht to pick up speed, and it left the CG cutter behind.[38]

Although the CG failed to capture any mother ships, Rum Row was almost deserted after six days of the blockade. "The dry navy has won a complete victory in the war with the wet fleet," a newspaper reported. Only six liquor freighters rode at anchor near New York harbor, and another three were positioned off Atlantic City, New Jersey. CG officers speculated that the other rumrunners had sailed south, looking for friendlier ports.[39]

Foggy weather protected the rumrunners on the seventh night of the blockade. A dense, swirling fog limited visibility, giving the contact boats an opportunity to slip past the Dry Navy. Anticipating visits from the Whiskito Fleet, the mother ships weighed anchor and moved closer to the shore. The Guards on the government cutters watched for contact boats but failed to spot any in the foggy darkness.[40]

While the blockade continued, fog proved to be the rumrunners' best friend. On foggy nights with limited visibility, speedboats broke through the blockade, picked up booze on Rum Row, and safely returned to shore. The contact boats landed substantial amounts of liquor at Highlands, New Jersey, and at Easthampton, New York, on the eastern end of Long Island.[41]

Despite obstacles, shore runners hauled cargos to New York's Fire Island, a barrier isle south of Long Island. "They are now forced to slip in close to the Fire Island sandbar and let their liquor float ashore in lots of ten cases, wrapped with rope," said a Prohibition official. "This is dragged across the sandbar by horses and is carried across Great South Bay in flat-bottomed boats and then up small creeks for distribution."[42] Obviously, this delivery system was neither speedy nor efficient. But it kept the shore runners in business.

After ten days of the blockade a CG officer sailed from Nantucket, Massachusetts, to Barnegat Bay, New Jersey, looking for rumrunners. He saw only 12 liquor freighters scattered around the sector. The scarcity of rumrunners "undoubtedly means the end of that picturesque method of liquor smuggling," he said. He seemed to be right when the number of mother ships dropped even lower over the next few days.[43]

To escape the blockade, some rumrunners took refuge in Canadian waters. For access to New England, liquor freighters lay at anchor in the Bay of Fundy between Nova Scotia and New Brunswick. Canadian fishermen jumped at the chance to make money hauling liquor from the mother ships to ports in Maine and Massachusetts. The fishermen turned virtually anything seaworthy into a contact boat. "Tales, lurid and otherwise, are being told of fortunes made overnight by boatmen willing to run a cargo to the American shore. It beats carrying sardines," wrote a Canadian.[44]

Nova Scotia seaports also attracted vessels fleeing the blockade. "Halifax Harbor has been rapidly filling with liquor-carrying steamers and schooners, many of them reporting that their run to port was occasioned by the intensified activity of the United States 'dry' fleet," a Canadian newspaper stated. At least two mother ships fled to Glace Bay, Nova Scotia, where they tried to sell their liquor but had no luck because Canadian revenue cutters kept them under surveillance.[45]

Not all the mother ships headed north. The Deep South hosted rumrunners "who managed to escape the sharpshooting Coast Guardsmen's campaign to break up" Rum Row at Ambrose Lightship. They ferried liquor from Cuba and other islands to Florida, Louisiana, Alabama, Georgia, and South Carolina. Southern drinkers welcomed the influx of imported whiskey, and the rumrunners found it easy to land their cargos, especially in Florida. The Coast Guard reported that five mother ships avoided the blockade by sailing all the way to San Diego, California, to sell their wares.[46]

The CG brass had reason to celebrate as the blockade approached the three-week mark. Only five mother ships lurked off the coast from New York City to Atlantic City. Then, an influx of mother ships arrived and anchored off New Jersey between Sandy Hook and Asbury Park. The rumor mill said that contact boats were routinely getting through the blockade to these ships. But CG officers scoffed at the gossip. They claimed the cordon was as tight as ever.[47]

Over the summer, observers saw the Whiskito Fleet swarming around the liquor freighters on Rum Row. Nevertheless, the CG brass denied that Liquor Lane even existed. The commander of the New York Coast Guard Division declared that "not a single steamer, trawler, schooner, or fishing smack" was selling liquor in his sector. "Rum Row is dry!" he crowed.[48]

The commander vigorously denied reports that the CG had withdrawn vessels from the blockade, making it easier for contact boats to slip through. However, some CG vessels were out of service because they needed repairs and had gone into port for extensive maintenance. Other CG vessels had been transferred to areas where the rumrunners had moved to avoid the blockade. In New England, rummers were very active along the Maine-Massachusetts coastline, so more CG resources had to be deployed there. The CG also urgently needed to beef up enforcement in the South. The situation called for "particular attention … to the Florida coast and to the countless bayous and inlets on the Gulf Coast from Florida west to the Rio Grande."[49]

The Coast Guard's "navigation protection" mission also pulled vessels away from the blockade around Ambrose Lightship. A large portion of the service's resources had to be allocated to keeping the waterways safe. The shipping industry put pressure on Congress to limit the CG's role in Volstead enforcement, so more CG vessels could be deployed for navigation safety, especially during stormy weather when sailing was riskier.[50]

Bribery played a major role in disrupting the blockade. The Guardsmen were paid low wages for long hours and hard work. Of course, some of them took bribes from the rum rings. Although the CG brass bristled at accusations of corruption, bribery was often the only logical explanation when boats breached the blockade. Nineteen Coasties from the Staten Island unit were jailed and "charged with dishonest practices in connection with Prohibition enforcement." But most corrupt Guards were never arrested.[51]

By autumn 1925 the blockade had large gaps, which allowed the rumrunners to operate freely in some areas. The revitalized liquor traffic was especially heavy on Long Island, where the shore runners found it easy to unload their cargo. Trucks with heavy loads of liquor "were lumbering nightly" along the island's roads with no interference from lawmen. "I am reliably informed that they are trucking liquor through Long Island as much as they ever did," said an attorney.[52]

The rumrunners were delivering vast quantities of liquor to the Northeast. Even CG officers "admitted that Rum Row, which for a time had been wiped out, existed again," a newspaper reported. However, the Coast Guard's official assessment disagreed. The service's annual report for 1925 stated, "The notorious Rum Row, formerly lying off the entrance to New York, and off Long Island and New Jersey, has been effectively scattered."[53]

Although the news report and the Coast Guard's official statement seemed contradictory, both were true. The blockade hadn't destroyed Rum Row, but fewer mother ships anchored around Ambrose Lightship. The liquor freighters spread out over a wide area, and many stayed far outside the rum line. Rumrunning continued to be a primary source of illegal alcohol in the Northeast and other coastal regions.

After ten years of Volstead, Prohibition officials estimated that rumrunners were bringing four million gallons of liquor into the United States each year. They called this an "irreducible minimum." The Coast Guard reported that 138 foreign mother ships smuggled liquor into the United States in 1930. According to the head of the CG Intelligence Unit, "the Coast Guard on the West Coast was practically impotent, and on the East Coast it could do little more than annoy the rumrunners."[54]

4

Cut to the Chase
Speed Plus Agility

Rumrunners relied on fast, agile motorboats to haul liquor from the mother ship to the shore. The crewmen on these small feeder boats had a dangerous, adrenaline-rush job. They were far more vulnerable to arrest than the sailors on Rum Row's liquor freighters. If a mother ship had foreign registry and stayed outside the rum line, international protocols restricted the Dry Navy's power. But the contact boats didn't have the luxury of staying in international waters. Sooner or later, they had to cross the rum line to land their liquor. Contact-boat skippers became adept at outrunning and outmaneuvering the larger, slower CG vessels. When the Coast Guard pursued a contact boat, the chase might last for minutes or for hours. To avoid capture, he contact-boat skipper needed nerve, skill, and fortitude.

Initially, buyers sailed out to Rum Row in any watercraft that could make the trip. But it soon became apparent that certain types of boats had advantages for rumrunning. Men intent on making large profits ordered boats that were designed and built especially for hauling liquor. A low-hulled speedboat with a sharp chine line, an almost flat bottom, and a pillbox-style pilothouse made an ideal shore runner.[1]

"There are lean boats that take the seas like a flash of the sun, fat boats that wallow through the trough with the grace of a tub, and real, sure enough rum runners, built to order," an observer wrote. The best booze boats "are fine products of the nautical art, slung low in the hull so that the liquor rides below the water line and keeps the boat down on the horizon, hard to see and almost impossible to hit."[2]

A speedboat with a low profile could race under drawbridges. This provided an advantage over Coast Guard patrol boats, which had to wait for the bridges to open because they had tall masts. CG commanders complained that the bridge tenders aided the rumrunners by responding slowly when a patrol boat signaled for the bridge to open.

To outrun the Dry Navy, many contact boats relied on Liberty, Fiat, or Packard aircraft engines converted for marine use. After World War I the U.S. government sold thousands of surplus Liberty airplane engines at bargain prices. Rumrunners snapped up the aircraft motors because they offered a lot of power at low cost.

Rumrunning created such a strong market for aircraft engines that manufacturers advertised them in boating magazines. The engine prices rose, largely due to demand from rummers. Enterprising mechanics bought aircraft engines, modified them for

Coast Guard rum chasers are docked in the harbor at East Boston (courtesy Boston Public Library, Leslie Jones Collection).

marine use, and sold them for a substantial profit. In 1924 a Fiat direct-drive aircraft engine with 300-horsepower cost $500. A few years later a Fiat engine equipped with a clutch cost $3,000. In 1928 a Liberty engine cost $4,000, a steep increase over the fire-sale prices paid earlier in the decade. To buy a high-powered Packard aircraft engine, a rumrunner had to shell out $7,000 or more in the late Twenties.[3]

Rumrunner Johnny Schnarr had two 400-horsepower Liberty engines in *Kit-nayakwa*, which scooted along at 30 knots. One night the Coast Guard set a trap to capture *Kitnayakwa* at Discovery Bay, Washington. When Schnarr sailed into the bay to deliver a load of liquor, a CG cutter followed him. The Guards opened fire with their machineguns. A tracer bullet whizzed past Schnarr's nose. He swung the wheel around hard, turning his boat in a tight half-circle. He accelerated and flashed past the cutter. But he wasn't home free. Five more CG boats lay in wait for him. He managed to dodge all of them and race away, leaving the Coasties behind.[4]

A veteran rumrunner designed *Kagome* expressly for carrying liquor cargos from Mexico to California. The plans called for two Liberty engines plus an auxiliary diesel motor. Without cargo or full fuel tanks, *Kagome* flew across the water. However, on its maiden voyage with a cargo of liquor, the engines failed to produce enough speed. In fact, the vessel performed so poorly that the captain returned to port. The captain and engineer determined that the engines weren't the problem. The propellers were too small. After larger propellers were installed, *Kagome* raced along at a fast pace and made many successful rumrunning trips.[5]

In Florida rumrunners liked boats built by Louis Nuta, Sr. His bestselling booze boat, powered by two Liberty engines, had a speed of about 20 knots when fully loaded. It could outrun the Coasties' fastest rum chaser and made the trip from Bimini to Miami in roughly two hours. A topnotch rum boat, built from the keel up in Nuta's shop, cost as much as $14,000.[6]

Although aircraft engines were popular, many rumrunners chose to equip their boats with powerful automotive engines built for luxury cars. *Skedaddle* roared along with two 400-horsepower, straight-eight Dusenburg gas engines. The owner claimed it could do 65 knots. *Moonbeam* sported a six-cylinder Marmon automotive engine, which had double ignition in each cylinder. When both sets of sparkplugs were firing, *Moonbeam* easily outran the Coast Guard cutters. *Revuocnav,* propelled by two Packard automobile engines, could run at 40 knots with a cargo of liquor onboard.[7]

Rumrunning boats needed to be silent and stealthy, but high-powered engines roared. To reduce the noise, a rummer could install a silencer or muffler. One simple method for reducing noise used an L-shaped exhaust pipe extension. When attached to the regular exhaust pipe, this extension diverted the exhaust underwater, muffling the engine sounds. The booze boat could move quietly across the water, like a ghost ship.[8]

Powerful motors were essential in producing speed, but they weren't the only factor. Weight and balance also played a role. "Each boat must weigh just so much and no more, barely enough to counterbalance the engine, which is huge for these small craft," a writer explained. "Every cleat and sheet of copper that goes into these boats is weighed with the nicety of a jeweler's scale."[9]

To make a respectable profit, a liquor smuggler needed a boat at least 30 feet long, and vessels twice that length were common. Syndicates with deep pockets bought custom-built boats with special options for rumrunning. For $100,000 a rum ring could buy a 150-foot vessel with diesel engines, shortwave radio, armor plating, and Maxim silencers. The price tag was high, but the vessel carried a big payload, so the syndicate could quickly recoup the cost.[10]

Liquor smugglers with fat wallets bought expensive boats, but novice rumrunners often had to improvise. An aspiring rummer could start by turning an old flat-bottomed, high-bow dory into a contact boat. Since a dory equipped with a single-cylinder engine was too slow for the liquor traffic, the rummer had to rip out the old motor and replace it with something faster, like a high-powered automobile engine. The renovated dory with an automotive engine had enough speed to be a moneymaker. After a few successful trips to Rum Row, the rumrunner could afford to buy a better boat.[11]

Many fishermen decided to become rumrunners because booze sold better than flounder. A fisherman who owned a boat could easily modify it for his new venture. He could devise a false bottom, double holds, secret compartments, or partitions to hide liquor. Layers of fish and ice could cover burlocks filled with whiskey bottles. In the Northeast a rumrunner could pose as a lobsterman. When the Coasties were watching, the rummer lowered slatted wood boxes into the water, going through the motions of a lobsterman setting his pots.[12]

At least one shore runner flew red caution flags, which signaled that his boat carried dynamite or another explosive. If a Coast Guard patrol boat or a strange vessel ventured near, the rumrunner hollered warnings to keep away. "Dynamite aboard!" scared off everyone, including the Coasties.[13]

Tricks of the Trade

The rumrunners had a toolbox full of ruses and maneuvers to use against the Coast Guard. The Coasties had their own weapons and tactics, which often doomed the rummer to capture. During the CG build-up in the mid–Twenties, both sides added firepower. Chases and gun battles became common during Volstead's latter years.

Contact-boat skippers learned to work together to foil the Coast Guard. In a favorite stratagem, several contact boats would converge on a mother ship at the same time. The slowest feeder boat took on no liquor while the other boats loaded up. If a CG cutter approached the mother ship, the slow boat became a decoy, sailing toward the Guards' vessel to attract their attention. The decoy sailed close to the cutter, virtually daring the Coasties to a showdown. When the Guards took the bait, the chase began.

While the decoy boat led the Guards away from the mother ship, the other contact boats raced to shore at top speed. In most cases, they safely landed their cargo. If the CG vessel caught up with the decoy boat or fired warning shots that came too close, the rummy skipper stopped and let the Guardsmen board. No matter how hard they searched, the Coasties found no booze.[14]

In a dangerous variation on this tactic, several feeder boats sailed out to the mother ship. The crews loaded liquor on all except one contact boat, which carried guns and shooters with itchy trigger fingers. The contact boats headed for shore at the same time. If a Coast Guard vessel confronted the rum convoy, the men on the heavily-armed boat unleashed their firepower. The gunfight kept the Guards busy while the contact boats dashed to shore.[15]

In a nonviolent ploy, a mother ship would radio a distress signal to the Coast Guard, giving the position of a sinking craft. While the Guards searched for the nonexistent sinking vessel, contact boats ran from Rum Row to the shore. In one incident, coastal stations received a radio distress signal about an emergency at the Frying Pan Shoals Lightship near Cape Fear, North Carolina. CG vessels hurried to the lightship, leaving the shoreline unguarded. Contact boats ran their liquor cargos into Cape Fear River without hindrance.[16]

Off Fire Island, New York, ships on Rum Row cooperated in a maneuver that usually foiled the Coast Guard. The line of mother ships engaged in a kind of drill, tacking to port and starboard, spreading apart, then closing ranks. The CG patrol boats stayed close, trying to hem in the rummers. At an opportune moment, one or two mother ships bolted from the line and headed toward shore at top speed. The CG vessels had to change course and try to catch up with the breakaway ships. Barely outside the rum line, contact boats met the breakaways. Working with quick precision, the crews transferred liquor to the small boats. Then the contact boats raced to shore ahead of the Coast Guard.[17]

Rumrunning skippers had a standard maneuver for escaping the CG destroyers, which couldn't make quick, sharp turns. When a destroyer chased a blockade runner, the rummy skipper charged ahead at full speed, leaving the warship as far behind as possible. Then the rum boat pivoted around and sped past the destroyer headed in the opposite direction. The destroyer captain summoned full speed and, with hard-over rudder, tried to follow the rumrunner. The rum vessel took advantage of its maneuverability, twisting and turning, making a zig-zag trail difficult for the warship to follow. If the destroyer managed to stay close, the rummy captain might tire of the game and head out to sea to await a better time to do business.[18]

When picketing a mother ship, it was standard procedure for a CG destroyer or six-bitter to circle continuously around the rum vessel, staying as close as possible. Sometimes the rumrunning skipper decided to follow suite, so the vessels ran in concentric circles. If the CG vessel left too much room between itself and the mother ship, a fast contact boat might sneak through. At night, the circling Guards kept a searchlight focused on the rum ship to let the skipper know he was under constant surveillance. The rummy crew often retaliated by trying to shoot out the light. Tragically, the shooter sometimes wounded or even killed the searchlight operator.[19]

At least one rummy crew fooled the Guardsmen by burning a riding light all night. A CG cutter had *Maid of Orleans* (AKA *Old Maid No. 2*) under constant surveillance just beyond the rum line. The Coasties planned to seize the booze boat when it sailed into U.S. waters. At sunset, the rummy skipper hoisted a riding light to mark his location. The Guards saw the light and kept an eye on it after nightfall, to make sure the booze boat didn't escape. When the sun rose, they were surprised to discover that the riding light was mounted on an anchored raft. *Maid of Orleans* had slipped over the rum line during the night, without running lights, and safely delivered her cargo of whiskey.[20]

In some cases, a rumrunner being chased by a CG cutter or destroyer took advantage of shoal water. Since the typical booze boat drew a fathom or less and the CG ships drew significantly more, the rummy skipper headed for a bar or shoal. The rummer could maneuver his boat over the shallow bottom where the CG vessel dared not go, due to the risk of running aground or sanding the condensers. In northern waters, Nantucket Shoals was a favorite place for this tactic.[21]

To confuse and thwart the Coast Guard, rumrunners sometimes moved the markers that helped sailors navigate tricky waters. For example, the water level in the channel into Florida's Soldier Key was dangerously shallow on one side. This channel was marked with arrows on posts pointing to the deep water, so boats wouldn't run aground. Rumrunners would change the direction of the arrows, causing unsuspecting CG vessels to get stuck.[22]

On occasion, rummers paid a high price for misjudging the depth of the water. *Elizabeth K*, a fast booze boat, led the marine police on a marathon chase along the New York–New Jersey waterfront. For several hours the speedy boat raced around the Upper Bay, repeatedly circling Governors Island and Bedloe's Island. Finally, running slightly ahead of the police boat, it headed for the shallow, rocky flats at Greenfield, New Jersey. The rummy skipper miscalculated and hit the rocks, ripping open the boat's hull. When

Mary, a contact boat, sits at the dock after the Coast Guard captured it with a liquor cargo in Dorchester Bay (courtesy Boston Public Library, Leslie Jones Collection).

the police boat caught up, the rummy crew was standing knee-deep in water, easy prey for the lawmen.[23]

The rumrunners' ploys didn't have to be complicated, In fact, some of the most successful were quite simple. Sailing in the shadow of a larger vessel could provide cover for a booze boat. A West Coast rumrunner routinely used this simple tactic on trips from Canada to the United States. On moonlit nights he lurked around the San Juan Islands, waiting for the Vancouver-Seattle passenger steamer. When he spotted the vessel, he moved his liquor-laden boat into position and cruised in the shadows, keeping pace with the steamer. The motorboat's dark green paint helped it blend into the darkness, and the Maxim silencers on the exhaust line allowed it to skim along quietly.[24]

Even after the Coast Guard learned about this rumrunner's ploy and began watching for him, he repeatedly escaped by outrunning the government boats. But the Guards were determined to catch him. One night four CG picket boats surrounded his booze boat. He darted through a gap between two vessels and raced away at full speed. The picket boats fired at the rum boat, fore and aft. One-pounders pierced the booze boat's armor plate, and machinegun fire smashed the pilothouse windows. The rummy skipper ducked down in the wheelhouse and steered blindly. The bullets kept whistling overhead. He soon realized he couldn't escape, so he surrendered.[25]

To put more liquor onboard a boat, rumrunners sometimes stacked burlocks in the head and used a bucket on deck for a toilet. When Guards on a picket boat saw a rummer sitting on a bucket, it was the perfect opportunity for a little harassment. The skipper of the CG vessel would ring up full speed and lunge at the rum boat. The abrupt wash would cause the bucket's occupant to fall off, knocking it over and spilling its contents on deck—usually accompanied by loud cursing.[26] Although this didn't actually enforce Volstead, it gave the Coasties a chuckle.

Another unsanctioned Coast Guard tactic used garbage. Guards on a picket boat would make a giant slingshot by hanging a tire inner tube between two davits on deck. They then filled the slingshot with garbage and lobbed it at the nearest rum boat. After a Canadian rumrunner was hit with an especially nasty barrage of garbage, the irate skipper insisted that Ottawa file a formal protest with the U.S. government. A diplomatic tempest in a teapot ensued. To prevent such rows, the CG brass officially discouraged garbage-flinging, and the practice fell into disrepute.[27]

Friend or Foe

Law enforcement confiscated thousands of rumrunning vessels during Prohibition. The rumrunner who lost his mother ship or contact boat suffered a serious financial setback, but the loss wasn't always permanent. The rummer could petition the court to return his property. Generally, he argued that it had been seized illegally, either because there was no liquor onboard or because law enforcement hadn't followed the proper procedures. If the court ruled against the rumrunner, the confiscated vessel would be sold at a government auction.

The auction gave the rummer an opportunity to reclaim his boat at a low price. The rules required at least three bids, so the rummer could submit bids under aliases or ask two friends to underbid him. The auction prices tended to be outrageously low. For example, rummers in Florida "fixed the maximum bid for a seized small boat at $10 and the maximum for larger vessels at $50." Law-abiding citizens generally shied away from bidding on rumrunning vessels at an auction. If an unwise bidder outbid the rumrunner, he might be subjected to verbal abuse or even violence. At least one rummer who lost his boat to a higher bidder later located it and blew it up.[28]

The government auctions became a revolving door for rumrunning vessels. After the Dry Navy seized a rumrunner's boat or ship, he bought it at auction and returned it to the Wet Fleet. Some boats went through this cycle multiple times. The oceangoing tug *Underwriter* hauled illegal booze in New England waters. The Coast Guard captured *Underwriter* four times in one year; after each seizure it was sold at auction and went back to work in the liquor traffic.[29]

The Guardsmen often saw a vessel they had "caught red-handed … released on some technicality or condemned, sold, and bought back by her same owners for a nominal sum." After the rummer reclaimed his boat, he could easily recoup his financial loss "by running a few cases of whiskey ashore any dark night." The Guards became frustrated because they risked their lives to capture vessels that returned to the rumrunning game again and again.[30]

The Coast Guard needed a large fleet of fast boats to chase the rumrunners, but Congressional appropriations for the Dry Navy always fell short. The CG brass argued that adding seized vessels to the Dry Fleet would be a cost-effective alternative to building more patrol boats. Officers could inspect the confiscated rum boats and choose those that would be suitable for Volstead enforcement. In 1925 President Coolidge signed a bill streamlining the legal process used by the CG to claim confiscated boats.[31]

The Coast Guard took advantage of the streamlined process to substantially enlarge its fleet. Over the course of Prohibition, the CG acquired roughly 650 rum boats and added 232 of them to the Dry Fleet. When the CG claimed a vessel but ultimately decided not to use it, it was sold, sunk, or transferred to another government agency.[32]

Underwater Smuggling

Submersible tanks were a popular means of transporting liquor, especially for short distances. The tank, typically 12 feet or longer, could be filled with hams of liquor and towed behind a motorboat. Or it could be keel-hauled, chained beneath a vessel. If a rumrunner pulling a submersible spotted a CG patrol boat, he quickly cut the tank loose. With a little luck, he could return later to reclaim the sub before the Coasties or someone else found it.[33]

A submersible captured off the coast of North Carolina had an engine and "a pilot room fitted for human occupancy." The sub had enough power to propel itself across the surface of the water but couldn't travel long distances underwater. To hide from the Dry Navy, the pilot could submerge for short periods of time. In 1922 newspapers reported that a submarine was plying the waters along the West Coast, carrying liquor from British Columbia to Washington and California. Similarly, Prohibition agents believed that a reconditioned German U-boat was hauling hooch off the coast of California. The sub reportedly belonged to a rum ring that operated out of Vancouver, Canada, and Ensenada, Mexico.[34]

When Coast Guard officials heard reports of submarines smuggling liquor into New York, they investigated with the help of aerial photographers. Pilots who were supposedly collecting data for maps flew over the Hudson River, taking aerial photos with telescopic lens. The photos showed two long, cigar-shaped, underwater craft opposite Sing Sing Prison, but the CG couldn't prove that they were smuggling liquor.[35]

A federal attorney in Boston stated that a German U-boat was operating near Cape Cod in 1924. He said that coastal towns were "flooded" with German beer and French wines delivered by the submarine. According to press reports in January 1925, a submarine with a German crew was ferrying liquor between a mother ship and contact boats that serviced New York City. Every night the sub carried up to two thousand cases from a mother ship south of Asbury Park to the feeder boats anchored near New York harbor. That same month, police in Philadelphia and Trenton noted an upsurge in the flow of liquor to their cities; the supply reportedly came from a rumrunning sub.[36]

Although submarines had obvious advantages for rumrunning, law enforcement could confirm only a few instances of their use. Searches for subs usually turned up something else. For example, when fishermen said that subs were delivering liquor to

Long Island's south shore, the Prohis sent agents to hunt for the vessels. After a week of patrolling the area in a boat, the federal agents spotted a suspicious dark object, possibly a periscope, near Fire Island. As the agents sailed toward the object, it submerged, resurfaced, and disappeared again. When the agents got closer, they identified the object as the dorsal fin of a porpoise.[37]

On the West Coast, a rumrunner devised a clever method for underwater smuggling that didn't require a submarine. In the Pacific Northwest, lumberjacks lashed logs together with wire or cable to make rafts, which were towed by boat from lumber camps in Canada to sawmills in Washington State. The innovative rumrunner saw that log rafts could be a cheap, efficient way of transporting liquor. He began by stringing burlocks onto a sturdy wire, much like stringing pearls to make a necklace. He secured the wire diagonally across the bottom of the raft and shackled it at the corners. After a boat towed the raft into U.S. waters, the rumrunner cut the wire loose and removed the burlocks.[38]

Going Overboard

When the Coast Guard chased a contact boat and closed in, the rummy skipper might jettison his cargo to lighten the load and get rid of evidence. The wise skipper planned ahead just in case he needed to toss booze overboard. Some rummers strung their burlocks together with a sturdy rope and tied a cork or buoy to the end. If the liquor were dumped overboard, the cork or buoy floated, allowing the rumrunner to find his cargo later.[39]

Salt could be a means of finding liquor that had been jettisoned. The rumrunner strung his hams together, filled a burlap bag with a block of salt, and tied the bag to his string. If he had to toss his hams overboard, the salt would melt in the water and the bag would rise to the surface. When the rumrunner found this empty bag, he could haul in his whole string of burlocks. In a variation, the rummer put a case of bottles inside a crocus bag and finished filling the bag with salt. If he threw his cases overboard, the salt dissolved and the bags slowly rose to the surface.[40]

A rumrunner could pile his burlocks on a raft or barge, which he towed behind his boat. If he spotted a Coast Guard patrol boat, he cut the raft loose, shoved it toward the shore, and hoped for the best. The obvious drawback to this method was the lack of control over the raft. The rumrunner couldn't steer his cargo to a safe landing, and the Guards might seize the raft before he could retrieve it.[41] If the Guards didn't confiscate the raft, beachcombers or pleasure boaters were likely to find it and pilfer the booze.

The rumrunner jettisoned his liquid cargo as a last resort. The longer a chase lasted, the more likely he was to sacrifice his payload. The Coast Guard's *Gresham* once chased the black ship *Albatross* for four hours along the East Coast. When *Gresham* came too close for comfort, the *Albatross* crew threw the liquor overboard. *Gresham* stopped briefly to recover two cases of Scotch and then resumed the chase. Finally, the Guards pulled within firing distance and aimed shots across the *Albatross* bow, nearly hitting the pilot-house. The rummy skipper stopped and allowed the Guardsmen to board. A search uncovered no liquor. The CG captain had been wise to stop long enough to scoop up evidence of the crime.[42]

On a busy night near Sea Bright, New Jersey, the captain of a CG vessel spotted a shore runner approaching the channel marked by Ambrose Lightship. The CG boat pursued the rumrunner, trying to cut him off as he headed toward Prince's Bay, Staten Island. The rummy crew frantically heaved cases of liquor overboard. The Guards drew alongside the rum boat, boarded, and searched. But they found no liquor. Without evidence, they couldn't arrest the crew or seize the boat. Later that same night, the CG vessel nearly collided with a mosquito boat. The rummers hastily changed course and threw burlocks overboard as they sped away. The Guardsmen watched the contact boat recede into the distance.[43]

When rumrunners ditched their liquor, lucky beachcombers often snapped up the bottles or burlocks. If a lost cargo washed ashore, the news spread quickly along the waterfront. Even in the middle of the night, a crowd of locals would suddenly appear to claim the liquid treasure. On a frigid winter night, the schooner *Madonna V* ran aground near the Napeague Coast Guard Station at South Fork, Long Island. As the schooner broke apart, the crew abandoned ship, leaving behind several hundred cases of good booze. But the cargo wasn't lost. "Lifelong teetotalers and even deacons of the church risked pneumonia in the December surf to bring it ashore."[44]

On a balmy August night federal Prohibition agents in speedboats chased a contact boat at Jones Inlet, Long Island. The rumrunners hurriedly tossed their whiskey cargo overboard and escaped. Later that night, the waves swept the cases ashore at Long Beach. Most people had gone to bed, but a few night owls saw the cargo wash up on the beach. "Like magic, the word spread about the resort." It didn't take long for all the bottles to disappear. "Only the local bootleggers, reflecting on their loss of business for a few days, and the local prohibitionists were unhappy."[45]

A rumrunning trawler ran aground one night near Black Fish Rock at Montauk, Long Island. Trying to refloat the vessel, the crew jettisoned hundreds of burlocks to lighten the load. Nevertheless, they were forced to abandon ship. Coast Guards came to inspect the wreckage and keep people from stealing burlocks. Despite the Guards' vigilance, at least one local resident managed to salvage some booze; a Guardsman found him "lying on the sand, unconscious … passed out from too much of the contraband liquor." At dawn a group of local men came to the beach with eel spears, clam rakes, and fishing nets. Before they could retrieve any burlocks, two Coast Guard cutters fired volleys at the beach. The thirsty men abandoned their quest.[46]

At Laguna Beach, California, gunfire awoke the locals early one morning. Coast Guards were firing rifles and a machinegun at a shore runner. The small boat stayed close to the rocks at the southern end of the bay. Suddenly the morning tide swept it against the rocks, ripping the hull open. The crew jumped into the water, swam to shore, and ran away. Local men hurried to the beach and claimed the gummy sacks full of liquor. That evening the denizens of Laguna Beach enjoyed bourbon, scotch, and Canadian whiskey, courtesy of the rumrunners who had absconded.[47]

Near Key Biscayne, Florida, a fisherman hauled burlocks of liquor out of the water after rumrunners threw them overboard. The fisherman invited his friends to an impromptu party to help him consume the hooch. The rummers went looking for their lost cargo, heard about the party, and crashed it. When they demanded their booze back, the fisherman refused, saying he would "rather give it to Andrew Volstead." To the rummers' dismay, he gathered up the unopened bottles and carried out his threat. He turned the hooch over to the sheriff.[48]

Rumrunners on the contact boat *Tuna* bought booze from a mother ship on Rum Row and headed for Cape May, New Jersey. When they had trouble, *Tuna* ran aground on the bay side of Cape May. To avoid arrest, the rumrunners disappeared into the night, leaving their valuable cargo behind. Thirsty locals soon appeared to rescue the cases of liquor. A tipster alerted the Cape May County sheriff, who hurried to the beach with a posse. The sheriff confiscated the liquor that the locals hadn't already carted away.[49]

Shortly after sunrise one hot summer morning, vacationers began emerging from their bungalows at Rockaway Beach, New York. They could hardly believe what they saw: thousands of cases of whiskey stacked up on the sand. The stacks were positioned at intervals in a line that stretched for a half-mile along the beach. The tourists quickly sized up the situation and embraced a childhood maxim: finders keepers, losers weepers. The happy finders rushed to claim a share of the free booze. Some took whole cases; others were content with a few bottles. They stowed the treasure in their cottages or cars for safekeeping.[50]

In a remarkably short time, hundreds of people were swarming over the beach. As the line of cases shrank, people began to argue over the remaining booze. They shouted profanities at one another, and fistfights broke out. A police sergeant from a nearby station arrived at the beach for a routine check. When he saw the chaos, he ran to a telephone and called the station for help.[51]

When the reinforcements arrived, the lawmen broke up the fights, arrested several people, and confiscated the remaining whiskey. Two of the arrestees were not tourists who had happened upon the scene by accident. They were bootleggers who had driven trucks to the beach to pick up their share of the cargo.[52]

In an ideal transfer, the rumrunners and the bootleggers arrived on the beach at the same time and quickly moved the liquor from the boats to the trucks. But something had gone awry at Rockaway Beach. The boats had arrived during the night, but the trucks hadn't come. The rumrunners unloaded their liquor cargo on the beach, expecting the bootleggers to pick it up before morning. The leggers paid a high price for being tardy.

5

Coast Guards
The Good, the Bad and the Drunk

Before Prohibition, the Coast Guards had a sterling reputation as honest public servants dedicated to saving lives. During the Arid Era, the Guards' public image evolved, becoming more complicated. Both wets and drys had strong opinions about the Coast Guard's mandate to enforce Prohibition. Drinkers didn't like the Guards because they disrupted the flow of foreign liquor into the United States. Dry activists criticized the Coast Guard because it stopped only a tiny fraction of the illegal liquor traffic. Both sides agreed that they didn't like paying high taxes to enforce the dry law. The wets wanted to eliminate the Coast Guard's funding for Volstead enforcement. The drys wanted the service to do a better job on a tighter budget.

Both wets and drys decried the rampant bribery that corrupted thousands of lawmen sworn to enforce Volstead. The extent of corruption in the Dry Navy was unknown. When Prohibition agents and police officers went on trial for corruption, the press covered the proceedings, which were open to the public. However, the Coast Guard had the option of closing a court-martial to the press, so its corruption cases were usually treated as internal matters and were, more or less, secret. The press covered the trials when Coast Guards were indicted in civilian courts, but those cases exposed only a fraction of the corruption in the Dry Navy.

Since the Coast Guard could seriously disrupt the liquor traffic, the rum rings offered hefty bribes to the underpaid Coasties. In the mid–Twenties, Guards earned $36 per month while CG officers were paid $99 per month. Naturally, they were tempted by offers of easy money. A federal attorney said, "Image them after days at sea in a small patrol boat, wet, uncomfortable, exhausted, returning to port to discover that, for an easy service they could live like kings, enjoy the so-called good things of life, and forget their past financial difficulties."[1]

Rum rings paid Coast Guard skippers to chase contact boats at less than top speed, so the rummers could reach shore unscathed. Corrupt CG captains took their vessels in for repairs or refueling at a prearranged time, so contact boats could land liquor without interference. A few skippers accepted money to escort booze boats safely into harbor. In New York at least one rum ring sent its own operatives to enlist in the Coast Guard. This gave them inside information as well as ample opportunity to bribe Guards.[2]

A dishonest CG captain in Washington State added a new dimension to corruption.

At the request of a Canadian liquor exporter, rumrunner Johnny Schnarr agreed to deliver a load of whiskey to a rendezvous point near Barnes Island, between East Point and Anacortes, Washington. He was stunned when he learned that a Coast Guard cutter would be waiting for the booze. Bootleggers, who knew that the Guards on the cutter would be on leave, had persuaded the CG captain to haul liquor for them. A bootlegger met Schnarr at the wharf, and they picked up the cargo. When they reached the rendezvous, they verified that the CG captain was alone and transferred the booze to the six-bitter.[3]

Many times malfeasance was passive, rather than active. In one egregious case, Coast Guard patrol boats chased a booze boat toward the shore, forcing the rummers to run aground near the Blue Point Coast Guard station on Fire Island. The CG skippers returned to patrol, expecting the Guards at the station to take over. Although the beached booze boat sat within sight of the station, the Guards did not arrest the rumrunners or confiscate the liquor cargo. Moreover, the Guards ignored the trucks that arrived to pick up the liquor. When the booze was safely aboard the trucks, the rumrunners set fire to their damaged boat and absconded. The fire department arrived to keep the flames under control. Law enforcement investigated the incident. Subsequently, 20 Coasties faced courts-martial for taking bribes up to $200 per man. However, the CG brass refused to give details of the case to the press.[4]

Although money was generally the reward for aiding rumrunners, some Guards were paid with gifts, such as tickets to baseball games, boxing matches, or Broadway shows. The most popular gift was liquor. The commander of the CG base in New London admitted that liquor bribes were a common, somewhat puzzling problem. "A man who would not think of stealing $10 and who is generally honest will consider it within his right to take liquor," the commander said. He found it surprising that "the gift of a little champagne or whiskey will turn men." He stated that "whole crews become corrupted" and "the strange, popular attitude of the men toward liquor is what makes them susceptible to advances by the rumrunner."[5]

Whenever Guards searched a boat and found liquor, they had a duty to seize the cargo and take it to a warehouse for safekeeping. But they didn't always take the booze to storage. They drank it. Or sold it. Rumrunners complained that this was unfair. The rummers braved the high seas, sailed to a foreign port to buy liquor, and paid substantial overhead costs. "Coast Guard crews, on the other hand, got their booze for free; Uncle Sam picked up the tab for gas and maintenance." In fact, Uncle Sam paid the Coasties a salary while they were seizing the illegal booze and selling it.[6]

The Sidewalk Spitters

Guardsmen became unpopular in ports where rumrunning stoked the local economy. Drinkers didn't like them because they were killjoys who enforced the Volstead law. On the other side of the issue, the drys assumed Coasties were corrupt and therefore untrustworthy. Negative feelings about the Guards led to a general shunning in coastal towns. When the Coasties went ashore, no one welcomed them. "Law-abiding persons in some communities don't even dare be civil to our men," complained a high-ranking CG officer.[7]

Rear Admiral Frederick Billard, USCG Commandant, led the Dry Navy in the war against the rum-runners from 1924 to 1932 (Library of Congress).

In unfriendly ports, local lawmen watched the Guards closely and harassed them. Sometimes the police arrested them for misdemeanors—real or imagined. "Twenty of our men were arrested in one day in one coast city for spitting on the sidewalk," said an angry CG official in Florida. "Nearly a dozen others were picked up at another Florida town on the pretext of minor infractions."[8]

The animosity toward the Coast Guard also led to arrests in Atlantic County, New Jersey. A CG cutter chased a shore runner, fired shots, and captured the boat. After boarding the vessel, the Guards found cases of liquor. This seemed like an open-and-shut case against the shore runner, but the county attorney chose to prosecute the

Coasties, too. He charged the Guards with abuse of authority for shooting at the rum-runner.[9]

After being arrested, a Guardsman often faced a hostile judge and jury when his case went to trial. "Commanding officers have had to protect their men from some of the courts," a newspaper reported. The federal courts were generally regarded as fairer than local jurisdictions. "Only the most vigorous measures in some instances have obtained federal court trials for accused Coast Guardsmen and thus assured them against being 'framed' or 'railroaded.'"[10]

Party, Party!

On more than one occasion, an incident that began well for the Coast Guard turned into a debacle. One triumph that turned sour began when a CG vessel pursued *Flor del Mar*, a sub chaser converted to a mother ship. To avoid capture, the *Flor del Mar* crew set their ship on fire and escaped in lifeboats. The Guardsmen did what they were trained to do: they fought the fire and saved the liquor freighter. Then they towed the vessel, with its four thousand cases of whiskey, to the CG station at New London.[11]

The damaged *Flor del Mar* was in danger of sinking at the pier, so the Guardsmen hastily removed the cases of liquor and stacked them in a storeroom onshore. At least a few of the Coasties found the liquor too tempting to resist. Many bottles disappeared during the transfer to the storeroom, and more vanished later. Predictably, the missing hooch showed up at parties, in speakeasies, and even on Navy destroyers. New London residents reported that liquor was flowing freely, and most of it bore the Golden Wedding label—the same as *Flor del Mar*'s cargo.[12]

The town buzzed with gossip about plastered Coasties. New London police were called to a boardinghouse to quell a drunken brawl among Guards, who admitted that their hooch came from *Flor del Mar*. The CG basketball team attended a party where the players broke training and drank their fill. After the party, drunken Coasties slugged it out with sailors from the nearby Navy base. Two men were seriously injured. The rowdy drinkers had imbibed booze from *Flor del Mar*.[13]

The CG brass moved quickly to punish the Guardsmen who broke the law. The first general court-martial began only days after *Flor del Mar*'s liquor disappeared. Fifteen Guards were charged with stealing confiscated cargo and/or possessing liquor on CG property. Two dozen more were charged with being under the influence. The accused faced serious punishment, including dishonorable discharge, up to ten days on bread and water, and a maximum of 30 days restriction.[14]

The Guardsmen at New London weren't the only ones who succumbed to the lure of free liquor. On a sunny Sunday afternoon, a CG cutter chased the rumrunner *Louise* along the South Florida coast. The Guards opened fire with their machinegun. When the Guards' bullets came too close, *Louise*'s skipper headed for the shore at Miami Beach. He knew the CG would stop shooting because the beach was crowded with people. He ran his boat aground, causing mild panic among the beachgoers. The rumrunners jumped out of the boat and quickly vanished.

When the CG captain saw that the rummers had escaped, he left two Guardsmen on the beach to secure the booze boat while he went back on patrol. For an unknown reason, the Guards decided to open a bottle of the liquor; perhaps they were simply thirsty. Some of the beachgoers wanted a taste, too, so more bottles were opened and passed around. After a while the Coasties dozed off. When they awoke, the entire cargo had disappeared! (Although the evidence of rumrunning had vanished, *Louise's* owner abandoned his boat and never came forward to reclaim it.)[15]

Tucker, a CG destroyer with a large crew, operated out of Key West, Florida. One night Guards on *Tucker* spotted the schooner *Conch Belle*, a known rumrunner, speeding from Gun Cay toward Miami. The Guards fired warning shots, but the schooner didn't stop. The CG skipper decided to escalate the battle; he ordered his gunners to shoot at the schooner's stern. *Conch Belle's* hull was soon riddled with bullet holes, and it began to take on water. The rumrunners surrendered.[16]

Conch Belle, heavily damaged and in danger of sinking, was securely tied up alongside *Tucker*. The CG skipper ordered his men to quickly transfer the cargo of two hundred burlocks to the destroyer before the schooner sank. A chain of Guards began relaying the burlocks of Canadian whiskey to *Tucker's* machine shop for safekeeping. It was a dark night with low visibility, so larcenous Guards seized the moment to open burlocks and steal bottles. As the sacks moved along the chain, the men found handy hiding places to stash bottles.[17]

When the cargo had been removed from *Conch Belle*, a count revealed that a substantial number of sacks hadn't made it all the way to *Tucker's* machine shop. The irate CG captain ordered his officers to conduct a search for the liquor. They did but found only a small fraction of the missing booze. The skipper threatened dire consequences, including courts-martial, if he didn't find two hundred burlocks in the machine shop when he arose the next morning. Then he retired to his cabin.[18]

In the morning, the captain learned that the machine shop still had a shortage of burlocks. He saw that many of his sailors appeared to be hung-over. Even worse, some were staggering drunk, incapable of doing their duty. The captain ordered his officers to conduct another, more thorough search for the liquor. This time they found bottles of booze under pillows and mattresses, behind the boilers, in the ventilator, in the paint locker, and in bilges under the turbines. In the commissary, they discovered bottles buried inside sacks of sugar and flour. In the vegetable lockers, onions and potatoes covered purloined whiskey. The officers even found bottles stashed in the bore of a deck gun and in the magazine hold where ammunition was stored. The sailors had actually tossed ammo overboard to make room for the booze![19]

Honor Guard

The media heavily influenced the public perception of the Coast Guard's efficacy in Volstead enforcement. The press printed reports favorable to the CG more often than unfavorable ones, but the negative stories tended to be more sensational. Malfeasance, corruption, and glaring ineptitude made exciting headlines on the front page. Scandals often generated long-term investigations and extended press coverage. Thus, they made a lasting impression on the public.

The cutter *Acushnet* battled rumrunners off the coast of Massachusetts and Rhode Island (Naval History and Heritage Command).

Counterbalancing the negative publicity, the media printed stories about honest Guards who served diligently and even heroically. Headlines trumpeted chases where the CG captured rum ships and seized big cargos of liquor. But these success stories were often undermined by the failure of the criminal court system. Most rumrunning cases never went to trial. Those that did tended to end with an acquittal or dismissal on technical grounds.

In all vocations, some individuals stand out because they go above and beyond the call of duty. Boatswain Alexander Cornell, who commanded 75-foot patrol boats, excelled at his job. Although the CG six-bitters weren't as fast as the contact boats, Cornell was an expert at outmaneuvering his prey. He captured at least ten notorious rumrunning vessels, including *Audrey B, Idle Hour, Penguin, High Strung, Yvette June, Vinces,* and *Black Duck*.[20]

On Christmas Eve 1930, Cornell scored a major coup despite horrendous weather. Driving sleet, gale-force winds, limited visibility, and rough seas made sailing dangerous around Long Island. However, rumrunners liked bad weather because it reduced the probability of getting caught. Shortly before midnight, Cornell sailed *CG-290* into Fort Pond Bay, Long Island. The six-bitter's searchlight penetrated the driving sleet to reveal hectic activity on a small pier. Men were transferring burlocks of liquor from a large shore runner, *Audrey B*, to bootleggers' trucks.

When the rummers saw the CG six-bitter, the *Audrey B* skipper maneuvered away from the pier, trying to make a run for open water. Cornell lowered armed men in a dinghy, telling them to seize the liquor on the pier. Then he ordered his gunner to fire *CG-290*'s one-pounder at the rum boat. He used *CG-290* to cut off *Audrey B*'s escape route, trapping the shore runner. With nowhere to run, the rumrunners surrendered.[21]

Law enforcement confiscated *Audrey B*, but that wasn't the end of the vessel's smuggling career. After *Audrey B*'s owners posted bond for the ship, it was released and sailed into international waters. The chronic offender picked up a cargo of liquor in Bermuda and traveled through the Panama Canal to Southern California. From that time until the end of Prohibition, *Audrey B* worked as a rumrunner on the West Coast.

In Florida, Boatswain Harvey Parry became a legend—a lone wolf praised by dry activists, hated by rumrunners. In less than a year he singlehandedly captured four booze boats, arrested their crews, and confiscated their liquor. He once jumped from a canal bridge onto the deck of a rum boat passing beneath him. The addled crewmen, too startled to resist arrest, immediately surrendered. In an incident that turned violent, Parry seized a booze boat at Caesar's Creek, arrested three men, and took them aboard his patrol boat as prisoners. When they tried to escape, a gunfight broke out. Bullets killed two of the prisoners, and the third suffered a gunshot wound.[22]

Once when Parry was driving along the beach, he saw a speedboat enter the channel at Dinnes Cay. When the motorboat moored alongside a skiff, he stopped his car because he suspected the sailors would transfer liquor from one vessel to the other. He waited onshore, watching as the rumrunners moved the cargo. When the skiff headed for the shore, Parry positioned himself to take action. He leapt aboard the boat when it reached shallow water. He didn't have his gun, so he had to fight with his fists. He quickly knocked one man into the water, destabilizing the skiff, which capsized. Parry landed in water up to his neck, but that didn't stop him from nabbing the rumrunners.[23]

Parry singlehandedly captured five men and two booze boats near Coconut Grove. Two trucks, three cars, and a shore crew were waiting for a load of liquor to arrive from Gun Cay. Parry kept watch, and in the wee hours of the morning, he saw a boat in the distance signal to the men on the beach. Then two boats, one towing the other, traveled through the narrow canal to the yacht basin. Parry jumped onto the first boat, took control at gunpoint, and ordered the skipper to sail to Miami. There he turned his prisoners and their illegal cargo over to Coast Guards on a patrol boat. A count of the cargo showed one thousand burlocks filled with bottles of liquor.[24]

Although Parry had street smarts, he was duped at least once. One night in Fort Lauderdale an informant told him about a load of liquor scheduled to land on the beach at 2:00 a.m. Well ahead of time, Parry went to the appointed place and hid so he could watch the landing. When he saw a vessel coming from the west, he assumed it was the booze boat. As he watched, someone sneaked up behind him and hit him with a blunt weapon, probably a blackjack. He fell on the beach, unconscious, and did not regain his senses until daylight. He caught no rumrunners that night.[25]

Not every honest Guardsman made headlines, but the press counterbalanced reports of corruption with stories of Guards who did their duty. One officer who refused bribes was Capt. Christopher Benham of Townsend's Inlet Coast Guard Station near Cape May. The skipper of *Mulhouse*, a liquor freighter, visited Benham and offered him $70,000 if he would "turn his back" while the rumrunners unloaded 35,000 cases of booze. The rummy skipper assured Benham that he would be a millionaire in less than a year if he would "get in the game." Benham flatly refused, saying he would choose poverty rather than betray his oath of service.[26]

Benham said he deserved no special credit for spurning the bribe. He knew numerous CG officers who had also rejected big bucks from rummers. "I thank God, for the Coast Guard men are true to their oath of allegiance," he said, "even if they are as poor as church mice."[27]

6

Volstead Enforcement
Tragedy and Controversy

On December 17, 1927, the Coast Guard destroyer *Paulding* was hunting for rum-runners near Provincetown, Massachusetts, on the northern tip of Cape Cod. Demand for liquor always soared during the winter holidays, and roughly three hundred booze boats were active off the New England coast.[1] CG vessels patrolled the waterways on a dry mission: protect Americans from potent, illegal Christmas cheer.

The waters in Cape Cod Bay were choppy that afternoon, but visibility was good. The *Paulding* commander ordered an ensign to keep the destroyer on a line parallel to two littoral buoys off Long Point. When the ensign noticed something protruding out of the water, he thought it was a "fish stick," a device used by fishermen to mark the location of their nets. Seconds later, the ensign realized that he was looking at a submarine's periscope. The commander, who also saw the periscope, reacted quickly to avoid a collision. He ordered "full speed astern" and sounded the general alarm.[2]

Only moments later *Paulding* rammed into the U.S. Navy's *S-4* submarine as it surfaced. *Paulding* hit the sub's conning tower, ripping a long hole in it. The force of the crash thrust *Paulding*'s bow up out of the water. Like the fin of a huge fish, *S-4*'s stern rose above the water and briefly hung there. Then the submarine rolled over and sank beneath the water's surface, its bow going down first. In only minutes the sub vanished in deep water roughly a mile offshore from the Wood End Coast Guard station.[3]

Paulding's radioman immediately sent out distress calls to summon help. The commander ordered the crew to launch a lifeboat. Guards hurriedly lowered the boat into the water to start the search for survivors. Only an oil slick and a little debris floated on the water's surface as evidence of the horrendous accident. To keep the search focused in the right area, *Paulding* dropped a buoy to mark the spot where *S-4* sank.[4]

The collision had crushed *Paulding*'s lower hull, causing serious damage and forcing the captain to head for shore to save his ship. He anchored the destroyer near the mudflats at Long Point Lighthouse. Water was rushing into the destroyer through a big hole in the lower hull, and the ship needed stopgap repairs to prevent flooding. Crewmen manned the pumps, working feverishly to keep the ship afloat.[5]

For hours the Guardsmen in *Paulding*'s lifeboat fought the choppy seas to stay afloat. As they shivered in the damp, cold air, they knew anyone fighting for life in the frigid waters wouldn't survive for long. Vessels from nearby Navy and Coast Guard bases hurried to the scene to join the rescue effort. In the waning daylight they searched but found no survivors in the water. If the *S-4* men were alive, they were trapped inside the sub.[6]

The disabled submarine carried five officers, 34 sailors, and a civilian draftsman who worked for the military. Navy officials said the men could survive for at least 40 hours inside the sub, so a rescue was feasible. Experts began formulating a plan, but the actual work couldn't begin until the necessary equipment arrived from bases in New London, Portsmouth, Boston, and New York City.[7]

After nightfall sailors in small boats kept watch, circling the spot where the submarine went down. People onshore could see the sailors' flares, bright pinpoints of light in the frigid, ominous darkness. A sub tender joined the flotilla of small boats and used its sounding devices, trying to communicate with the trapped crewmen. The *S-4* didn't respond. As the hours passed, more sub tenders, minesweepers, and Coast Guard cutters arrived, but the rescuers had to wait for daybreak, when operations would get underway in earnest.[8]

When morning came, Navy rescue divers plunged into the icy waters, looking for the disabled sub. They found it more than one hundred feet below the surface. The hull was smashed amidships; the stern and the battery room had heavy damage. Yet there was reason for optimism; the submarine was divided into six watertight sections and the forward compartments appeared to be intact.[9]

As the first step in the rescue plan, a diver attached an airline to the sub's forward ballast tanks, and a minesweeper used its powerful compressors to begin forcing air into the tanks. The experts planned to increase the sub's buoyancy, upend the bow, and use cranes to raise the vessel. Huge pontoons would be attached to keep the sub afloat while the rescuers drilled through the thick armor plate to cut an escape hole for the trapped men.[10]

Taps

To locate the men inside *S-4*, a diver went down to try communicating with them. Using a hammer, he tapped out Morse code on the sub's hull. He hammered again and again, moving slowly along the exterior, hearing nothing in response. Then he thought he heard a faint noise. As he strained to listen, he heard a noise from inside the sub's long, narrow torpedo room. He listened intently and caught snatches of sound. He hammered again.[11]

Tapping out dots and dashes, he asked, "How many are you?"

"Six," came the reply. "Please hurry."[12]

The diver, moving as fast as he dared, returned to the surface with his exciting news. Although the urgent need for a rescue could not be denied, experts said the trapped men could live for at least five days. To survive, they must keep their muscular activity to a minimum, moving as little as possible. They must also inhale shallowly, pacing their breathing at long intervals to conserve oxygen. A reporter likened this to performing Houdini's famous coffin trick.[13] But the sailors weren't magicians.

The second morning after the collision, bitter winter weather seriously hampered

This team of U.S. Navy divers tried to rescue the men trapped on the *S-4* submarine (National Archives and Records Administration).

the rescue effort. The temperature was 20 degrees, a northwest gale was blowing at 46 mph, and the seas were churning. A tug moving pontoons from the New York Navy Yard to the shipwreck had to stop at Buzzards Bay until the weather improved.[14]

Later that same day, Navy signalmen made another attempt to communicate with the trapped sailors. The submarine *S-8* used its oscillator signaling system to try to reach its sister ship. The men in the *S-4* torpedo room had no receiving equipment, so the *S-8* crew could only hope that their fellow sailors would somehow hear the signals, press their ears against the *S-4*'s metal hull, and understand the code. Defying the incredibly long odds, the two groups managed to communicate.[15]

"Is there any hope?" asked the men in the sunken sub.

"Yes, there is hope. Everything possible is being done," replied the operator in *S-8*.

About three hours later, the desperate men in the disabled *S-4* tapped out their question again, asking if they dared hope for a rescue. The *S-8* operator responded with a reassuring message, despite growing pessimism. The rescue effort was on hold due to the raging winds and rough seas. Even the big ships were rocking a little, buffeted by rolling waves and blustery, cold gusts of wind. The freezing water washed over the ships. Ice coated the decks, masts, derricks, funnels, and rigging. The sailors struggle to control their vessels, and rescue ships narrowly avoided colliding with one another.[16]

Almost 74 hours after *S-4* sank, the oscillator signaling system on the *S-8* picked up a very faint series of taps. The *S-8* signalmen couldn't make sense of the noise. They couldn't even be sure it came from the sunken vessel; yet the noise offered hope that someone was still alive on the *S-4*. Sadly, the bad weather continued to thwart the rescuers. A gale was forecast, so no relief was in sight.[17] The *S-4* torpedo room seemed destined to be a death chamber.

Four days after the crash, calmer weather finally allowed the rescue workers to resume operations. To pump fresh air into the *S-4* torpedo room, Navy divers worked in shifts, attempting to attach hose pipes to the sub's hull. Late at night they finally succeeded. A Navy tender began pumping clean air into the *S-4*. Once again there was reason for hope; the rescuers believed they could save their comrades.[18]

To reassure the trapped men in the torpedo room, Navy divers descended to the wreck, tapped out code on the sub's hull, and listened for a response. No one answered.[19]

Five days after *S-4* sank, Navy officials admitted they had no hope of rescuing anyone from the submarine. The mission changed from saving the trapped sailors to raising the wreck. The sense of urgency evaporated. Officials said the winter weather would hinder the salvage work, so *S-4* might remain on the bottom for weeks or even months. The grieving families faced prolonged agony.[20]

Three and a half weeks after *S-4* sank, divers tethered to a thick line descended to the shipwreck; they carried a dog wrench and an underwater light. After removing the external kingbolt that secured the strong-back, which supported the hatch, they entered the engine room. There they found three victims, who had drowned in the flooded compartment. These would be the first bodies carried to the surface. More bodies would be removed over the next few days, but others would remain in the sub until it was raised and towed to Boston.[21]

Authorities convened a Naval Court of Inquiry to investigate the tragic accident. *Paulding*'s commander stated that his vessel was hunting for rumrunners when the crash occurred. "We had knowledge that very day that one of our most astute enemies was in those waters," he said stiffly. He stated that the accident was "unavoidable" because he didn't see the *S-4* until moments before the crash. "Submarine signals described in the monthly pilot charts, warning us of submarines in the vicinity, were not displayed," he said.[22]

High-ranking Navy officers took the witness stand to give expert testimony. A submarine commander said that *S-4*, which had two periscopes up, should have seen the *Paulding* approaching several minutes before the crash. He also stated that *S-4* was traveling along a test course that had been used by subs for many years, even though it lay in the path of ships entering Provincetown Harbor from Cape Cod Bay. Navy officials admitted that *S-4* was not accompanied by a submarine tender, but they disagreed about whether an escort was necessary.[23]

After evaluating all the testimony, the Naval Court of Inquiry decided that the commanders of *S-4* and *Paulding* shared responsibility for the tragic accident. The court advised the Navy to publish more detailed pilot charts, to operate submarines "less obscurely," to improve safety procedures, and to acquire better rescue equipment. The court also found that the rear admiral who directed the rescue effort had mismanaged the mission. He was "unfitted to continue in command of the Control Force of the United States Fleet."[24]

The Naval Court of Inquiry's findings caused an uproar in Washington. Several Congressmen and top Cabinet officials expressed outrage. The Secretary of the Treasury objected to placing even part of the blame on the Coast Guard commander, because the absence of proper submarine warning signals had caused the collision. The Navy brass argued that the *S-4* captain had followed the correct procedures and the evidence didn't prove his guilt beyond a reasonable doubt. The court's harsh words about the rear admiral angered the Secretary of the Navy. He ordered the naval panel to reconvene and reconsider the whole case.[25]

Following orders, the Naval Court of Inquiry met and issued a new report. In a reversal that seemed to be dictated by politics, the court found that the rear admiral had acted properly and was fit for his command. The Secretary of the Navy indicated that he was highly pleased with the admiral's vindication and showed scant interest in other aspects of the case.[26]

The Coast Guard Board of Inquiry conducted its own investigation and issued an official report. After reviewing the evidence, the board placed "full responsibility" on the Navy because its flawed policies and procedures had caused the accident. The board

The American flag flies at half-mast as the *S-4* submarine is towed to port after colliding with *Paulding* (National Archives and Records Administration).

commended the CG commander for his leadership on that tragic afternoon. "The *Paulding* was keeping a sharp and efficient lookout as required by law, Coast Guard regulations, and the practice of seamen," said the report. "It was the duty of the *S-4*, under the international rules for the prevention of collisions at sea, to keep clear of the *Paulding*." Since *S-4* had its periscopes up, the Navy captain should have seen *Paulding* and avoided the crash. The Secretary of the Treasury, who had ultimate responsibility for Volstead enforcement, agreed with this assessment and put his stamp of approval on the report.[27]

Three months after *S-4* sank, the Navy finally raised the sub and towed it to the Boston Navy Yard. Naval personnel removed the bodies of the dead, including six inside the torpedo room. Chisels, wrenches, and other tools lay in the debris scattered throughout the sub. In the engine room, the tiller room, and the torpedo compartment, the walls bore marks and dents made by the trapped sailors trying to batter or cut their way out.[28]

Limited repairs were made to *S-4*, so it could be moved and used to test rescue procedures. On December 17, 1928, exactly one year after *S-4* sank, the vessel submerged again—this time in the Great Salt Pond, Block Island, south of Rhode Island. Crews and divers worked diligently to attach lines to *S-4*'s new lifting bolts, which would be used to raise it. At 3:37 p.m., they paused for a minute of silence to remember the men who had lost their lives in the disaster. Then they returned to their duties. After 49 hours of intense effort, *S-4* was lifted to the surface. Naval experts lauded the effort but said this would be too slow to save lives in the typical submarine disaster.[29]

The tragic, unnecessary deaths of the law-abiding, dutiful men on *S-4* intensified public debate about Prohibition enforcement. Many Americans felt strongly that no one should be killed in order to enforce a law of dubious value. Congressman Frederick Britten (R-IL), a member of the House Committee on Naval Affairs, called for appropriations to improve safety at sea. "Certainly, Yankee ingenuity and American gold should prevent another *S-4* disaster," he opined. He condemned the ruthless enforcement methods "employed in the interest of a fanatical law." He spoke for countless Americans when he said the *S-4* tragedy "causes us to wonder if Prohibition is worth this awful price."[30]

Black Duck

Black Duck, a speedy New England rumrunner, joined the Dry Fleet after gunplay led to tragedy, controversy, and scandal. Two days before New Year's Eve 1929, the Coast Guard captured *Black Duck* with a large cache of booze intended for the holiday market. Under normal circumstances, the public would have applauded the Coasties for their good work. But violence and misconduct turned the triumph into a fiasco.

In the wee hours of the morning, Boatswain Alexander Cornell was at the helm of *CG-290*, a six-bitter patrolling the eastern passage to Narragansett Bay, Rhode Island. Near the Dumpling Rock Bell Buoy, Cornell heard the distant, low roar of powerful engines. As the sound came closer, he peered into the foggy darkness and saw the outline of a speedboat moving swiftly, without lights. He focused *CG-290*'s searchlight on the boat and immediately recognized *Black Duck*, a chronic offender. The rummy vessel with dual 300-horsepower engines had outrun the Coast Guard many times.[31]

Black Duck was pulling a load of booze in a rowing dory behind the vessel. The crew had picked up nearly four hundred cases of liquor from the British oil screw *Symor*. If the Coast Guard came close enough to be a real threat, the *Black Duck* sailors would quickly untie the dory and launch it toward the beach. If the Guards boarded *Black Duck*, they would find no liquor and sail away. Then *Black Duck*'s crewmen would hurry to retrieve their floating cargo before someone else found it.[32]

Boatswain Cornell sounded his klaxon horn, signaling for *Black Duck* to stop. The defiant rummy skipper raced away. Cornell followed closely and hollered at the rum-runners, demanding that they surrender. *CG-290*'s searchlight swept over *Black Duck*'s deck, silhouetting figures in the pilothouse. Cornell ordered his gunner to fire warning shots with the Lewis light machinegun mounted on the foredeck. The gunner swung into action, and bullets flew over the water. In only a few seconds the machinegun spit out 21 rounds. Then it jammed.[33]

Boatswain Cornell peered into the darkness, searching for *Black Duck*, but he couldn't see it. Then at slow speed the booze boat emerged from a fog bank, coming toward *CG-290*. Cornell saw that *Black Duck* was moving erratically, yawing slowly, clearly in distress. Smoke billowed up from the rum boat's afterdeck; the engines ground to a halt. The Guards saw a man staggering around on *Black Duck*'s deck.[34]

When *Black Duck* bumped into *CG-290* on the starboard quarter, Guardsmen scampered onto the booze boat. They found a lifeless body on the deck near the wheel and two more dead men in the pilothouse. Only the skipper was alive, but he hadn't escaped bullet wounds. His arm was bleeding, and his thumb had been shot off. The gunfire had left bullet holes in the dory, the wheelhouse, and the engine hatch. Flames lapped at the burlap bags holding the dory's highly flammable cargo. The Guards reacted quickly, extinguishing the fire.[35]

Boatswain Cornell ordered his men to carry the *Black Duck*'s crew aboard *CG-290* and then tow the booze boat to Newport's Fort Adams. In Newport a doctor treated the wounded skipper. The other crewmen were pronounced dead. Coast Guardsmen searched both *Black Duck* and the rummer's clothing for weapons but found none.[36]

The deaths of the unarmed men on *Black Duck* infuriated wet activists. They accused the Guards of using unnecessary force and violating the CG's own rules of engagement. A regulation, issued several months before the incident, stated that machineguns must never be used to fire warning shots. Live machinegun fire must be used only with the intent to injure or kill. Thus, Cornell had erred by ordering his gunner to shoot the machinegun as a warning.[37]

Anti-Volstead sentiment engulfed New England, a region where rumrunning money supported many families. In a fiery sermon on New Year's Day, the minister at the Newport Seamen's Church Institute denounced the Coast Guard for killing unarmed men. He placed the ultimate blame squarely on dry fanaticism. "Let us not forget that those three men were murdered right off our shores," he said. They were "shot like rats in a trap, to satisfy frenzied fanaticism and smug hypocrisy."[38]

U.S. Senator David Walsh (D-MA) called for a thorough investigation of the *Black Duck* shooting to determine if the Guards had "exceeded their authority and used their official position to needlessly kill their fellow citizens." He said, "It is a murderous act to kill the unarmed whose attempted crime is aided and abetted and encouraged by overwhelming numbers of our citizens." The senator demanded that federal law officers be prohibited from using guns to enforce Volstead unless they knew with certainty that they were facing men with weapons.[39]

In Boston wet leaders held a mass meeting that drew an overflow crowd at historic Faneuil Hall. One speaker likened the *Black Duck* shooting to the killing of Crispus Attucks by the Redcoats in 1770. "The Constitution commands our respect, but the Eighteenth Amendment is inconsistent with the Constitution and deserves no respect whatsoever," declared a local politico. "When stark wholesale murder stalks abroad under the guise of any law, in God's name repeal that law!" An angry spokesman for the Liberal Civic League called the *CG-290* skipper a "miserable skunk" and accused him of failing to warn the rumrunners before ordering his gunner to shoot.[40]

Black Duck's crewmen were "bringing in liquor for New Year's Eve celebrations," said John Fitzgerald, former mayor of Boston and grandfather of future President John F. Kennedy. "They knew it would be consumed by governors of states, mayors of cities, selectmen of towns, judges of the Supreme Court, judges of the Superior Court and the Municipal Court—in fact, by public officials everywhere," he said. He called the incident a "murderous shooting" and claimed that the Guards had no right to fire at *Black Duck*.[41]

After listening to the speakers, the irate crowd passed a resolution urging President Hoover to order "a thorough and searching investigation into the facts surrounding this deplorable incident." They demanded an impartial probe that would not be a "whitewash." Then the angry wets poured out of Faneuil Hall onto Boston Common, where an unlucky petty officer manned a Coast Guard recruiting booth. The wets tore down his recruiting posters and threatened him but stopped short of attacking him. He fled in a taxi.[42]

For months after the tragic shooting, Boatswain Cornell and the *CG-290* crewmen received death threats. A group of men threw stones at the houseboat where the Cornell family lived. The attack terrified Mrs. Cornell and her children, who were alone on the boat moored at a wharf in New London, Connecticut. In another incident, a gang of thugs "bent on avenging" the deaths on the *Black Duck* attacked two Guardsmen near the New London CG base.[43]

The heated debate over *Black Duck* focused on the rationale for firing the machine-gun. Wet leaders stated that the rumrunners were attempting to surrender when the Guards opened fire. However, Boatswain Cornell said that *Black Duck* was running away. He insisted that he had acted properly when he ordered warning shots. Rear Admiral Frederick Billard, the Coast Guard commandant, defended Cornell's decision to shoot. "The Coast Guard has the job of stopping liquor smuggling at sea," he said. "It is not a job that can be handled with soft words and amiable gestures."[44]

Coast Guard investigators examined the bullet holes on *Black Duck*, looking for evidence to justify the shootings. They found that the bullets had struck at an oblique angle, coming from behind on the rum boat's starboard side. The bullets' trajectory seemed to show that the CG gunner had not fired warning shots intended to miss *Black Duck*. Rather, he had fired directly at the booze boat, trying to cripple it. Moreover, when the bullets hit, *Black Duck* was not running away from *CG-290* but was headed toward it.[45]

The Coast Guard released a report putting the best possible spin on the bullet-hole evidence. The document stated that *Black Duck* had been fleeing and had turned hard left at the wrong moment, putting it directly in the line of fire. Investigators had found bullet holes in the tender on the afterdeck, the after hatch, the rear door and walls of the wheelhouse, and the pilothouse windshield. The CG rejected the argument that the rumrunners were killed while trying to surrender.[46]

The controversial nature of the shooting guaranteed that there would be more than one inquiry. Rhode Island's attorney general held an inquest, and a special grand jury was convened to review the evidence. After hearing 22 witnesses, the jurors declined to indict Boatswain Cornell or his crew. The same grand jury evaluated rumrunning charges against the *Black Duck* skipper, the only rummer who survived the shooting. The panel decided not to indict him. A special Treasury Department committee investigated the *Black Duck* incident and concluded that "the Coast Guard patrol boat acted within the law when fire was opened up on the smuggler."[47]

The headlines about *Black Duck* turned it into a tourist attraction. A crowd gathered to see the boat after the CG towed it into the harbor at Providence, Rhode Island. A customs guard, who had a "spotless record," was assigned to keep the sightseers at bay. Unfortunately, he had a cold that he was treating with medicinal whiskey. He wobbled when he walked. He staggered around and fell, breaking a bottle of whiskey and staining his uniform. With difficulty he got to his feet to resume his guard duties. To assert his power, he brandished his service revolver and another pistol. Waving his guns, he threatened to shoot the crowd. He poked terrified sightseers in the stomach with the muzzle of a gun.[48]

The inebriated guard made his way to a telephone, called the Treasury Department field office, and demanded reinforcements to help him protect *Black Duck* from hijackers. He claimed he had already repulsed one hijacking attempt. Policemen and a Customs Service official responded to his call for help. The customs official quickly assessed the situation, suspended the guard, and told him to go "sleep it off." Later, the Customs Service gave the guard a chance to defend himself, but he "offered no denial of his reprehensible conduct."[49]

The Coast Guard brass decided that *Black Duck* would be a valuable addition to the Dry Navy. Repainted and rechristened *CG-808*, the former booze boat became the pursuer instead of the pursued. Equipped with one-pounders and Browning machineguns, *CG-808* patrolled the waters of Narragansett Bay and the Sakonnet River. On occasion, it was deployed to chase rumrunners at sea.[50]

From time to time *CG-808* sailed into the media spotlight. *Good Luck*, one of the fastest contact boats on the East coast, made headlines when it outran *CG-808* in a chase near Newport, Rhode Island A few months later, the Guards on *CG-808* captured *Mardelle*, a speedboat with a cargo of liquor. The gunner on *CG-808* peppered *Mardelle* with machinegun bullets, wounding a rumrunner and setting the boat on fire. The *Mardelle* gunfight occurred very near where the *Black Duck* crewmen had been shot.[51]

The speedboat *Artemis* was a fast shore runner that often outran the Coast Guard vessels. One summer night when *CG-808* was patrolling Long Island Sound, the Guards heard the low rumble of diesel motors in the distance. The CG skipper ordered his crew to cut the engines, douse the lights, and drift. When the diesel sound came closer, the Guards trained a spotlight on the vessel, which they recognized as their familiar foe *Artemis*.[52]

Relying on its superior speed, *Artemis* raced toward *CG-808*, rammed into the bow, ripped a hole in the cutter, and roared away. The CG captain ordered his crew to fire at the fleeing vessel. The *CG-808* machinegun quickly spit out more than five hundred rounds. The bullets damaged the shore runner but didn't stop it. *Artemis* sped into the darkness, leaving the Coasties behind.[53]

In the following days, Guardsmen went looking for the damaged speedboat and found it in a boatyard at Port Jefferson, Long Island. The hull had already been repaired, but evidence of the battle littered the boatyard. The Guards found planking riddled with bullet holes and a plank torn off *CG-808* when *Artemis* rammed it. Law enforcement had enough evidence to arrest *Artemis'* owner and crew. When the rumrunners came to the boatyard to reclaim their property, they were taken into custody. Subsequently, they were indicted and convicted in federal court. After the government impounded *Artemis* and put it up for sale, a rumrunner purchased it. The speedboat rejoined the Whiskito Fleet, and the familiar cycle of the Rum War went on.[54]

Far from Alone

During the Rum War, few battles generated as much controversy as the fight between the U.S. Coast Guard and *I'm Alone*, a mother ship built in Canada and registered as a British vessel. Three days of combat in March 1929 ignited a firestorm that didn't subside until January 1935, more than a year after Prohibition had ended.

I'm Alone was a sleek, two-masted knockabout schooner with twin engines and cargo space for six thousand cases of liquor. It was among the first rumrunning vessels equipped with illegal radio transmitters to keep in touch with onshore stations along the U.S. coast. The radio operators onboard and ashore used code to exchange information about rendezvous points, the position of Coast Guard cutters, and other vital matters.[55]

For several years *I'm Alone* sailed on the Atlantic Ocean, hauling liquor from St. Pierre to spots along the New England Coast and as far south as the Virginia Capes. With some regularity, observers spotted it in the waters off Boston. The schooner assiduously stayed beyond the rum line, preventing the Coast Guard from capturing it. However, international law allowed CG cutters to picket *I'm Alone* to keep contact boats from picking up liquor.[56]

On one trip *I'm Alone* experienced engine trouble off the coast of Massachusetts. The crew couldn't fix the problem, and the schooner's fuel supply ran low. The captain feared that his vessel would be confiscated if he went into a Massachusetts port for repairs. He dumped his liquor cargo into the ocean and returned to St. Pierre. After this substantial financial loss, the owner decided to sell *I'm Alone*.[57]

Prohibition officials noted changes in *I'm Alone's* operations and suspected that it had been sold. The schooner had a new captain, John Thomas Randell, an experienced seaman and decorated veteran of the British Royal Navy. With Randell at the helm, *I'm Alone* shifted its base of operations to the Gulf of Mexico, sailing to nearby Belize or distant St. Pierre whenever the liquor supply had to be restocked.[58]

Typically, *I'm Alone* rode at anchor off the coast of Louisiana, and contact boats came out to pick up booze. After the shore runners landed the liquor, bootleggers took it to Abbeville or Gueydan, Louisiana, where it was hidden in shipments of rice in railroad freight cars. The railcars took the booze to Chicago, New York City, or another urban market.

In March 1929 Randell planned to rendezvous with contact boats at a point south of Trinity Shoal, off the coast of Louisiana below Marsh Island. After sailing *I'm Alone* to the designated site, he waited for the contact boats to come out. He was annoyed when the Coast Guard cutter *Wolcott* appeared and began picketing *I'm Alone*. For two days the CG cutter stayed close to the rumrunner, scaring away the contact boats.[59]

Frustrated, Randell decided to leave in order to shake the Coast Guard cutter. He cruised to Belize, then sailed east to Nassau, and finally returned to the rendezvous spot off Trinity Shoal. The CG cutters were busy elsewhere, so *I'm Alone* was alone and shore runners came out to buy liquor.[60]

At daybreak on March 20, the CG cutter *Wolcott* reappeared, steaming toward *I'm Alone*. When Randell spotted the cutter, he set sail, putting the mother ship on a southerly course. The CG captain checked his position and pinpointed it at 10.8 miles from shore, within the rum line. He then hailed Randell via megaphone and asked permission to board the mother ship.[61]

"You can shoot and sink me," Randell bellowed, "but I'll be damned if you will board me!"[62]

The CG skipper hoisted flags on the signal halyard, ordering *I'm Alone* to heave to. Defiantly, Randell yelled that he would shoot any Guardsman who tried to board his ship. The CG captain ordered his crew to man the deck gun and to hand out the small firearms, including a Thompson submachine gun.[63]

After the Guards fired blank shots at the mother ship's bow, Randell decided not to fight. He shouted that the CG skipper could climb aboard if he came unarmed. Leaving his weapon behind, the Guard commander boarded *I'm Alone* and advised Randell to surrender. The rumrunner refused. Choosing to err on the side of caution, the CG skipper returned to *Wolcott*. *I'm Alone* sailed south, with the CG cutter following it.[64]

The CG skipper awaited orders from his superiors and, via radio, received permission to "use all force to seize" *I'm Alone*. Once again he hailed Randell and ordered the mother ship to stop, but the rumrunning captain refused. The CG skipper warned Randell that the Guards would start firing if he didn't surrender in the next 15 minutes.

When the time limit expired, the gunners on *Wolcott* opened fire with blanks. The Thompson submachine gun spit out wax bullets. One hit Randell in the thigh, causing him acute pain, but he didn't surrender. The Guards switched to firing live rounds aimed over the deck. Bullets ripped through the schooner's sails and tore holes in the Union Jack. *I'm Alone* sailed on, with *Wolcott* following, until the vessels were more than two hundred miles south of the Mississippi Delta.[65]

The weather turned nasty, a middling gale blew in, and the sea was choppy. *Wolcott's* skipper sent an update on the battle to division headquarters: "Will not allow black to escape. Will try again to seize her when weather improves. Have shot through sails, also British flag.... Master appears desperate. Have not enough men to board her. Will take long chance if other boats do not arrive tomorrow."[66]

The next morning another CG cutter, *Dexter*, appeared on the southwest horizon, coming to *Wolcott's* aid. *Dexter's* skipper ordered *I'm Alone* to heave to. By semaphore and megaphone, Randell replied that *Dexter* had no jurisdiction over the mother ship. With bravado befitting a booze buccaneer, he yelled that the Guards could commence firing whenever they wanted.[67]

Dexter's crew fired warning shots with blanks and then changed to live ammunition. The Guardsmen shot at *I'm Alone's* sails before aiming at the hull. Roughly four hundred rounds of small-arms fire shredded the deck house and bulkheads on the mother ship. The Guards' deck gun blew a hole in *I'm Alone's* hull below the waterline under the forward mast. The engine room flooded. *I'm Alone* couldn't stay afloat much longer.

Captain Randell ordered his crew to abandon ship. Then he went over the side, too. He grabbed a cabin door floating on the water and clung to it, bobbing in the water. *Dexter* picked up the rummy crew, including the captain. When the Guards hauled the rumrunners aboard, they discovered that one sailor was unconscious and couldn't be revived.[68]

The Coast Guard cutters carried *I'm Alone's* crew to New Orleans. The customs service took custody of the men, who were held under heavy guard in the Orleans Parish Prison. American civil and military officials interrogated them; so did the British vice consul at New Orleans. U.S. Attorney General William Mitchell defended the Coast Guard for sinking *I'm Alone*. Nevertheless, he ordered the rummy crew's release. The sailors were small fry, and Mitchell knew that prosecuting them would anger both Ottawa and London.[69] As the situation developed, releasing the sailors wasn't enough to avert an international uproar.

Because *I'm Alone* sank far outside the rum line, Ottawa and London accused the Coast Guard of violating the international treaty that allowed the Dry Navy to enforce Volstead on the high seas. U.S. military officials argued that *Wolcott* had first confronted *I'm Alone* inside the rum line. When Randell had refused to heave to, the rules of engagement allowed the CG cutter to chase the rumrunner, even beyond U.S. territorial waters. The U.S. State Department supported the Coast Guard, saying that it had complied with the international treaty.[70]

The Canadian government conceded that *I'm Alone* "had unquestionably been engaged for a number of years, under various owners, in endeavoring to smuggle liquor into the United States." Nevertheless, Ottawa filed a formal protest in Washington, arguing that "the essential elements of the international doctrine of 'hot pursuit' were lacking." In Ottawa's view, the Coast Guard had violated the international laws governing a chase on the high seas. *Dexter's* role in the battle was clearly illegal. Even if *Wolcott* had first confronted *I'm Alone* within the rum line, *Dexter* joined the chase far out at sea, calling into question its right to shoot at the Canadian vessel. Ottawa argued that sinking *I'm Alone* constituted "too severe" a remedy under the terms of the treaty. Washington and Ottawa agreed to appoint arbiters to review the incident and resolve the dispute.[71]

Meanwhile, federal investigators searched for the owners of *I'm Alone*. Since black-ship owners went to great lengths to hide their identity, they weren't easy to track down. The New Orleans Customs Bureau uncovered a series of coded telegrams that appeared to be messages sent from *I'm Alone* to a rum ring in New York City. After a crypto-analyst decoded the messages, Prohibition agents found the black ship's owners, Marvin Clark and Dan Hogan, U.S. citizens who had used a straw man to obtain British registry for *I'm Alone*. Clark signed an affidavit admitting that he was part owner of the mother ship. He seemed willing to help the feds, but someone murdered him to ensure that he didn't talk too much.[72]

Federal attorneys struggled to find enough evidence to convict Dan Hogan of heading the rum ring. Their case improved when two rumrunners agreed to testify against him. The men had their own legal problems and hoped to reduce their punishment by cooperating with the feds. Hogan stood trial in two separate cases related to *I'm Alone*—first in Lake Charles and later in Opelousas, Louisiana. He was convicted of conspiring to smuggle liquor into the United States and sentenced to federal prison.[73]

After exchanging many official memoranda, the international arbiters finally convened to settle the dispute over *I'm Alone*. Ottawa demanded $386,000 in compensation because the vessel had flown the Union Jack, even though the true owners were U.S. rumrunners. In international law, American ownership reduced the severity of the incident to a "flag insult," which could be settled by a formal apology and a cash indemnity.[74]

After reviewing the evidence, the arbiters decided that Washington owed Canada an official apology plus monetary compensation of $50,666. The ruling stated that "the United States ought formally to acknowledge its illegality and to apologize to His Majesty's Canadian government." The arbiters specified that the cash settlement would be shared by the Canadian government, the surviving *I'm Alone* crewmen, and the deceased sailor's heirs. On January 21, 1935, U.S. Secretary of State Cordell Hull issued a formal apology to Canada. He promised to send a check as soon as Congress appropriated money to pay the cash judgment.[75]

In the aftermath of the controversy, the Coast Guard cutter *Dexter* was transferred to the U.S. Navy and stationed in Buffalo, New York. After it was decommissioned in 1936, civilians bought it and sailed it on the Great Lakes. Although *Dexter* was famous for enforcing Prohibition, the vessel became *Buccaneer*, a pirate-themed party boat with a well-stocked bar. In 2010 *Dexter/Buccaneer* was scuttled, going to its final resting place at the bottom of Lake Michigan.[76]

7

Bill McCoy
Rumrunning Pioneer

Bill McCoy looked exactly like a rumrunner should look. He was tall, lean, and sinewy. He had alert eyes, a sly smile, and the tanned, leathery skin of a man who worked outdoors. "He has a strong face, with clear gray eyes that never flinch," an admirer wrote. "Altogether, he is what the novelists would call a rugged fellow, and the tan of the sea and the tropical sun is embedded deep within his cuticle."[1]

McCoy was a skilled sea captain with enough grit to command a crew through the roughest storm or battle. He had a reputation as a square shooter, a man who kept his word. He treated his crewmen fairly and paid them a decent wage; in return, he expected them to be loyal and to follow orders. He had great respect for lawmen who didn't take bribes. Utter contempt for those who did.

William Frederick "Bill" McCoy was born in Upstate New York in 1877. He seemed to inherit wanderlust from his father, who had served in the Union Navy during the Civil War. The elder McCoy stirred Bill's imagination when he recounted his seafaring exploits during the war. After the McCoy family moved to Philadelphia, young Bill spent many hours watching the boat traffic along the Delaware River. He attended the Pennsylvania Nautical School and trained aboard USS *Saratoga*. For several years he served on merchant marine ships. Then he settled down in Florida and went into the boat business at Holly Hill, near Daytona Beach.[2]

In a boatyard on the Halifax River, William F. McCoy and Company built superior watercraft. McCoy's clientele included millionaires Andrew Carnegie, Frederick Vanderbilt, and John Wanamaker. In addition to building boats, Bill McCoy partnered with his brother Ben to operate motorboats carrying freight and passengers. The McCoy Brothers' Indian River Line ran from West Palm Beach to Daytona and St. Augustine. Their Everglade Line took inland waterways from Palm Beach to Ft. Myers through the Everglades, Lake Okeechobee, and the Caloosahatchee River.[3] This business prospered for a time but waned as Florida built better highways and bus service became more reliable.

Shortly after Volstead became the law of the land, a boat owner tried to hire Bill McCoy to sail liquor cargos from the Bahamas to the United States. McCoy declined because he didn't like the man's shabby old boat. However, he found the idea intriguing because he had reached a point in his life where he needed a change. A series of unfortunate events had left him restless and lonely. His wife had walked out on him. His widowed mother had recently passed. His devoted, beloved dog had died. He needed purpose and excitement in is life, so he decided to return to his first love—the sea.[4] Rumrunning would supply all the adventure he desired and also make him rich.

When Bill McCoy embarked on his new career in rumrunning, he recruited his brother Ben to help. Bill sailed the ships; Ben handled the business on land. Both became nomads. Bill spent most of his time in Nassau or at sea. Ben moved around to be near Bill's mother ships in the Northeast. He handled the money and kept the ships supplied with necessities, like food and fresh water.

In August 1920 Bill McCoy purchased a fishing schooner, *Henry L. Marshall*, in Gloucester, Massachusetts. He transferred ownership to Charles Albury, a British subject who claimed residence in Nassau. Subsequently, Albury switched *Henry L. Marshall* from U.S. to British registry. Despite the transfer, McCoy retained control of the vessel. The exact nature of his agreement with the new "owner" was secret, but Albury probably received a share of *Henry L. Marshall*'s profits in return for being the straw man.[5]

Before Prohibition, Albury had served as chairman of Nassau's development board. During the Twenties he lived in Miami, where he became a partner in a shipping firm. The company, which specialized in the Florida-Bahamas trade, grew at a rapid pace. Authorities suspected that contraband liquor accounted for the firm's big profits. An investigation led to Albury's indictment on Volstead conspiracy charges, but the case was dismissed on a technicality.[6]

To launch *Henry L. Marshall*'s smuggling career, McCoy took a load of liquor from the Bahamas to St. Catherine's Sound near Savannah, Georgia. The man who bankrolled the shipment assured McCoy that he had arranged to keep law enforcement away from *Henry L. Marshall*. While the booze cargo was being unloaded, McCoy spotted a Coast Guard cutter. He watched warily as the cutter passed by without stopping. On that first trip, McCoy made $15,000—more than the average American earned in six years. His rumrunning venture was off to a stellar start.[7]

McCoy quickly made a name for himself in the rumrunning game. Bootleggers sought his services, and he contracted with a group to deliver a cargo of booze to Norfolk, Virginia. He picked up the liquor in Bimini and sailed *Henry L. Marshall* to the rendezvous spot. But the buyers had changed their plans. They said his liquor was too expensive for the small-town markets in Virginia, so they wanted him to take it to New York. He obliged, and they paid him with a $15,000 bank draft.[8]

When a rum ring wanted McCoy to transport five thousand cases from Nassau to New York, he had a problem because *Henry L. Marshall* couldn't carry that much booze. However, he was making money, so he felt a second boat would be a sound investment. He didn't shop around because he knew the vessel he wanted. On a trip to Gloucester, he had seen *Arethusa*, a three-jibbed fishing schooner named for a mythological nymph. McCoy loved *Arethusa*'s graceful lines and low, sleek oak hull. Luckily for him, the schooner was on the market because the owners had gone bankrupt. He snapped it up at a bargain price, paying cash with his rumrunning money.[9]

While McCoy sailed his new schooner, he chartered *Henry L. Marshall* to an acquaintance who used Atlantic City, New Jersey, as a rumrunning base. Under the new captain, *Henry L. Marshall* smuggled liquor from the Bahamas to the Northeast. Bill's brother Ben went to Atlantic City for an extended stay, to keep an eye on their new rumrunning colleague. Ben probably knew that he wasn't the only one watching *Henry L. Marshall.* Lawmen kept it under surveillance, too, because they wanted to prove it was a black ship.[10]

In the summer of 1921 a large number of liquor freighters were doing business off the New Jersey shore. The Coast Guard ordered the cutter *Seneca* to picket the mother ships, especially *Henry L. Marshall,* because lawmen had seen contact boats buying liquor from it. One day *Seneca* spotted *Henry L. Marshall* and headed toward it, even though the schooner was positioned beyond the rum line, flying the British flag. When the rum-runners saw *Seneca* coming, they began throwing cases of liquor overboard. As the Coast Guards watched, the rummers put a small motorboat over the side. The captain and first mate climbed into the launch and sped away.[11]

When the Guardsmen boarded the schooner, they found all the crew, except one man, totally intoxicated. The drunken sailors were rowdy but didn't resist arrest. They readily confessed that they had brought a cargo of liquor from the Bahamas. Despite their clumsy attempt to toss the evidence into the sea, the Guards found a large quantity of whiskey onboard. *Seneca*'s commander placed a prize crew aboard *Henry L. Marshall* and towed it into port.[12]

New Jersey authorities moved quickly to procure arrest warrants for the rumrunning skipper and his crew. They also planned to arrest three men reputed to own the schooner and its cargo. They identified the trio as Bill McCoy, John Crosland, and Dr. Holden (first name unknown). Crosland was a millionaire fish wholesaler in Miami, but author-ities believed much of his wealth came from the illegal liquor traffic. They suspected that he had bankrolled *Henry L. Marshall*'s recent rumrunning trips.[13]

The seizure of *Harry L. Marshall* quickly became an international issue because the schooner was a British vessel captured outside the rum line. Legal experts argued over whether the Coast Guard had violated U.S. and/or international law by capturing the mother ship. Despite this controversy, federal prosecutors indicted Crosland and McCoy for conspiracy to violate the Volstead act. According to the indictment, the conspiracy had begun six months earlier in Jacksonville, Florida.[14]

Lawmen couldn't find McCoy to arrest him, but they had better luck locating the millionaire fish mogul. After Crosland was arrested in Miami, he fought extradition and used other delaying tactics to avoid trial. He was eventually transported to New Jersey for his day in court, where he was convicted on Volstead charges. He appealed all the way to the U.S. Supreme Court, which refused to hear his case. After serving a short term in the federal prison in Atlanta, he returned to the business world as president of the Miami Fish and Ice Company.[15]

Despite the international uproar over the seizure of *Henry L. Marshall,* the Treasury Department formally confiscated the ship and its liquor cargo. Treasury filed writs asking the federal district court to order the sale of the schooner and cargo. The district court obliged, the U.S. Circuit Court of Appeals affirmed the decision, and the ship went on the auction block. Bill McCoy sent a surrogate to the government auction, where he paid the hefty sum of $3,000 to reclaim *Henry L. Marshall.* McCoy then sold the schooner to a friend in the fishing business in Massachusetts.[16]

Years later, McCoy explained why *Henry L. Marshall* had been seized. He said his chartered schooner "was manned by a crew and officer with little discipline, who ran liquor off Atlantic City." He called the captain "a cheater" and the crew "a bunch of bad men." He said, "Owing to the fact that there was little discipline aboard, these men were arrested in a drunken condition." The man who leased *Henry L. Marshall* had contracted to sell his liquor cargo to "a political group in New Jersey for $40 a case." However, another buyer offered $60 per case, so the man reneged on his contract. To get revenge, the politicos arranged for the Coast Guard to capture *Henry L. Marshall*, even if the mother ship stayed outside the rum line.[17]

Catching McCoy

After buying *Arethusa*, McCoy spent a substantial sum to customize the vessel for rumrunning. He installed a powerful auxiliary motor for speed and refurbished the fish pens to maximize the cargo space. He mounted a Colt-Browning machinegun on the deck, in case pirates tried to hijack him. In order to transfer the schooner from U.S. to

The Coast Guards on the cutter *Seneca* captured rumrunner Bill McCoy on *Arethusa*, his favorite schooner (Naval History and Heritage Command).

British registry, he formed the Ocean Trading Company of Halifax, Nova Scotia, with a British subject as his partner. Officially the vessel was renamed *Tomoka*, but McCoy continued to call it *Arethusa*. So did most everybody else.[18]

McCoy anchored *Arethusa* beyond the rum line off Noman's Land, a tiny island south of Massachusetts, in the summer of 1921. After fishermen spotted the sleek, handsome *Arethusa*, the news spread quickly in the seafaring towns. Customers sailed out to buy liquor, and local yachtsmen went to take a look at McCoy's pride and joy. "She is certainly a beautiful craft, trim, well-fitted, well-handled," a sailor told a reporter.[19]

McCoy sold hooch to all comers, whether they were ordinary citizens or bootleggers. A newsman, who hitched a boat ride out to *Arethusa*, joined the steady stream of visitors. After waiting his turn, he climbed aboard and looked over the cargo, which included brandy, cognac, champagne, and several types of whiskey. Burlocks of liquor were piled high in the "whiskey room." The reporter found that he could buy scotch by the bottle, but Irish whiskey was sold by the case only. He could also purchase a barrel of whiskey or a single drink served by a "sailor bartender."[20]

The waters "off New Bedford were never so alive with small craft of all kinds, most of them carrying customers," a reporter wrote. Some of *Arethusa*'s customers bought liquor to replenish their personal stock. Others loaded their boats with hundreds of burlocks for resale. *Arethusa* was supplying Block Island, Martha's Vineyard, New Bedford, and Fall River "with what the residents of those places seem to want the most," stated a Boston paper. Drinkers in Rhode Island were also guzzling booze from *Arethusa*.[21]

Federal Prohibition agents in Boston heard about *Arethusa* but didn't try to seize the floating liquor store. A newsman asked why the federal authorities were ignoring the rumrunner. A Prohibition administrator replied that he didn't have a "floating force" to patrol the seas; his agents enforced Volstead on land.[22]

Since Boston's federal Prohibition Unit didn't have boats, the agents worked onshore to stop the flow of liquor from McCoy's ship. They raided speakeasies and other sites in coastal towns, hunting for rum brought ashore from *Arethusa*. Only one raid yielded any booze—a mere 20 quarts of whiskey, although thousands had been landed.[23]

The collector of customs in Boston said he didn't have "definite proof" that *Arethusa* was smuggling liquor. Then he went a step further and questioned whether *Arethusa* actually existed. He declared that a "thorough search" in waters near New Bedford had found "no sign of any vessel answering to the description of the *Arethusa*." Moreover, customs inspectors had failed to uncover "any evidence showing any wholesale landing of liquor" in or around New Bedford. The collector called the reports about *Arethusa* "propaganda ... at least ninety percent fiction and imagination."[24]

Despite the collector's skepticism about *Arethusa*, dry activists clamored for law enforcement to stop the liquor sales. In response to public pressure, federal officials sent the revenue cutter *Ossipee* to search for McCoy's mother ship. Customs inspectors expected to find *Arethusa* off Martha's Vineyard, but they couldn't locate it. Two days later Dry Navy vessels caught up with *Arethusa* near Thatcher's Island off Cape Ann. But McCoy had sold all his booze, so he couldn't be arrested. He sailed away to pick up another load.[25]

McCoy was raking in the money, so he decided to expand his liquor business. He bought three more boats and chartered them to other rumrunners. But he hit a jarring bump in the road when the government seized two of his chartered ships. The revenue cutter *Taylor* captured *M.M. Gardner* off the coast of Long Branch, New Jersey, even though it had British registry, flew the Union Jack, and was outside the rum line. The ship's papers showed that it had sailed from Nassau with two thousand cases of liquor and had sold almost the entire cargo. When the revenue men searched the liquor freighter, they found $50,886 in gold. (By demanding payment in gold or silver, a rumrunner avoided the risk of being paid with counterfeit money.)[26]

After keeping *M.M. Gardner* in custody for almost two months, Washington admitted that it had been seized outside the rum line. London demanded the ship's release, and Washington obliged.[27] *M.M. Gardner* was soon back on Rum Row. The government had better luck with McCoy's other captured charter boat. The feds formally confiscated the ship and put it up for auction. McCoy paid $20,000 to buy it back.

Due to the setbacks with his charter boats, McCoy had cash flow problems. To turn a quick profit, he sailed *Arethusa* to Nassau, bought a liquor cargo, and took it to Rum Row off Fire Island Lightship. Sales were slow so he moved down the coast to a point off New Jersey's Highlands. Despite bad weather, he quickly sold all his liquor at this new stand, replenishing his cash reserves.[28]

McCoy regularly anchored *Arethusa* on Rum Row at Ambrose Lightship, even during the winter when harsh weather increased the risk. In January 1923 nasty weather forced the liquor freighters to abandon Rum Row. Severe storms followed one another in rapid succession, making it impossible for the contact boats to take liquor ashore. The bad weather forced McCoy to leave Rum Row before he sold all his liquid cargo. Even so, the trip added $127,000 to his cash assets.[29]

McCoy called the summer of 1923 "the busiest and happiest" part of his rumrunning career. *Arethusa*'s roundtrips between Nassau and Rum Row ran on a regular schedule: one week to load the cargo, one week to sail to Liquor Lane, one week to sell the booze, and one week for the return trip to the Bahamas. To satisfy customs regulations, officials in Nassau cleared *Arethusa*'s alcoholic cargo for shipment to Halifax, Nova Scotia. When McCoy returned to Nassau, he signed an affidavit stating that he had changed his plans and sold his cargo at sea without stopping in Halifax or any other port.[30]

McCoy's success in the rumrunning game made him a celebrity of sorts—a wily booze buccaneer who always sailed away with a safe full of money. His notoriety also made him a high-value target for the lawmen who enforced Volstead. The Treasury Department assigned undercover agents to watch his ships and track his movements. He had fun outsmarting the federal agents and outrunning the government boats sent to capture him. But formidable forces were arrayed against him.

Arethusa rode at anchor near Sea Bright, New Jersey, in November 1923. McCoy had sold four thousand cases of whiskey and had only two hundred left to sell. Acting on information from federal agents, the Coast Guard sent two vessels, *Seneca* and *Lexington*, to hunt for McCoy's schooner.[31]

After several days of searching, *Lexington* sighted *Arethusa* and radioed *Seneca*, which zeroed in on the target. The *Seneca* skipper hailed *Arethusa* and ordered McCoy to heave to, so Guardsmen could board the schooner. *Seneca* launched a surfboat with an armed boarding party, led by Lt. L.W. Perkins, to take control of *Arethusa*. McCoy sped away, leaving the surfboat behind. The *Seneca* skipper called his gun crew to quarters and cast loose the number one gun. After warning shots, he ordered McCoy to permit the boarding party to climb aboard *Arethusa*. McCoy allowed Lt. Perkins to come onboard while the rest of his party waited in the surfboat. Perkins signaled that he had control of *Arethusa*, so *Seneca's* skipper headed to port, expecting the rumrunner to follow.[32]

Seneca sailed toward Ambrose Lightship, but *Arethusa* didn't follow. To the Guards' surprise, McCoy's gunner opened fire with a machinegun. The Guard boarding party on the surfboat hastily retreated, leaving Lt. Perkins behind. When *Seneca's* captain saw what was happening, he turned around and caught up with *Arethusa*. The Guard skipper warned McCoy that he would use his big guns to sink *Arethusa*, if it did not immediately head to New York harbor. McCoy's vessel moved in that direction. Then suddenly McCoy's crew started the engine, hoisted the fore staysail, and sped away. *Seneca* gave chase. The Guards fired warning shots, deliberately missing the black ship. Then they aimed directly at *Arethusa*.[33]

A shell landed only a few feet from McCoy's schooner, spraying water over the deck. *Arethusa's* engines stopped. McCoy was surrendering. His crew hauled down the fore staysail. The schooner headed into the wind, with its foresail flapping. Guardsmen on *Seneca* trained their rifles on McCoy's crew. The CG skipper ordered McCoy to haul down his foresail, and his crew immediately did so. A CG boatswain led an armed boarding party onto *Arethusa* and detained the schooner's crew below deck. *Seneca* led the captured vessel, now manned by Coast Guards, to Staten Island, where *Lexington* assumed the escort duties.[34]

After taking *Arethusa* to the Battery, Guards searched the schooner for contraband and seized large amounts of cash—mostly $1,000 and $10,000 bills—from McCoy's pockets and his cabin safe. Unofficial sources estimated the amount at $60,000–$108,000. Lawmen arrested McCoy along with his crew and took them to jail. McCoy immediately demanded the return of his cash, arguing that the Guards had seized it illegally. The collector of the port ordered the return of a burlap bag with $68,000 cash to McCoy, who used part of it to pay his bail.[35]

Federal prosecutors moved quickly to arraign McCoy on a variety of charges. The major ones were smuggling liquor into the United States and being a fugitive from justice in the *Henry L. Marshall* conspiracy case. Because *Arethusa* had British registry, the British Vice Consul attended McCoy's arraignment but refused to comment on the case.[36] Legal experts expected McCoy to argue that *Arethusa* was flying the British flag in international waters at the time of its capture.

At a preliminary hearing, McCoy was asked what defense he planned to make. "I have no tale of woe to tell you," he said. "I was outside the three-mile limit, selling whiskey, and good whiskey, to anyone and everyone who wanted to buy and had the price. That's going to be my defense." He denied being a profiteer or price gouger. He viewed himself as an honest businessman making a fair profit. He said his business was "selling liquor only of a high quality and giving everyone a square deal." An observer wrote, "McCoy altogether is the most picturesque and delightful man ever put behind the bars in New York City."[37]

McCoy disputed allegations that his crew had fired at *Seneca* and other Coast Guard vessels. "All that talk about fighting and firing on the revenue cutters goes for Sweeney," he said. "I am an American citizen. Do you think for one moment I would permit that

British crew of mine to fire on the American flag?" Despite McCoy's indignation, GG skippers stated that *Arethusa*'s crew had, in fact, shot at government vessels on more than one occasion.[38]

McCoy denied reports that he had held Lt. Perkins at gunpoint on *Arethusa*. Far from mistreating the officer, McCoy claimed he had been hospitable. "I helped him over the side and offered him some coffee and a heavy overcoat that he could be warm," the rumrunner said.[39]

British officials, acting upon a request from Ottawa, asked the U.S. government to release the *Arethusa*'s British and Canadian crewmen. After investigating, British authorities concluded that *Arethusa* was owned by a Canadian company in Nova Scotia. The Canadian owners wanted both the schooner and its cargo returned to them. However, the U.S. State Department argued that the schooner was owned by a bogus company, and the board of directors consisted of clerks in a ship chandler's office. The State Department also said it could prove that McCoy was "a heavy investor in the vessel, if not its actual owner."[40]

After McCoy made bail, he decided to make a little money while he waited for his trial to start. He stocked *M.M. Gardner* with a large supply of liquor and anchored it off Jones Inlet, Long Island. Contact boats sailed out to buy booze for the always thirsty New York market. To keep McCoy's mother ship well stocked, two schooners regularly brought fresh inventory from Halifax, Nova Scotia.[41]

To McCoy's profound disappointment, the U.S. courts refused to validate *Arethusa*'s suspect British registry. Hence, the ship and its owner were subject to U.S. laws. The federal government sold McCoy's beloved schooner at an auction in New York City. The buyer paid only $7,200 for the famous mother ship; his "first act" was purchasing an American flag and running it up the mainmast. The new owner had probably been McCoy's surrogate at the auction. He quickly sold *Arethusa* to McCoy, making a small profit.[42]

McCoy returned his favorite schooner to action as a supply ship in his rumrunning fleet. He sent *Arethusa* on trips to St. Pierre to pick up liquor to restock *M.M. Gardner*, which anchored for extended periods off Long Island. In 1925 McCoy regretfully sold *Arethusa*, by far his favorite boat, to protect it from being confiscated again. The new owner turned it into a seal hunter, and eventually it was lost in the Arctic ice.[43]

McCoy lived in legal limbo for more than a year after being arraigned. He was repeatedly interrogated by lawmen and federal attorneys. He was summoned to appear at tedious legal hearings. He paid large sums of money to his attorney, but nothing happened. Although the wheels of justice seemed to be turning, McCoy's case went nowhere. Unbeknownst to him, his lawyer was an unethical shyster under investigation by the Department of Justice. Finally, a friendly Treasury agent advised McCoy to change lawyers, and he did so.[44]

McCoy's new lawyer soon arranged for *Arethusa*'s crewmen to go free, with all charges against them dismissed. The charges against McCoy relating to *Arethusa* simply seemed to evaporate, and the case never went to trial. However, both Bill and his brother Ben still faced Volstead conspiracy charges related to the smuggling on *Henry L. Marshall*. A rumrunner serving time in the Atlanta federal prison turned informant and gave the feds strong evidence against the McCoy brothers.[45]

When the *Henry L. Marshall* case went to court, the disposition smacked of a plea deal: the charges against Ben were dismissed and Bill pled guilty. It appeared that Bill had saved his brother by agreeing to take all the blame and the punishment. Bill hoped to pay a fine and walk out of court a free man, but he was sentenced to nine months in the Essex County Jail in New Jersey.[46]

The Essex County Jail held many rumrunners, so McCoy found that he had friends there and time passed quickly. Serving his sentence became even easier when he was moved to a jail in New Brunswick. This facility was bursting at the seams with petty criminals. To alleviate the overcrowding, prisoners who could pay rent were allowed to live in a nearby apartment hotel. McCoy moved to the hotel, slept in a comfortable bed, ate decent food, and even attended sporting events. When "a couple of moralists" spotted him at a prizefight in New York, they were livid. They accused the authorities of malfeasance, and the embarrassed officials moved McCoy to a jail in Trenton. He was released on Christmas Eve 1925.[47]

After his release, McCoy returned to Florida to enjoy a safer lifestyle. The rumrunning game had changed from blood-stirring adventure to coldblooded business. The rapacious mobs had taken over, and McCoy didn't want to work for them. Although he claimed he had spent all his money on lawyers, he lived comfortably. He built boats with his brother Ben and bought an apartment house for rental income. In 1938 officials in the Dominican Republic chose him to build a special boat, a mahogany fishing sloop for President Franklin D. Roosevelt. It was presented to FDR "to show the high regard of the island" for the U.S. President.[48]

When asked about his rumrunning days, McCoy sounded sentimental and even a little poetic. "There was all the kick of gambling and the thrill of sport ... the open sea and the boom of the wind against full sails, dawn coming out of the ocean, and nights under the rocking stars," he said.[49] What more could a sailor want?

The rumrunning pioneer died at age 71 aboard the *Blue Lagoon of Coral Strand*, a vessel built in the McCoy brothers' boatyard. Food poisoning combined with a heart attack dealt the fatal blow.[50]

The Original "Real McCoy"

Many sources attribute the phrase "the real McCoy," meaning the genuine article, to Bill McCoy's reputation as a rumrunner who sold quality liquor. However, the *Oxford English Dictionary* (OED) shows that the phrase dates back to the nineteenth century. The OED cites "the real McKay," referring to whiskey produced by the McKay distillery in Edinburgh as early as 1856. In 1872 Elijah McCoy, an oilman for the Michigan Central Railroad, patented an automatic lubricating device for trains. When others imitated his invention, his became known as "the real McCoy."

In the early 1900s, sports reporters called boxer Selby "Kid" McCoy "the real McCoy." On one occasion a sportswriter went to interview a man claiming to be the boxer. When the man proved to be an impostor, the reporter wrote that he was definitely *not* "the real McCoy." Boxer Marvin Hart claimed he had invented a new kidney blow, "a haymaker, swung with the English reversed." A writer said the new punch contained "the stuff the sleep tablets are made of." Another boxer praised Hart's innovation, saying it was "the real McCoy."[51]

Although Bill McCoy didn't coin the phrase associated with his surname, he was the real McCoy in the rumrunning game. He came as close as any rumrunner to being an honorable outlaw—a criminal entrepreneur who sold a good product at a fair price.

8

Gertrude Lythgoe
The Bahama Queen

Although women could be found in all sectors of the illegal liquor trade, very few females joined the rumrunners' club. Over the course of Prohibition only a handful of women sailed in mother ships on the high seas. Court records and press reports documented the exploits of Gertrude Lythgoe and Edith Stevens, making them the most famous women rumrunners. The two had little in common. Lythgoe was a level-headed career woman who ran an import-export business in the Bahamas. Stevens was a bored housewife looking for excitement. She fell in love with a rumrunner and became his daring, devoted helpmate. She embraced rumrunning as a thrilling romantic adventure.

"No Skirts!"

Gertrude Lythgoe, a women's libber long before the term was coined, played the rumrunning game with gusto. Unlike the typical woman of her era, she chose a career in business and competed with men on an equal footing. She relied on hard work, common sense, and perseverance to succeed. She exuded great self-confidence and seemed to fear nothing. At a time when society believed a woman needed a man's protection, she lived alone, traveled alone, and relished her independence.

The press dubbed Lythgoe the Bahama Queen, the Rumrunning Joan d'Arc, and Queen of the Booze Buccaneers. An admirer said she was "a woman of cultivated tastes" who read widely, enjoyed "the best music," and danced "divinely." She had "a wonderful personality" and "artistic taste in dress." Summing up Lythgoe's career, a reporter wrote, "Girls have envied her alluring beauty; men have admired her sheer courage; motion picture magnates have sought after her, and the government has endeavored to send her to prison."[1]

Lythgoe had high cheekbones, dark eyes, and a strong jaw line. Many people found her to be exotic looking and speculated about her ethnic heritage—believing her to be Russian, French, Spanish, Egyptian, or Native American. Photos show that she was a slender woman who wore fashionable, flapper-style dresses. The hemline of her dresses went up and down as fashions changed in the Twenties. In a photo taken on a beach, her hair was blowing in the wind and she wore the latest style swimwear: a body-hugging, one-piece suit. In most photos she was smoking, with her cigarette in a holder like those used by the *femme fatale* in silent movies.

Lythgoe had a sad childhood that taught her to be resilient and self-reliant. She was born in 1888, the youngest child in a family of ten siblings in Bowling Green, Ohio. Her mother had chronic health problems, so the older children looked after the younger ones. While her father was away on a long trip, her mother died of tuberculosis. Her widowed father was unable to care for all the children so he placed the three youngest ones in institutions. Gertrude was sent to an orphanage. After a time, she went to live with a "spinster" aunt in Greenfield, Indiana.[2]

Lythgoe's father, who owned a glass factory, drank heavily after his wife's death. He became unreliable and suffered serious financial setbacks. Gertrude's oldest sister took over the parenting duties and placed Gertrude in a parochial school in Anderson, Indiana. Gertrude excelled in school, especially in her music classes. She had a fine singing voice and learned to play the piano, violin, and pipe organ. She performed in school programs and at community concerts. To make money, she sang for the slide shows at the cinematograph.[3] (In the silent movie era, theaters showed slides between the motion pictures. During the slides, a pianist or organist played music, and a vocalist sang or led the audience in a sing-along.)

After Lythgoe graduated from high school, she went to a business college where she studied secretarial science. When she finished her education, she worked in Indianapolis and saved her money so she could travel. In 1915 she settled in San Francisco, where she supported herself as a public stenographer in a hotel. She worked for businessmen who had offices in the hotel or were staying there while in town on business.[4]

During World War I, Lythgoe became acquainted with a British businessman staying at the hotel. He had big plans for the postwar future. He was starting an import-export firm and expected to reap huge profits selling lumber to help rebuild war-ravaged France. When he offered Lythgoe a job, she accepted and moved to London to work in the home office. She became the firm's liaison with timber suppliers in Maine, Oregon, and other American states. She gained valuable experience in sales, shipping, and international finance. She found London exciting yet dreary because the city was still recovering from the war. Her job gave her the chance to travel extensively in Europe for business and pleasure.[5]

When the import-export firm opened an office in New York City, Lythgoe moved to the Big Apple to run it. Disruptions in shipping turned the venture into a "grand fiasco," and the new office closed after a few months. Despite this setback, Lythgoe's bosses saw rosy prospects for trade in the United States. But whiskey, not timber, would be the path to profits. To circumvent the Volstead law, the firm would ship liquor from the British Isles to an offshore locale and sell it to smugglers headed for Rum Row.[6]

When Lythgoe's bosses asked her to run this new operation, she took the job and packed her bags again. This time she moved to New Providence Island in the Bahamas. She was very displeased when her bosses sent a young Englishman to help her manage the new venture. Liquor licenses were normally issued to men, but Lythgoe didn't want the young man to have the upper hand. She insisted that they procure a joint liquor license.

Sadly, the young man proved to be both inept and dishonest. After cheating the firm out of a sizeable amount of money, he sailed away. Without him, Lythgoe needed her own liquor license, but she faced an uphill battle to get one because she was female. At a public hearing, a local official stated that she was "unfit" to hold a license. He based his harsh judgment on gossip about her love life and the fact that she carried a revolver. She stated that she didn't own the gun but was merely keeping it for a friend. She heatedly argued that her love life had no relevance to getting a liquor license. She answered the licensing board's questions with candor and common sense. She convinced the men that she was an honest, competent woman who could manage a business.[7]

Armed with her new liquor license, Lythgoe set out to find buyers for her whiskey. Once again her gender complicated matters. The liquor wholesalers were expected to show the booze buccaneers a good time while they were in port. The male wholesalers took the rummers to see scantily-clad shimmy dancers in the bars. They hosted beach parties where liquor flowed freely and native women danced naked around bonfires.

As a respectable woman, Lythgoe couldn't host, or even attend, a wild party. But she thought she had a solution to this problem. As a rule, the money to buy a liquor cargo came from a rich investor, either a mob boss or a legit businessman who stayed in the shadows. Lythgoe decided to bypass the booze buccaneers and contact the men who bankrolled the black ships. She would rely on her sales skills and business acumen to negotiate good contracts.

Lythgoe was stunned when she ran into a brick wall. The money men refused to deal with her. "They were ultraconservative, suspicious, and very prejudiced towards a woman in the game," she said. "As they put it: 'No skirts!'"[8]

Lythgoe's luck changed when Bill McCoy sailed *Arethusa* into port to pick up a cargo of liquor. When they met, the legendary rumrunner dazzled her. He had a warm personality, an agile mind, and extraordinary strength of character. She felt sensations that she couldn't explain. Sounding like the heroine in a romance novel, she said, "Something hit me, hit me hard. I could not analyze just what it was." Whether it was love or lust, she was smitten. And so was McCoy. She instinctively trusted him and knew he would treat her right. He couldn't take his eyes off of her. He found her to be a fascinating, plucky spitfire—the kind of spirited young woman he admired.[9]

McCoy knew that Lythgoe's business was faltering because she was a skirt in a man's game. Although she had a warehouse full of superior, aged whiskey from famous distilleries, she was making few sales. McCoy advised her to cut out the middleman. He told her to take her whiskey to Rum Row and sell it "over the side" to contact boats. He had already loaded his cargo of liquor and was preparing to sail, but he had a little space left on *Arethusa*. She could put some whiskey on his schooner and sail with him.

Although life on a mother ship had inherent dangers, Lythgoe didn't hesitate. She quickly agreed on the business terms with McCoy and arranged to have her cargo loaded onto his vessel without delay. Her liquor was piled high on the deck and stowed in every available space below deck.[10]

When McCoy set sail, a launch took Lythgoe to board *Arethusa*. As the schooner headed out to sea, she watched the sailors go about their chores. She barely knew McCoy and had never met any of his crewmen. She felt "horribly alone and useless." She had acted with haste. Now she was having second thoughts. But she couldn't turn back. She had inventory to sell, and this was her best bet.[11]

Lythgoe had been in such a hurry to take advantage of McCoy's offer that she hadn't inquired about the sleeping arrangements on *Arethusa*. When bedtime came, McCoy told her that she could share the captain's quarters, which had two bunks. He gave her first choice of bunks and assured her that she would have plenty of privacy because he would only come to the cabin to sleep. Moreover, the cabin boy would sleep on the floor between the bunks, acting as a sort of chaperone.[12]

Although Lythgoe enjoyed sailing, she suffered a brief bout of seasickness due to rough seas. After the seas calmed down, she savored the trip and her time with Bill McCoy. They had fun, talking, laughing, and sharing meals. They even found a little time to be alone together. She admired his strength, his sailing skills, and his expertise in handling the crew.

Upon reaching Rum Row at Ambrose Lightship, *Arethusa* joined the formation of liquor freighters waiting for the Whiskito Fleet to come out.

"Each evening about five o'clock we would search the horizon through the binoculars for the little speedboats," Lythgoe wrote. "To me they resembled little skimming bugs with white-spray wings, speeding towards us on the water." Up to a half-dozen boats would converge on *Arethusa* at one time. The smallest of the mosquito boats carried only five cases, but the standard shore runner could hold 250 cases. Around New York City a motorboat named *Cigarette* was the fastest as well as the biggest contact boat, with space for six hundred cases.[13]

Lythgoe found that life on Liquor Lane alternated between boring and exciting. Many hours were spent waiting for the next onslaught of mosquito boats. For amusement during the idle hours, *Arethusa* carried a gramophone with a stack of jazz records. To entertain the crew, Lythgoe sang popular songs, accompanied by the cook, who played the violin. The crewmen and Lythgoe often practiced target shooting, aiming at bottles or other objects floating in the water.[14]

Lythgoe usually slept during the day because the nights were hectic. When the contact boats converged on *Arethusa*, the men worked quickly to transfer the liquor. The crewmen on the small boats brought newspapers, magazines, and fresh produce to the mother ship. Sometimes they also delivered soft drinks to supplement the ship's water supply. McCoy, a teetotaler himself, never allowed the crew to drink whiskey onboard.[15]

To avoid monotony, McCoy and Lythgoe took a dory to visit other ships on Rum Row and talk business with their peers. They made frequent trips to *M.M. Gardner*, a schooner that McCoy owned and leased to another rumrunner. McCoy's mother ships exchanged inventory and provisions as needed to be well supplied at all times.[16]

On one occasion *Arethusa*'s crew challenged another ship to a race. The two vessels sped across the water, neck in neck. *Arethusa* surged ahead, then lagged behind. The lead seesawed back and forth. In the heat of the race, McCoy came dangerously close to crossing inside the rum line. A revenue cutter spotted *Arethusa* and headed toward it at full speed. McCoy instantly conceded the race so his crew could hoist the sails and turn the ship seaward, leaving the cutter behind.[17]

At all times the rumrunners kept watch for the Coast Guard patrol boats. One evening when a CG cutter came closer than normal, five contact boats were alongside *Arethusa*, each loading liquor or waiting its turn. To avoid capture, the speedboats scattered, racing away to a safe haven. But the shore runners didn't give up their mission.

Two Navy nurses accused of rumrunning posed with their attorneys in 1925. They were acquitted at their trial, which was the first court-martial of women in the history of the U.S. Navy (Library of Congress).

They waited until the night became pitch black so they could sneak back to *Arethusa* unseen. One by one, each contact boat returned to load up.[18]

The following night when the contact boats surrounded *Arethusa*, the CG sent out two launches, each with a machinegun mounted on the bow. The launches were able to sneak up on the mosquito boats, and the Guards opened fire. Lythgoe, who stayed on deck to watch the action, heard a man yell that he had been hit, but she couldn't see him. The CG launches trained their searchlights on *Arethusa*'s deck. Machinegun fire crackled above the water. Lythgoe felt a bullet whiz by, too close for comfort.[19]

Amid the barrage of bullets, the contact boats sped away. The CG launches chased after the motorboats, and Lythgoe lost sight of them. For the next few days a CG cutter hovered near *Arethusa*, stopping all sales because the contact boats dared not come out. Then the CG cutter steamed away, and the mosquito boats resumed their regular trips.[20]

When Lythgoe had sold all her liquid cargo, she reluctantly left McCoy, not knowing when she would see him again. She took a launch to Sheepshead Bay, New York, and a taxi to Manhattan. Then she sailed to London to meet with her bosses at the import-export firm. Because her rumrunning trip had made a stupendous profit, the board of directors upped her compensation and gave her more responsibility. When she left London, she went to Havana temporarily to supervise liquor shipments there. Then she returned to Nassau to manage the Bahamas trade.[21]

After several years of rumrunning with impunity, Lythgoe had two major mischances. She chartered a schooner called *Venturer* and sailed on it, taking a cargo of liquor to Bimini to sell to tourists and rumrunners. After nearly capsizing in nasty squalls, the vessel anchored off Bimini, and Lythgoe stayed onboard to keep an eye on her valuable cargo. A fierce storm blew in. The winds ripped *Venturer's* sails into tatters and tossed the schooner around. Water flooded the engine room. *Venturer* was thrown against sharp rocks and hung there, listing to one side. Lythgoe and two others scrambled off the schooner and escaped in a dory, hanging onto the tiny boat as the seas rose and fell, threatening to swallow them.

When the storm subsided, Lythgoe hurried to save her investment. *Venturer* lay on its side atop a reef near the shore. Lythgoe paid islanders to salvage the burlocks of liquor that had somehow survived the shipwreck. The men formed a line from the beach to the ship and, like a bucket brigade, passed the sacks of liquor bottles from hand-to-hand. Lythgoe counted the sacks as the men loaded them onto carts for the trip to the warehouse. After recovering most of her cargo, she left the remainder for the natives to scavenge later. Due to continued bad weather, few buyers came to Bimini and it took almost a month for Lythgoe to sell her liquor.[22]

After her misadventure in Bimini, Lythgoe traveled to Miami. She expected no trouble, but her visit turned into an ordeal. Police officers arrested her on rumrunning charges in a case that would be prosecuted in New Orleans. Guards traveled with her on a train to a small station near New Orleans; there federal agents took custody and guarded her to prevent her "assassination" by her accomplices.

The indictment charged that Lythgoe and her accomplices had smuggled a large cargo of whiskey from Havana to New Orleans aboard the British steamer *Gladys Thornburn*. She admitted that she had purchased the whiskey in Cuba. However, she claimed she was not involved in the New Orleans plot because her assistants had stolen the liquor from her. After they made a shady deal to sell it in the Big Easy, law enforcement had nabbed them. When the case went to trial, Lythgoe testified against her underlings and the court dismissed all charges against her.[23]

Lythgoe, who was superstitious by nature, viewed the shipwreck and arrest as bad omens. She decided to quit rumrunning because her luck had turned sour. She changed vocations, using her management skills to build a new career in the rental car business. She continued to move around, living in Miami, Detroit, Los Angeles, and New York City. She died at age 86, after enjoying an unconventional and eventful life.[24]

9

Edith Stevens
Love and "Reckless Courage"

Antonio Cassese smuggled booze into New York via boat, truck, and airplane. In the early 1920s the busy liquor trafficker owned at least three mother ships. His flagship was *Edith*, an impressive steam yacht that cost $250,000—a major outlay, even for a rich liquor lord. *Edith* boasted luxurious cabins, rosewood and mahogany woodwork, shiny brass fittings, and a snow-white hull.[1]

The yacht's name honored Cassese's girlfriend, Edith Stevens, a young woman with "quick wit and reckless courage." The petite, nineteen-year-old Stevens weighed about one hundred pounds and wore size-two shoes. She had dark eyes, reddish-brown hair, and tiny hands. She had the "large, farseeing eyes of the dreaming visionary … the sort of person who writes poetry in a freezing garret with crackers and milk for a diet," an admirer rhapsodized. Although the dainty young lady seemed fragile, she had a daring, steely spirit. She looked like "a clinging vine, but there would come flashes of the determination which made her the intrepid partner of Cassese," a reporter said.[2]

When Stevens met Cassese, her life took a dramatic turn. Before their accidental meeting, she had felt overwhelming discontent. She wanted something different, but she didn't know exactly what would make her happy. Rumrunning lay far outside her life experience. She had enjoyed a normal, happy childhood until her parents divorced and her wealthy father disappeared, leaving her mother destitute. As a teenager, Stevens needed to earn money, so she found a job as an adding-machine clerk. Desperate for financial security, she married a vaudeville actor who was old enough to be her father.[3]

Alas, marriage disappointed Stevens. Both her husband and housewifery proved to be dreadfully dull. She was a young woman, full of vitality, yearning for romance and excitement. But she was trapped in a boring, loveless marriage. Life with a vaudeville actor wasn't as glamorous as she had expected. Dreary days of cooking, cleaning, and drudgery loomed ahead of her.[4]

One day Stevens went to the cemetery to visit her grandmother's grave. As she was walking home, a car almost hit her. The handsome driver, Antonio Cassese, jumped out of his auto and apologized profusely. The glib young rake had dark eyes, wavy black hair, and a bright smile. He was "a tall, dark, athletic Romeo" who could've been a matinee idol. When he flirted with Stevens, her pulse raced. She smiled and laughed at his banter. He asked if he could call on her. She consented.[5]

The two began meeting secretly because both of them had spouses. Stevens found Cassese to be the most charming, irresistible man she had ever met. She soon fell madly in love with him and succumbed to his advances. He took her away from her dreary routine, seducing her with his "forceful manner and his promises." Her dull husband and tedious housework couldn't compete with the spirited rogue. She left her husband, and Cassese kept her in style in a luxury apartment on Riverside Drive in New York City.[6]

Initially, Stevens didn't know Cassese's true occupation. To explain his wealth, he claimed to be a millionaire tobacco tycoon. He took her on exciting, fun trips to Florida and the Bahamas. They stayed at grand hotels, partied at glitzy speakeasies, and ate at the finest restaurants. They enjoyed first-class accommodations on trains and ships. Cassese introduced Stephens to his rich friends who also lived the high life. Although he talked vaguely about his big business deals, she didn't see any evidence that he owned farmland or factories that made tobacco products. On their second trip south, she put two and two together. She realized that her lover wasn't selling tobacco. Rather, he "was engaged in rumrunning on a gigantic scale."[7]

Stevens embraced the romantic idea of being in love with a bold young rumrunner. She was eager to share Cassese's lifestyle because she craved glamor and adventure. "My honest impulses told me that I must obey the call of the sea and rumrunning," she wrote. From the first minute, she loved "the uncertainty of it and the utter freedom from conventionalities and hide-bound routine." With more than a touch of melodrama, she vowed, "I will not be prosaic and cautious. I will do and dare as my heart and impulses tell me to."[8]

Stevens, who had total confidence in Cassese, saw him as a natural leader, someone born to command other men. "Antonio is essentially a man's man," she wrote. "Men always like him." Although he was an outlaw, she saw him as an ethical man with great integrity. In her eyes, "he was absolutely on the level, never lied to a friend, and never betrayed an enemy." She said that men instinctively knew that Cassese "was the most dangerous man in the world to double-cross."[9]

Stevens wanted to be Cassese's helpmate as well as his mistress. She took an interest in his business, entertained his guests, and helped him avoid arrest. On one trip aboard *Edith* they docked in Port Royal, South Carolina, to pick up coal. Strangers admired the sleek, handsome yacht in the harbor. The mayor's son came aboard for a visit and showed no inclination to leave. After several hours he was still enjoying their hospitality when an officer from a federal revenue cutter joined them. Stevens chatted with the visitors and did her best to mislead them. She told them the yacht was headed south on a pleasure trip, even though it was going north with a cargo of whiskey.[10]

Inevitably, the federal officer asked, "Any liquor onboard?"

Stevens said they kept liquor onboard for personal use and offered him a drink. He accepted. She pulled out a bottle of Johnnie Walker and poured a round of drinks for the men. As the officer sipped his whiskey, she barely breathed, fearful that he would ask prying questions. Or, even worse, decide to search the yacht. She wasn't sure what Cassese would do if the federal officer tried to search the boat. She feared there would be a fistfight or gunplay.

As the officer drained his glass, Stevens hoped he wouldn't ask for another drink. Her nerves were at the breaking point. She wanted him to leave.

The federal officer didn't ask for more whiskey, but he did take time to examine the yacht's papers. Stephens' heart thumped wildly while he scanned them. Without fanfare, he pronounced the papers okay. Stevens breathed easy and smiled as he departed.

"When at last he stepped down to his launch, I was about ready to collapse with the sheer joy of our triumph," she wrote.[11]

But her relief was fleeting. When the mayor's son also departed, she realized that the yacht was too quiet. She and Cassese were all alone. The crew had jumped ship!

Fearing that the federal officer would arrest them, the sailors had hopped onto a nearby coal barge. Cassese went to the barge and coaxed the crewmen back onto *Edith*, but they were in a mutinous mood. Speaking for the whole crew, the young captain argued that they were destined for jail if they stayed on the black ship.

"If we aren't searched here, you know as well as we do what will happen to us up the line," the captain said. "We don't mind taking a chance at being caught, but this isn't a chance. This is a sure thing!"

Cassese assured the crew that he had the situation under control. He was an old hand at rumrunning, and he knew they were in no danger of being arrested. Stevens admired Cassese for taking charge and standing up to the roughnecks who worked for him. She felt that he commanded just the right balance of respect and fear.

Despite Cassese's reassuring words, the crew wanted to scuttle the contraband. "The liquor has to go!" the young captain declared. "So we have decided, and we believe you

The destroyer *Henley* was painted with "dazzle camouflage" before the Navy transferred it to the Coast Guard to fight liquor smugglers (National Archives and Records Administration).

will agree, that we should take the liquor ashore tonight and bury it in the woods. We can come back and get it when this trouble blows over."

Cassese flatly refused to unload the liquor. He told the crew that *Edith* would sail as planned with all its cargo. "This is a strong man's game," he said. "This is no time to weaken."

Unconvinced, the young captain continued to voice his misgivings. He fully intended to unload the illegal cargo.

"You took your chance when you signed up," Cassese told him. "You are honor-bound to live up to your obligations."

Neither the captain nor Cassese budged. The impasse continued for hours as they argued about leaving the liquor behind. Cassese grew frustrated and angry. Stevens saw that he was only a hair's breadth from violence. Fearing that the standoff would escalate into fisticuffs, she tried to defuse the tension. She told the crewmen they wouldn't be arrested because she had a "hunch" that everything would be okay.

"Do you think that revenue officer would miss a chance to get a gold stripe on his arm for capturing a rum vessel?" she asked. "If he thought this was a ship to take, he would get the credit for it himself. He wouldn't give the glory of the capture to some other officer up the line, would he? And if he were going to capture it himself, he would have lost no time about it."

Watching the crewmen's facial expressions, she felt that she was being persuasive.

"Let me tell you, I am a girl, and as a girl I have more at stake than any of you, or all of you put together," she said. "It doesn't matter as much about what happens to a man as it does to a girl. And, if I honestly believed that revenue officer could possibly have any design on our cargo, I would be getting off this boat so fast that the draft would give you pneumonia!"

Stevens' convoluted appeal to the double standard somehow persuaded the men to stay onboard. They crowded around her, shook her hand, and promised to protect her.[12]

But the crisis wasn't quite over. The next morning the young captain had "another severe attack of buck fever" because he saw the revenue cutter sailing toward *Edith*. Although Stevens was also worried, she ordered the skipper to calm down. She watched anxiously as the cutter neared the yacht. Her mind raced. Maybe she had misjudged the federal officer. Maybe he was coming back to arrest them.

Abruptly the government boat swerved and headed out to sea. Stevens wanted to shout for joy. She had handled the situation just right. She knew how to manipulate men.

After leaving Port Royal, *Edith* continued on its course to New York and delivered its expensive cargo without a mutiny or an arrest.[13]

The Ripple *Effect*

On a quiet night in March 1922, Antonio Cassese stood on a Long Island dock, awaiting the arrival of his yacht *Edith*. Although he was an old pro in the rumrunning game, he felt tense because unloading a cargo of illegal liquor always entailed a certain amount of danger. A convoy of trucks waited onshore, but he was irritated because there was one less truck than he needed. He had ordered the drivers to be there when the booze arrived. Where was the missing truck?[14]

When *Edith* docked, swampers quickly began transferring the liquor to the trucks. The late truck finally arrived, and Cassese was furious because the driver had a lame excuse: he had gotten lost. Cassese cursed at the tardy driver and ordered all the men to hurry up. They were vulnerable on the beach. Hijackers or lawmen might swoop down at any moment.[15]

Cassese would soon have even more reason to yell at the tardy truck driver, who had stopped at a gas station to ask directions. The driver had told the station attendant that he and his crew were going to pick up a load of furniture. Picking up furniture on the dock in the middle of the night? The attendant thought that sounded suspicious, so he eavesdropped as the men talked. What he heard convinced him that they were picking up a load of liquor. When the truck left, the attendant called the sheriff, who notified the state police. The troopers jumped into action. As the swampers unloaded the last of *Edith*'s liquid cargo, the lawmen watched from a hiding spot near the dock.[16]

Suddenly, the jolting sound of gunshots rang out in the darkness. For a split second Cassese's startled men froze in place. Before they could scatter, the state troopers fired more shots into the air. In the dark the rumrunners couldn't see the shooters and didn't return fire. The troopers quickly swarmed around the rummers, trapping them. The lawmen arrested 33 men, including Cassese and *Edith*'s captain, and hauled them off to the Nassau County jail.[17]

When the authorities interrogated *Edith*'s captain, he accused Edith Stevens of being "the woman behind the bottle." He said she had directed the loading of the liquor cargo in Nassau and sailed with it to New York. However, she was not on the yacht when the troopers arrested the crew because she had taken a launch to shore.[18]

Stevens admitted that she had sailed on *Edith*, but her story differed from the captain's in a crucial detail: she claimed to know nothing about the cargo. She was merely Cassese's girlfriend and traveling companion. Law enforcement officials found the captain to be more credible than Stevens. She was arrested, jailed, and indicted on multiple criminal charges, including conspiracy to violate the Volstead law.[19]

In a separate indictment, Cassese was charged with smuggling liquor on *Edith* and another vessel. While he waited for his day in court, he asked the judge for permission to travel to Florida to collect affidavits that would strengthen his defense. The court granted his request. But Cassese didn't really want to interview witnesses in Florida. His actual destination was the Bahamas, where he planned to buy a cargo of liquor.[20]

Stevens, who was out of jail on bail, joined Cassese on the trip. They traveled by train to Jacksonville, Florida. There they chartered a small yacht named *Stranger* to take them to the Bahamas. Cassese had ordered one of his mother ships, *Ripple*, to meet him in Nassau to pick up a load of booze.[21]

What should have been an easy voyage from Florida to Nassau turned into a series of mishaps. *Stranger*'s captain lost his way and steered the yacht onto dangerous shoals. Cassese, always a man of action, took command, treating the captain like just another crewman. Cassese ordered the crew to pole the boat away from the shoals, but the situation was tricky. "We were on top of the peaks and plateaus of mountains in the sea—

jutting up here and there," wrote Stevens. "At one minute we could get out and wade in water up to our knees. In another minute we were in deep water."[22]

Under Cassese's direction, the crew extricated the yacht from the shoals—only to run into more shoals. Cassese snapped orders at the men, who struggled to move the boat into deeper water. At long last, *Stranger* escaped the shallows and lay at anchor overnight.

When the sun rose, Cassese spied a small island and steered the boat toward it. Stevens argued against going to the island because she feared that cannibals lived there. Her concern seemed to be warranted when she spotted "scantily-clothed brown men" on the beach. Despite her pleas, Cassese sensed no danger and insisted on going ashore.

The island's "white master" welcomed the *Stranger* party to his home. He seemed happy to have visitors to break up the monotony of life on an isolated island. He fed his guests and gave them water. Nourished and refreshed, the rumrunners were ready to resume their voyage. When they left, the white master put a native aboard the yacht to act as navigator.[23]

Stranger arrived safely in Nassau, where Cassese met up with the captain of his steam trawler *Ripple*. Cassese bought a cargo of liquor and watched it being loaded on the trawler. Then he and Stevens took a boat to Miami, traveled by train to New York, and waited for *Ripple* to arrive. After three days, Cassese received an urgent message from the trawler's captain, saying that the vessel was stranded off the coast of Virginia. Cassese rushed to Virginia and hired a tugboat to tow *Ripple* to shore. However, when the tug reached the area where the trawler was supposedly stranded, Cassese couldn't find his black ship.[24]

If Cassese suspected that he had been double-crossed, he was right. While he searched for his wayward trawler along the Virginia coast, *Ripple*'s captain sailed the vessel to New York and anchored near Ambrose Lightship. The captain planned to quickly sell the liquid cargo, pocket the money, and leave town before Cassese found him. But that wasn't his only reason for being in a hurry. *Ripple* had been at sea longer than expected, so the food supply was gone. The crewmen, who were subsisting on beer, were threatening to mutiny.[25]

While *Ripple* rode at anchor on Rum Row, the skipper of another vessel came alongside. He hailed the trawler's captain and made a deal to buy 250 cases of liquor. The crews worked quickly to transfer the whiskey from one vessel to the other. When *Ripple*'s captain tried to collect his money, the other skipper refused to pay. The heavily-armed crewmen on the buyer's boat drew their guns, and the skipper threatened to report *Ripple* to law enforcement. *Ripple*'s captain chose not to fight, so the thieves sailed away.[26]

Ripple's captain decided it would be safer to sell his liquor closer to shore. Due to the risk of being arrested inside the rum line, hijackers or pirates were unlikely to strike there. In the wee hours of the morning, *Ripple* entered the Barge Canal leading into Erie Basin near Clinton Street, Brooklyn. Contact boats darted out of the shadows and surrounded the mother ship. *Ripple*'s crew began tossing hams of liquor to the men in the motorboats. Prohibition agents, who had been watching *Ripple* since its arrival on Rum Row, were waiting onshore. They jumped into a rowboat and rowed as fast as possible toward the black ship. When the rumrunners spotted the rowboat, the contact boats scattered. As they pulled away, the shore runners exchanged gunfire with the Prohis, who had no hope of capturing the speedy motorboats.[27]

The Prohis encountered no resistance when they boarded *Ripple*. The hungry sailors didn't feel like fighting. They threw their rifles overboard and welcomed the federal agents as rescuers. After being hijacked and going without food for days, the sailors were ready to swear off rumrunning. They meekly submitted to arrest and asked for something to eat.[28]

Cassese was not onboard *Ripple* when the Prohis captured it, but authorities knew he owned the trawler and indicted him on new Volstead charges related to his latest trip to the Bahamas. Cassese went into hiding to avoid arrest. He left Stevens to fend for herself, and law enforcement soon took her into custody. She was indicted on charges related to *Ripple*'s ill-fated trip from the Bahamas, even though she had played a minor role. She pled not guilty. Her bail was set at $20,000, but she couldn't pay it. She argued that the court had set bail too high, in order to keep her in jail. She accused federal authorities of incarcerating her so Cassese would come out of hiding to prove her innocence.[29]

"I am waiting now to see what kind of man Cassese really is," she said. "If he allows me to remain in jail, a victim of my friendship for him, if he does not come back and extricate me from this trouble into which I have been drawn through him, then he is not the man I thought him, and I will not shield him." Despite his disappearing act, she believed he would save her. "I have great confidence in him," she said.[30]

Alas, her confidence was misplaced. Cassese did not appear like a knight in shining armor to save her. He seemed to be more interested in saving his own skin. Strangely, his wife came to Stevens' trial but offered her no help.[31]

In the courtroom, prosecutors accused Stevens of rumrunning on both *Edith* and *Ripple*. One of Cassese's underlings testified that Stevens had been in Nassau, had watched the men load liquor onto *Ripple,* and had "checked" the containers. She took the stand to defend herself. She admitted going to Florida and the Bahamas with Cassese. She also admitted that she had counted the packages in Nassau but said she didn't know they held liquor.[32]

When the judge instructed the jury, he said the evidence clearly showed that Cassese had conspired to break the Volstead law and had, in fact, done so with Stevens' help. The issue was whether she "was conscious of her participation in the plot." Had she really not known she was counting cases of liquor? That was the question the jurors must answer.[33]

After brief deliberations, the jury found Stevens not guilty. Clearly disappointed, the judge said, "She deserved to be convicted."[34]

When Stevens talked about her rumrunning ventures, she sounded appropriately contrite. Her brush with the law had caused her to reassess her values. "It's the old story. I was deceived," she said. "Virtue and honor are more precious than money." She declared that "a home, a husband, housework are the things that really count." She advised teenaged girls to avoid her mistakes. "Don't marry too young—wait till you know your heart," she said. She firmly renounced rumrunning and pledged to live a simple, honest life. "I'm glad I'm out of it. I have had more than enough excitement to last a lifetime."[35]

Love Behind Bars

Although Stevens publicly swore off rumrunning, she was far from swearing off Cassese. He didn't show up at her trial to defend her, but she was still in love with him. After her acquittal she contacted him, and they rekindled their romance. Through her rose-colored glasses, she foresaw only bliss in their future together. She knew there would be a happily-ever-after ending for them. "We planned to go the Bahamas to live in peace and quiet the rest of our lives," she later wrote.[36]

Even though Stevens quit rumrunning, her name remained in the headlines. Her abandoned husband filed for "an absolute divorce" that would prohibit her from remarrying during his lifetime. He also sued Cassese for alienation of his wife's affections. He alleged that the handsome rumrunner had corrupted his teenaged wife at a hotel in New York and on the yacht *Edith*. When the husband's case went to court, he won because Cassese didn't show up to offer a defense. The court awarded the husband a default judgment of $50,000 to be paid by Cassese. But his chances of collecting the money were minuscule.[37]

Cassese, who was still a fugitive from justice, arranged to buy a new yacht, *Iris*. When it was ready to sail, the rumrunning lovers headed south with the Bahamas as their destination. Their journey ended abruptly when the yacht capsized in rough waters near Ossabaw Island, off the coast of Georgia. Everyone onboard made it safely to the island, where a friendly couple gave them shelter. Their host also took Cassese back to *Iris* so he could salvage valuable items, including a substantial amount of cash he had left onboard.[38]

After the tides washed *Iris* ashore, Cassese had the vessel towed to Savannah for repairs. The local grapevine hummed with the tale of the shipwrecked yacht, and a newspaper published the story. Somehow the news report came to the attention of New York investigators, who knew that Cassese had bought a new yacht. Combining the story of the shipwreck with other information, New York officials believed they had located the runaway rummer. At their request, lawmen in Savannah arrested Cassese. The Savannah lawmen didn't recognize Stevens as Cassese's notorious accomplice, so they didn't detain her. She fled Georgia, returning to New York City post haste.[39]

The federal authorities soon moved Cassese from Georgia to New York to stand trial. The court set his bail at $101,000—an astronomical sum for anyone charged with Volstead crimes, but he was definitely a flight risk. Unable to pay, he went to prison while he awaited trial.[40]

Stevens worried about Cassese and longed to see him, even if only for a moment. His wife was allowed to visit him in jail, but his mistress had no legal right to see him. When Cassese's trial started, Stevens couldn't resist the urge to go to the federal building to be near him. She hoped that she might talk to his lawyer or a court official and arrange a private meeting with the love of her life. Word quickly spread that she was in the building. The prosecutor immediately asked the judge for an order detaining her as a material witness for the state. The judge issued a subpoena, and Stevens was taken into custody. In all likelihood, she would be detained until the trial ended.[41]

Stevens was housed at the gloomy Raymond Street jail in Brooklyn. Since Cassese was in the federal prison next door, she found a silver lining in her new rat-infested home. She persuaded a guard to let her stand at a window overlooking the prison's exercise yard, so she could catch glimpses of her sweetheart as he walked around. She also saw him when they both went to the prison worship services on Sundays. Although the guards kept them from talking to one another, she felt close to him simply because they were in the same room.[42]

At Cassese's trial, the prosecution called sailors who had worked for him on rum-running trips. *Edith*'s former captain described a trip when he sailed the schooner from Long Island to the Bahamas and back. He admitted that the ship carried 1,800 burlap bags on the second leg of that trip but claimed he didn't know what the sacks held.[43]

As the trial progressed, Stevens became totally frustrated because she couldn't talk to Cassese. She couldn't get close enough to communicate with him, either in prison or in court. When she was taken to the courtroom, she could only watch the trial and wait to be called to the witness stand. Although the prosecution was holding her as a material witness, she didn't know when she would be called to testify. The uncertainty added to her frustration. (As it turned out, the state never put her on the witness stand.)[44]

When the judge turned Cassese's case over to the jurors, they quickly found him guilty of conspiring to violate the Volstead law. The court fined him $10,000 and sentenced him to two years in the federal prison at Atlanta.[45]

Before lawmen took Cassese to Atlanta, Stevens begged for time alone with him. After consulting Cassese's wife and getting her permission, officials granted Stevens a brief jailhouse visit to say good-bye.[46]

She felt overwhelming, crushing sadness. She knew that difficult, lonely days lay ahead of her. She would have to build a new life for herself while her lover served his time. Uncertainty loomed ahead of her, but she knew one thing for sure: their love would survive.

"Alone, I am facing the long anguish of my separation from the man I love," she wrote. "But through the blankness of the coming two years, there will rest with me the blessed conviction that he is mine—and he is strengthened by the knowledge that somewhere in the world outside, one woman waits and prays for his release."[47]

One woman's prayers weren't enough to reform Cassese. After he served his term in federal prison, he returned to his criminal career, running an illegal distillery and a speakeasy in Brooklyn. He also returned to his wife, who welcomed him home and forgave "his escapades."[48]

10

Long Island
The Rumrunners Next Door

In the 1920s Long Island was a sparsely-populated paradise for rumrunners. The island's sheltered inlets, harbors, and streams offered excellent hiding places for booze boats. "Every creek and inlet on both shores receives its quota of darkened powerboats stealing in at all hours of the night with their loads," an observer wrote. The rumrunners unloaded their liquor cargos on dark beaches, where men waited to put the booze on trucks. Isolated estates, waterfront inns, and vacation cottages made ideal storage depots for the illegal alcohol until it could be moved to the Big Apple.[1]

The illegal liquor traffic thrived in virtually every waterfront town on Long Island. The rumrunners on the south shore were mostly long-time island residents who had good boating skills because they grew up fishing and sailing. In contrast, "a great many foreigners from New York" engaged in the liquor traffic on the north shore. Big Apple rummers often leased offices or cottages on the north shore to be near their boats and crews.[2]

Mother ships rode at anchor outside the rum line along the coast of Long Island. As conditions changed, the number of liquor freighters fluctuated, but the typical count was eight to ten during Volstead's early years. At night scores of motorboats sped out to the ships and returned to shore "with gunwales awash from the weight of their cargos." Most of the contraband was scotch or rye whiskey.[3]

Long Island had many spots where liquor smugglers could safely unload their cargo. Shore runners often landed at Montauk Point on the eastern end of the island or at Orient Point on the North Fork. Good landing spots dotted both sides of Long Island Sound, the waterway separating the island from Connecticut. On the island's southwestern shore, Sheepshead Bay, Coney Island, Gravesend Bay, Rockaway, and Jamaica Bay attracted rumrunners who transferred their liquor to trucks for an easy trip across the Brooklyn Bridge into Manhattan.

Contact boat skippers timed their trips to reach Rum Row after dark, so they left Long Island in mid- to late-afternoon, depending on the season, the weather conditions, and the position of the mother ships. The rum rings deployed lookouts with binoculars to watch for Coast Guard vessels and signal the contact boats. At Long Beach the shore runners waited in an inlet until the lookout raised a flag to signal "all clear." This sometimes inconvenienced other boaters. "Damn those rumrunners," a game warden said.

Patrol boats like this one played an essential role in the Coast Guard's war against rumrunners (National Archives and Records Administration).

"They were so thick in Jones Inlet yesterday afternoon that I couldn't navigate my boat. Then the flag went up and they all started full speed out to sea. They nearly ran me down."[4]

Rumrunners hungry for a big payday sometimes took too many risks. More than one shore runner overloaded his boat and suffered the consequences. A careless skipper loaded 20 cases on his boat, which should have held six. The boat rode low in the water, and the choppy sea swept the skipper overboard. He lost half of his booze but, luckily, not his life. In a similar incident, two men disappeared after sailing to Rum Row and loading too many cases on their small motorboat. Before they reached shore, fog developed, followed by a snowstorm. Their families believed the boat had capsized or the men had lost their bearings and sailed too far out to sea.[5]

To ensure a steady supply of booze, "certain unwritten rules" governed Long Island's liquor traffic. Generally, the rum ring boss chose the spot where the contact boats would land the liquor. The smart boss scouted every inch of the Long Island coast and found several suitable landing spots, so he didn't use the same one too often. Each day the spot was "chosen with regard to the activities of local officials and rumors of federal raids." The "dock fixer" was an essential player in the process because he bribed local policemen to ignore the rumrunners.[6]

Whenever islanders spotted a new ship on Rum Row, they expected a burst of activity. "As soon as a new ship appears, and sometimes long before they appear, there is a great activity all along the coast and on the roads leading to it," a newsman said. "Automobile trucks and vehicles of every kind hurry to different towns ... and meet people who tell them where to park their cars and wait."[7]

After the skipper of a contact boat picked up his cargo, an onshore lookout signaled him when it was safe to land. Flares and bonfires were used as signals, despite their limitations for sending messages. For more precise messaging, lookouts sent Morse code with large flashlights that emitted different colors of light. "Almost every night as far as the eye can see, one can make out the flickering lights of the signalers," an observer said.[8]

When the shore runner landed his boat, he usually ran up on the beach until the keel dug into the sand. The swampers, who had been waiting for the boat, waded into the water and began unloading it. The booze was placed on trucks to be moved to the city or a storage depot on the island. The swampers worked quickly, often forming a bucket brigade to move the burlocks from boat to truck. On cold nights the water was frigid, but the high pay offset the harsh working conditions.[9]

While swampers moved the booze from boat to truck, gunmen stood guard, ready for combat against robbers or lawmen. From time to time, a shootout between rumrunners and hijackers shattered Long Island's peaceful night. The rummers also engaged in gun battles with the Coast Guards, who patrolled the beaches on foot and the waterways in boats. Although many shots were fired in the gunfights, fatalities were rare, largely because the darkness limited visibility and accuracy. To prevent bloodshed, the gunners on CG boats had the option of shooting blanks or firing into the sky.

Long Island residents grew accustomed to heavy nighttime traffic on the roadways. "Nightly the speedy powerboats, in increasing numbers, bring in their supplies from the distant rum fleet and nightly the great, heavily-loaded trucks thunder over every Long Island highway that leads to New York." The bootleggers' speeding trucks were both a nuisance and "a menace to all other motorists."[10]

Long Island residents with a will to live stayed inside their homes at night. Stray bullets and speeding trucks could be injurious to a person's health. One civic-minded rum ring cleared the public off the beach before its contact boats arrived to unload liquor. When the shore crew ordered the beachgoers to leave, the wise civilians would skedaddle.

The men driving the liquor trucks had to avoid honest lawmen, who might confiscate their cargo. They also had to protect their cargo from hijackers, who might steal it. An ambush by hijackers was the greatest threat. The thieves might block the road with stalled cars or big tree limbs, or they could intentionally crash their vehicle into a truck to stop it. For safety, the rum rings formed convoys of trucks protected by heavily-armed gunmen in escort cars. Cautious smugglers who feared hijackers more than lawmen transferred their liquor cargos in the daylight. They had to spend more money paying off local authorities, but they greatly reduced the risk of being hijacked.[11]

Volstead enforcement was lax and sporadic on Long Island. In general, island residents didn't like Prohibition and didn't view the rumrunners as criminals. In fact, many Long Islanders lauded the rummers for defying an annoying law passed by chaw-bacons and church women.

Due to chronic budget shortages, New York's federal Prohibition office didn't have enough agents to station a permanent force on the island. The Prohis expected local law enforcement to take up the slack, but liquor traffickers found it easy to bribe the underpaid police. Most often they paid the police to simply ignore them. A few lawmen actively aided the liquor smugglers, usually by standing guard and/or keeping the roads open. "Long Beach police stand guard along the ocean while boats are unloaded between three and four o'clock in the morning," an informant told federal officials. To clear the roads for the liquor trucks, the motorcycle police rerouted the traffic, sending the public on annoying detours.[12]

From time to time, federal Prohibition officials decided to send a squad of agents to dry up Long Island. With uncanny accuracy, the rumrunners could "prophesy the coming on of a burst of federal activity." Presumably, someone "on the take" forewarned them. For the most part, the liquor smugglers acted "with great discretion" until the feds' enforcement frenzy subsided.[13]

In a short-lived crusade to dry up Long Island in 1924, federal Prohibition agents made arrests and confiscated liquor cargos. Early one morning, the Prohis pursued a convoy of six liquor trucks racing down an island highway toward the city. Local police saw the speeding vehicles and joined the chase. The lawmen stopped the convoy, arrested six men, and seized liquor valued at $25,000. A few weeks later, federal Prohibition agents arrested two bootleggers and seized a large quantity of whiskey at a liquor depot on Long Island.[14]

During the same enforcement crusade, customs agents captured a rumrunning yacht, three sloops, and a motorboat off Long Island. They also arrested 16 rumrunners. Customs officers and Prohibition agents fought rumrunners in "the first real marine battle Long Island Sound has witnessed since Prohibition became effective." For more than four hours, the lawmen on two patrol boats "waged a fruitless battle" against the steam yachts *Fantesma*, *Sioux*, and *Helen*. *Fantesma* carried an expensive cargo of liquor; the other two vessels were "traveling light and acting as scouts for the rum carrier." The Prohibition agents shot many rounds at *Fantesma*, but the yacht was protected by armor plate.[15]

The Volstead enforcers lost the battle "due to the smallness of the marine patrol boats ... which were unable to withstand the sea kicked up by the powerful yachts.... The lives of the customs crew were continually in peril...; but the men stood up under the strain without flinching." The turning point came when the patrol boats ran dangerously low on fuel. As the government vessels returned to port, *Fantesma* escaped with all of her liquor cargo.[16]

Although the burst of Volstead enforcement made headlines, it didn't turn Long Island into a dry district. The island's illegal liquor traffic "reached unprecedented proportions" and suffered virtually no interference from law enforcement. Residents, whether they worked in the liquor traffic or not, didn't help the police enforce the dry law. A federal agent found that both money and the fear of reprisal kept Long Islanders from aiding the Volstead enforcers. "Whole towns are in on the risks and profits," he said. "The bootleggers have not the slightest compunction in getting rid of the first person who shows signs of speaking out." He noted that "mysterious fires" had destroyed barns and reinforced the islanders' reticence.[17]

The illegal liquor traffic brought new opportunities and prosperity to Long Islanders. Rumrunning paid so well that some residents acted "as if they had struck oil." In the early 1920s at least three hundred residents were operating contact boats and "many times that number" helped distribute the liquor after it came ashore. To reduce the risk for the islanders who hauled booze in their own boats, the rum rings guaranteed to buy a man a new boat if law enforcement seized his. So many fishermen switched to rumrunning that New York's seafood markets had a shortage of product.[18]

The Long Island grapevine hummed with "amusing stories of sudden prosperity." For instance, one man was so poor that "his wife and family were fed by neighbors." When he went to work for a rum ring, his fortunes greatly improved. After a few months, he bought an automobile and had a small fortune, more than $30,000 in his bank account.[19]

Long Islanders spent much of their rumrunning income to renovate their homes. "There has been a general improvement of property and increase of taxable values," a newspaper reported. Rumrunning money bought new furniture, pianos, phonographs, and other everyday luxuries. Some residents made enough money to buy an auto, a prized possession too expensive for the average workingman. But very few islanders were "spoiled to the extent of putting much money into fine clothes."[20]

Ironically, as liquor smuggling increased, booze consumption seemed to decrease on Long Island. "Many who used to drink heavily are said to have become sober and industrious since they entered the rumrunning business," a journalist wrote.[21]

Rumrunners and Hostages

One of Long Island's rumrunning gangs began by leasing a large house on the waterfront in Bayville. Since the place didn't have a dock, they improvised one: a large, flat lightering scow on the beach, fastened with cables to nearby trees. They bought a yacht suitable for rumrunning, hired a crew, and sailed to Grand Bahamas Island.[22]

When the rummers reached the island, they renamed their yacht and gave it a facelift. They painted the new name on the ship, hauled down Old Glory, hoisted the Union Jack, and changed the registry from American to British. They bought their first cargo of liquor from a wholesaler. After it was loaded onto their vessel, they obtained clearance papers showing that their British yacht was bound for Montreal, Canada, a popular bogus destination. "[I]f all the liquor clearing Grand Bahama for Montreal were to arrive at that city, it could wash the streets with booze every week and still have enough to keep all the drinking classes in a comatose condition," a reporter wrote.[23]

After leaving the Bahamas, the yacht sailed without incident until it rounded Montauk Point, Long Island, where a U.S. government patrol boat stopped it. An official on the boat chatted with the rumrunners but didn't search their vessel. After issuing a stern warning against smuggling, he sailed away. The rummers arrived at their waterfront house before dusk but waited for darkness to unload their cargo. To pass the time, they took friends abroad the yacht and cruised around.[24]

After sunset the guests disembarked, and the rumrunners unloaded their contraband. They lowered half over the side onto the improvised wharf and covered it. They lugged the remaining whiskey up the steep embankment to the house, where they stashed it in the cellar until it could be sold. A bootlegger took orders for the whiskey and made numerous trips to deliver it. While the bootlegger did his job, the rummers sailed their yacht to the Bahamas to buy another cargo.[25]

Long Island resident Rudolph Wylk led a successful rum ring that smuggled liquor into New York for nearly a decade. His criminal career began when he and two accomplices committed bank fraud in 1920. When the case went to trial, one defendant pled guilty; the jury acquitted a defendant; and the court dismissed Wylk's indictment on technical grounds. Insiders said that Wylk used his share of the stolen bank money to fund his first rumrunning venture.[26]

Wylk built a prosperous syndicate that owned mother ships, contact boats, cars, trucks, and real estate, including liquor depots. The ring operated a fleet of at least six auxiliary schooners, each with space for thousands of cases of liquor. The mother ships picked up their cargo at Canadian ports or at St. Pierre, where the ring owned a warehouse. They carried liquor to ports along the East Coast as far south as Florida. Small towns in North and South Carolina were favorite landing spots.[27]

To avert suspicion, each liquor freighter carried burlocks hidden under a legitimate cargo. Typically, the mother ship cleared from St. Pierre for a port in North or South Carolina, sailed to that destination, and unloaded its legitimate cargo. Another cargo, often lumber, was taken onboard as a decoy, and the ship cleared for New York. When it arrived, the clearance papers indicated that it had come from a U.S. port, not a foreign island notorious for rumrunning. When the rummers took the hooch ashore, they stashed it in one of the ring's liquor depots on Long Island.[28]

To stay a step ahead of the Volstead enforcers, Wylk equipped his mother ships with radio. Onboard ship, the radioman intercepted messages sent by the Customs Service and the Coast Guard. He deciphered the messages, utilizing the official U.S. Navy codebook used by all the vessels in the Dry Fleet. Wylk didn't reveal how he came to possess the secret government codebook, but he wasn't averse to theft or bribery.[29]

The winter holiday season was an especially busy time for liquor smugglers because people partied more than usual. In December 1922 the Dry Navy formed a blockade to prevent booze boats from landing liquor for the holidays. A few days before Christmas, one of Wylk's mother ships broke through the blockade and headed for Baldwin Harbor, Long Island. Wylk took a shore crew to meet the ship at the pier. The men unloaded four hundred cases of liquor, stacking the burlocks on the wharf. As the ship sailed away, the crew began loading the liquor onto trucks. Suddenly, state troopers and special deputy sheriffs arrived on the scene. The lawmen trapped the rummers on the dock and arrested them.[30]

Two of the arrestees claimed to be truck drivers who knew nothing about rumrunning. They said Wylk had hired them to drive loads of oysters and clams into the city. They had come to the pier on an innocent mission—to supply "harmless and delicious bivalves" for Christmas dinner. They didn't know they were smuggling liquor until the lawmen burst on the scene. The officers took all the rumrunners, including the truck drivers, to jail. Wylk arranged for a bond company to bail them out.[31]

Two months after the December arrest, Wylk went to court to demand the return of a large cache of whiskey that lawmen had confiscated from a private home on the outskirts of Baldwin, Long Island. Wylk claimed ownership of the liquor, and his attorney argued that the seizure was illegal because the lawmen had entered the house without a search warrant. Wylk pled guilty to liquor possession, and the court ordered him to pay a small fine. Due to insufficient evidence, the judge didn't rule on the legality of the seizure. Wylk paid his fine and left without a court order to reclaim his booze.[32]

While the CG cutter *Gresham* was patrolling the Long Island coast in October 1924, Guards sighted an improvised distress signal flying on *Dorothy M. Smart*, a schooner

The Coast Guard acquired *Upshur (CG-15)* **from the Navy. The destroyer picketed mother ships off the coast of New York and New Jersey (National Archives and Records Administration).**

belonging to Rudolph Wylk's syndicate. *Gresham* easily overtook the rumrunner, which "was wallowing in the heavy seas without anchorage." The anchor chain slapped against the pitching bow, the rudder swung with the waves, and the masts had no sails.[33]

Onboard the schooner, the Guards found barrels of brandy along with the skipper and four disgruntled crewmen who said they had been shanghaied. The exhausted, parched, and hungry crew had been held hostage for 22 days on *Dorothy M. Smart*.[34]

The hostages' misadventure began when they went looking for work at the Sailors' Institute South in New York City. They signed on to crew on the *Enterprise*, a brick carrier that sailed on the East Coast. A man named Rudolph, who claimed to be the ship's engineer, said he would take them to the vessel. He drove them to Rockville Center, Long Island; because the weather was stormy, he checked them into a small hotel to wait for calmer seas. In the morning, Rudolph and another man drove the unsuspecting crew to Jones Inlet, where they all boarded a motorboat.[35]

Rudolph took the helm of the motorboat and headed out to sea. When he spotted a Coast Guard cutter, he abruptly changed course and raced away. After leaving the CG behind, he stopped the speedboat at a schooner and unloaded some supplies. Then he sailed to another schooner and told the new crewmen to climb aboard. When they did, the old crew jumped off the schooner into the motorboat. Rudolph sped away, leaving the shanghaied men behind. The ship's only other occupant was the snarling skipper, a veteran seadog who looked like he had weathered many voyages.[36]

The new crewmen saw cases of champagne stacked on the deck. They discovered whiskey, cognac, kimmel, and brandy in the cargo hold. The ship's larder held little food, and the galley stove didn't work properly. The water tanks contained a small supply of smelly water tainted with rust and dirt. The men realized they were hostages on Rum

Row, stuck on a shabby liquor freighter riding at anchor within sight of Ambrose Lightship.[37]

The skipper, who was armed with pistols, shot a few seagulls to show off his marksmanship. The hostages got the message. However, they outnumbered him. They quickly formulated vague plans to take command of the ship and sail into port. When the skipper issued orders, they refused to obey. He seemed to know what they were thinking; he warned that they would be arrested for mutiny and piracy if they took the ship into port. He spoke with authority, and he had guns. The hostages were unarmed, so they decided to follow orders for the time being and wait for a chance to escape.[38]

That evening when the sun went down, contact boats raced out to Rum Row. The skipper put his prisoners to work transferring liquor from the freighter to the speedboats. The busy boat traffic continued until a fierce storm rolled in, shortly after midnight. The captain shouted orders at his hostages, who handled the sails as best they could. The liquor freighter "tossed and pitched" for hours, and the strong winds blew it away from Rum Row.[39]

When the storm subsided, the skipper ordered his hostage crew to sail the ship back to Rum Row, and they obeyed. That evening, the shore runners came in a steady stream. The champagne sold quickly because it was priced right and packed in easy-to-handle cases. Few buyers wanted the kegs of brandy because they were expensive, heavy, and hard to handle. Shore runners soon bought all the champagne, kimmel, and cognac. Substantial quantities of brandy and rye whiskey remained in the cargo hold.[40]

During the day the skipper put his hostages to work, painting and doing repairs. While painting the hull, the trapped men discovered that they were aboard *Dorothy M. Smart*, not the *Enterprise*. They longed for a chance to escape, but they feared both the skipper and law enforcement. They didn't know if authorities would believe their tale of misfortune. They didn't want to go to prison for piracy or rumrunning. One day a CG cutter passed near enough for the hostages to flag it down, but they didn't have the nerve because "jail looked too close."[41]

The shanghaied crew endured shortages of food and fresh water because supplies weren't delivered regularly. On one occasion, a ship came alongside *Dorothy M. Smart* and the hostages traded a few bottles of rye whiskey for meat. The following day, a CG cutter tried to intercept a motorboat carrying water out to the mother ship *Athena*. The motorboat skipper, unable to reach his destination, changed course, pulled alongside *Dorothy M. Smart*, and let the hostages have five tanks of fresh water. A few days later a contact boat delivered potatoes, turnips, cigarettes, and pipe tobacco.[42]

After 12 days Rudolph, who had tricked the hostages onto the liquor freighter, returned to the ship. When he came onboard, the trapped crew demanded to go ashore. Sounding sympathetic, Rudolph agreed to take them back to port and pay their wages. However, he asked them to stay onboard until he could find a replacement crew. He said the skipper wouldn't be safe alone on the ship. Pirates lay in wait, watching Rum Row; they would murder the lone man and steal everything of value. If the hostages would agree to stay only one more night, Rudolph promised to return the next day with a new crew.[43]

Rudolph appealed to their better nature, so the prisoners agreed to stay onboard. Unfortunately, they misplaced their trust. Rudolph didn't return as promised. The meager foodstuffs ran out, and the hostages went hungry. One night a strong gale drove *Dorothy M. Smart* off course. Winds battered the schooner, and the anchor chain snapped. Disaster threatened. To survive, the kidnapped crew followed the skipper's orders, worked together, and saved the ship.[44]

After the men had been held hostage for three weeks, Rudolph finally returned. He sailed out to the liquor freighter on a motorboat, bringing an armed gunman with him. To replenish the ship's larder, he brought chickens and apples but nothing else—not even potable water for the parched, exhausted men.

The hostages, desperate to go ashore, rushed to Rudolph's motorboat, hoping to climb aboard. The gunman reacted quickly, blocking the way. Protected by the gunsel, Rudolph tried to mollify his prisoners. He promised to return in two days to take them ashore. But they had heard his promises before. They demanded to go immediately. While they were arguing with Rudolph, one of the hostages saw a CG cutter in the distance and tried to signal it. Rudolph and the gunman yelled at him, threatening to kill him. The hostage backed off; Rudolph and his gunsel hopped into the motorboat and raced away.[45]

The following day the trapped crewmen sighted the CG cutter *Gresham*. Hungry for freedom, they vowed to stop it. The skipper was below deck, and a hostage went down to keep him busy while the others quickly hoisted an old, tattered blanket to the masthead. Although the blanket was flying on the mast, the cutter passed by without stopping. The hostages were stunned. Then they realized their mistake; they must fly the blanket at half-mast to signal distress. They could still see the cutter in the distance, so they had hope.

One of the prisoners climbed into the rigging, grabbed the blanket, and frantically waved it. The cutter changed course and headed for *Dorothy M. Smart*. Although the rummy skipper was below deck, he sensed something was afoot. He rushed onto the deck, but he was too late because the Guards had already seen the distress signal.[46]

Following protocol, the CG commander asked the rummy skipper if he wanted to put into port. The skipper replied that he didn't but would put into port if ordered to do so. The CG commander gave the order, and *Dorothy M. Smart* followed *Gresham* to Ellis Island, where a prize crew boarded the liquor freighter and took control.[47]

When questioned by the authorities, *Dorothy M. Smart*'s skipper claimed he had discovered the schooner on Rum Row, a derelict with a crew but no captain. He had taken command of the vessel, even though he didn't know the crewmen or how they came to be onboard.[48] His story made no sense, but an indictment seemed unlikely. Rudolph Wylk had done the dirty work, kidnapping the crew and carrying them out to the ship. Law enforcement needed to identify Rudolph and arrest him, but the hostages didn't even know his last name.

Authorities took the freed hostages to the Seamen's Institute, where they were paid a month's salary. Subsequently, they took legal action and successfully libeled *Dorothy M. Smart*. When the U.S. Marshal's office sold the vessel at public auction, the money went to the former hostages as compensation for their ordeal.[49]

After *Dorothy M. Smart* was sold at auction, the Wylk syndicate regained control of the vessel. Wylk began using *Dorothy M. Smart* in tandem with two other mother ships, *Vinces* and *Amaranth*. *Dorothy M. Smart* functioned as a tender or supply ship, delivering booze to the other two. On a regular basis, *Dorothy M. Smart* sailed to St. Pierre and picked up a large load of liquor. Then it sailed south, met *Vinces* in international waters, and transferred the entire liquor cargo. While *Dorothy M. Smart* headed back to St. Pierre, *Vinces* met *Amaranth*, usually off the coast of Virginia, and shared the cargo. *Amaranth* then sailed farther south to land the liquor in North or South Carolina. By using *Dorothy M. Smart* as a tender, Wylk kept both *Vinces* and *Amaranth* supplied with liquor cargos on a regular basis. If *Amaranth* sailed to St. Pierre, picked up liquor, and returned to North Carolina, the trip took 20 days. Under Wylk's system, *Amaranth* had a new cargo every ten days.[50]

Vinces often sold its share of the liquor cargo in the waters around Fire Island. While the mother ship lay at anchor, scallop fishermen came out and bought hooch. Then they went about their fishing as usual. After two or three days, the fishermen returned to port with the liquor concealed under the scallops they had caught.[51]

In 1927 Coast Guards patrolling off the coast of North Carolina saw *Dorothy M. Smart* transfer a liquor cargo to *Vinces*. Working on the assumption that *Vinces* would try to land the liquor, the CG sent the cutter *Mascoutin* to follow the mother ship. The cutter maintained radio silence to avoid detection by *Vinces*, which was equipped with a radiotelephone as well as a spark transmitter and receiver.[52]

Mascoutin's captain found *Vinces* inside the rum line and set a course to intercept the mother ship. When the rummy skipper saw the CG cutter, he quickly turned his ship around and headed out to sea. The CG captain swung his vessel around in an arc and came astern of *Vinces*. The Guards blew whistles, signaling for the mother ship to stop. But the rumrunner sailed on. The Guards fired a blank shot across *Vinces'* bow and then sent four service rounds over the mastheads.[53]

Mascoutin drew abreast of the mother ship, and the CG commander ordered the rummy skipper to stop. The rumrunner ignored the order. The Guards sent more shots over the schooner, lowering the elevation with each round. When the CG captain again demanded surrender, the rummy skipper bellowed that he wouldn't give up as long as his vessel was seaworthy. *Mascoutin's* captain accepted the challenge. He ordered his gunner to fire a solid shot across the rumrunner's bow. The shell crashed through *Vinces'* bulwarks and hit the rail, a hatch, and a dory. Although the damage was minor, it was enough for the rummy skipper. He surrendered.[54]

When the Guards boarded *Vinces*, they found malt, whiskey, and champagne worth more than $73,000. They arrested the crew, seized the vessel, and collected evidence that could be used in court. Strangely, they found no log book or manifest. The skipper showed his clearance papers and said he was not required to have a log book or manifest because he was sailing from St. Pierre to Nassau. He stated that he believed the CG had stopped him in international waters, but he had made no soundings to ascertain his exact position. He denied that he had been headed for the shore to land his liquor cargo. *Mascoutin* took *Vinces* in tow to the Charleston Lightship and then to Savannah.[55]

Although *Vinces* belonged to Wylk's syndicate, the owner of record was the Smart Shipping Company of Nova Scotia. Smart Shipping went to federal court, trying to reclaim the ship. The primary issue was whether the CG had illegally seized *Vinces*, which had British registry, in international waters. The arguments focused on the principles of navigation and the location of the vessels on the high seas. An expert who testified for the government stated that the CG cutter had first confronted the rumrunner in U.S. territorial waters and had pursued it beyond the 12-mile limit because it attempted to escape. The court ruled that the seizure was legal under the "hot pursuit" doctrine, which allowed the CG to capture a rumrunner in international territory if the chase had begun in U.S. waters. Thus, the federal government owned *Vinces* and could sell it.[56]

In a familiar rumrunning scenario, the federal government sold *Vinces* and it returned to Wylk's fleet. The CG kept it under surveillance as it sailed up and down the East Coast. Patrol boat *CG-290*, commanded by Boatswain Alexander Cornell, confronted *Vinces* off the Long Island coast, not far from Montauk Point, in September 1929. When *CG-290* sailed toward the mother ship, the rummy skipper didn't try to run away. Rather, he turned his ship's prow toward the CG cutter and sped straight ahead, intending to ram it. Cornell quickly maneuvered the cutter out of harm's way and ordered his gunner to fire blank shells at *Vinces*. The rummy skipper changed tactics and tried to outrun the patrol boat, but Cornell overtook the mother ship and captured it.[57]

This time, the government didn't auction *Vinces* off to the highest bidder. The CG brass decided that the schooner would be a valuable asset to the Dry Navy. Rechristened *CG-821*, the vessel switched sides in America's Rum War.[58]

Coast Guards stationed at Norfolk, Virginia, spotted Wylk's *Amaranth* hovering off the coast in 1927. An intelligence officer notified Washington that *Amaranth* was waiting for a "favorable opportunity to elude" the CG picket and unload a liquor cargo on the banks of the South Edisto River. "This vessel has succeeded in doing this many times during the past year, and it is only recently that we succeeded in finding the general territory," the officer wrote. He added that rumrunning vessels were "entering the Capes almost unmolested and proceeding up the Bay to the many different points available for discharge."[59]

Although *Amaranth* usually operated along the Southeast coast, the CG cutter *Boutwell* encountered it near Long Island in December 1929. While following the mother ship, *Boutwell*'s skipper saw a good opportunity to aggressively chase it. The cutter overtook *Amaranth* several miles off Long Beach. The Guards arrested the rummy crew and confiscated a cargo of gin and champagne. *Amaranth*'s captain was indicted, but the case never went to trial because he absconded to Canada, which rarely extradited fugitives accused of Volstead crimes.[60]

The customs service discovered *William E. Litchfield*, a Wylk ship, in the Hudson River off Yonkers in 1928. To avert suspicion, the liquor freighter had been painted bright green and white, rather than the dark colors typically used on black ships. Despite *William E. Litchfield*'s new paint job, customs officers recognized it as a veteran rumrunner. Upon inspection, they found a deck cargo of laths covering a huge stash of liquor valued at $400,000.[61]

The U.S. attorney's office appeared to have no interest in prosecuting Wylk. He seemed to have immunity, perhaps because he was paying large bribes to law enforcement. But the feds didn't actually give Wylk a free pass. Federal agents spent nearly a year investigating his rum ring, "adding link after link in the chain" of evidence against him. One valuable informant was the widow of a rumrunner who had died when a Wylk ship sank during a storm. She felt betrayed because she couldn't collect survivor's insurance money and Wylk gave her no financial help.[62]

When the U.S. attorney's office had sufficient evidence, the case went to the grand jury, which returned sealed indictments against 13 men, including Wylk. Subsequently, Wylk and several accomplices were arrested at an estate near Hempstead, Long Island. Customs agents searched the property and confiscated burlocks holding $300,000 worth of uncut whiskey. (St. Joseph's Sisterhood, an order of nuns, owned the estate but did not occupy it; law enforcement concluded that the sisters weren't involved in rumrunning.)[63]

Wylk and his henchmen went on trial in federal court in November 1929. One defendant turned state's evidence and testified against the other men. He stated that the rum ring operated a fleet of six schooners and numerous speedboats, which routinely landed cargos of booze in New York and North Carolina. Favorite landing spots were Montauk Point on Long Island; the Neuse River between Oriental and Morehead City, North Carolina; and Beaufort Inlet, North Carolina, between North Edisto and Meggett.[64]

A "boss stevedore" from Jacksonville, Florida, testified about loading timber on *William E. Litchfield*. He stated that the lumber was arranged aboard the schooner "in such a manner as to leave a large concealed hole amidships," which could be filled with

The Coast Guard cutter *Chelan*, launched in 1928, had cutting-edge technology, including modern radio communications (Library of Congress).

a cargo of illegal liquor. A lumber commission merchant from Miami confirmed that timber had been loaded on the schooner. A ship chandler from Jacksonville identified Wylk as the man who had paid him for repairs made to *William E. Litchfield*.[65]

A radio engineer also testified for the prosecution. He said he had sailed with Wylk to Halifax, Nova Scotia, and installed a radio on the mother ship *Amaranth*. Then the two men traveled to Liverpool, Nova Scotia, where he installed similar equipment on *Vinces*. Wylk demanded that the radioman sail aboard *Vinces* to monitor the equipment and assured him that he could go ashore near New York City. Although he didn't trust Wylk, he agreed to sail on *Vinces*. Due to a storm, the mother ship changed course, and the captain sent the radioman ashore in a small boat. He landed on an isolated stretch of coast in North Carolina. Although he had little money, he managed to make his way back to New York.[66]

The radioman didn't sail on *Vinces* again, but he agreed to do more work for the rum ring, building radio sets and stations. The radio sets had a radius of roughly five hundred miles and could be used to transmit voices as well as coded signals. The radioman set up land-based stations in several locations, including Brooklyn, New York, and Beaufort Inlet, North Carolina. He claimed he didn't know how the sets or the stations were used. He "surmised" that certain of Wylk's ships carried liquor, but he didn't know that for a fact.[67]

Before the case went to the jury, the defense argued that the various charges against the defendants should be consolidated into a blanket charge of conspiracy. The state agreed to bundle the charges, but that didn't help the defendants. The jurors found Wylk guilty of conspiring to violate the Prohibition and customs laws. His codefendants, with one exception, were also convicted. The judge sentenced Wylk to two years in federal prison; the other men received shorter terms.[68]

Father Knows Best

Antonio Romano, Sr., didn't want his sons, Michelangelo and Antonio Jr., to become rumrunners. He advised them to stay away from smuggling because it was risky business. He warned that they might be cheated out of money and would have no legal recourse. "This is a business in which you cannot make any claims afterward," he wrote in a letter. If they went ahead with their rumrunning scheme, they must make the buyers "pay before the discharge of the merchandise." He also warned them about the duplicity of their cousin, who had already involved them in a disastrous scheme to smuggle illegal aliens into New York.[69]

The father was alluding to a voyage when Michelangelo captained *Dori* (AKA *Zetti*), a ship that carried illegal immigrants. Approximately 150 men paid to be smuggled from Sicily to New York City. Their voyage was almost complete when *Dori* encountered a Coast Guard vessel off the coast of New York. Michelangelo panicked and refused to land his passengers in the United States. He made port in Nova Scotia and hastily put the Sicilians ashore. Canadian officials caught most of *Dori*'s Italian passengers and deported them.[70]

Despite this smuggling fiasco, the Romano brothers ignored their father's advice and set out to make money as rumrunners. They went into partnership with their shady cousin, who bankrolled the venture.[71]

On New Year's Eve 1924 the patrol boat *CG-234* (AKA *Red Wing*) put into Huntington Harbor, Long Island, because a storm was brewing. *Arco Felice II*, captained by Michelangelo Romano, lay at anchor inside the rum line at the entrance to the harbor. The *CG-234* skipper thought the four-masted schooner looked like a mother ship, so he went aboard for an inspection. When questioned, Romano stated that his ship, which flew the Italian flag, had cleared port in Honduras on its way to Havana, Cuba. At first he said *Arco Felice II* had been blown off course and never reached Havana. Later, he stated that it had stopped in Havana.[72]

Upon searching *Arco Felice II*, the Guards found a case of champagne, two cases of scotch whiskey, several guns, and a few bottles of liquor in the crew's quarters. The ship's manifest showed that it had sailed from Honduras with a cargo of more than eight thousand cases of liquor shipped by "Fred Smith." The clearance papers gave the ship's final destination as the island of St. Pierre. The log showed that *Arco Felice II* had encountered bad weather and tried to outrun the storm. Water rose in the bilges, sand clogged the pumps, and the vessel faced "serious danger."[73]

When questioned about Fred Smith's large consignment, Michelangelo claimed that the choppy seas and damage to the ship had forced him to jettison the booze off the coast of Newport, Rhode Island. He had ordered the crew to begin throwing the cases overboard on Christmas morning, and it had taken them more than 40 hours to finish the job.[74]

Law enforcement arrested the Romano brothers and their crew for rumrunning. Long Island residents told undercover agents that *Arco Felice II* had hovered offshore for a week before anchoring at Huntington Harbor. While the ship rode at anchor, armed men guarded the beach and contact boats spent three nights moving cases of liquor to shore. After the booze was loaded on trucks, "sullen-looking men" with rifles rode shotgun as the vehicles drove away in the direction of New York City.[75]

Long Island residents seemed to know a great deal about *Arco Felice II*, but they became strangely quiet when prosecutors looked for witnesses who would testify in court. Luckily for the prosecutors, the crewmen arrested on *Arco Felice* could be given immunity to testify against the Romanos. The state's case suffered a serious setback when all but one of the sailors disappeared before the trial began. The men forfeited their bonds, and the rumor mill said they had fled to Cuba or South America. The only remaining *Arco Felice* crewman was indicted along with the Romano brothers.[76]

When the *Arco Felice II* case went to court, the Romano brothers and their accomplice were charged with illegally importing alcohol into the United States. The prosecution relied heavily on the scant evidence found aboard the ship, arguing that the three cases of liquor were all that remained of more than eight thousand. The jury returned guilty verdicts for all of the defendants. The court sentenced the rumrunners to jail terms of nine to 24 months.[77]

The defense attorneys petitioned the appeals court to overturn the convictions. They argued that the discovery of three cases of liquor onboard *Arco Felice II* was not sufficient evidence for inferring that the ship had carried more than eight thousand cases. The appeals court agreed, stating, "We think no reasonable man could draw such an inference, and therefore it was error to let the jury speculate." Even if the ship had carried a large liquor cargo, there was no proof it was sold in New York. It could've been sold in international waters, unloaded in another country, "or even abandoned at sea." Therefore, the appeals court reversed the conviction and directed the lower court to dismiss the indictment.[78]

The Romano brothers beat the rap. They were free to take their father's advice or return to liquor smuggling.

11

"Big Bill" Dwyer
The Czar of Rum Row

Every night shore runners roared up to docks along the New York-New Jersey coast, delivering illegal liquor for the thirsty throngs. The Big Apple and its environs were a gargantuan market for booze. The populace wanted alcohol, and the proscription against it meant little. Everyone, from Hoboken's poorest rag picker to Gotham's richest financier, seemed to hate the Volstead law. The area's insatiable demand for whiskey spawned smuggling ventures that created rich, powerful liquor lords. Many rumrunners belonged to a syndicate led by William "Big Bill" Dwyer, known as the Czar of Rum Row.

"As Easy as Tomatoes"

In New York's underworld, it was common knowledge that Dwyer commanded the biggest fleet of booze boats in the Northeast. Like other liquor lords, he spent vast sums of money to bribe policemen, Coast Guards, and government officials. But he failed to corrupt at least one honest man: U.S. Attorney Emory Buckner, who put Big Bill at the top of his most-wanted rumrunners list.

Dwyer grew up in Hell's Kitchen, a seething urban cauldron that produced many gangsters. In his youth he worked as a stevedore and strong arm on the waterfront. He loved to gamble, so he started a two-bit illegal bookmaking racket. When Volstead came along, he had the nerve, the underworld contacts, and the waterfront savvy needed for rumrunning. His instinctive business skills quickly propelled him to the upper echelon of Gotham's alcohol aristocracy. He was a genial, free-spending man-about-town who liked nightlife and "action." He was equally comfortable with mobsters, blue collar guys, and society swells.

Dwyer invested part of his rumrunning millions in legal businesses, including restaurants, racetracks, and sports teams. He imported athletes as well as booze. In the 1920s, ice hockey crossed the Canadian border to become a sports sensation in U.S. colleges. Dwyer was among the first to see the potential for professional ice hockey in the United States. He bought a team of Canadian players, moved them to the Big Apple, and named them the New York Americans. He was so excited about hockey that he paid for Madison Square Garden's first ice-making machinery, in order to showcase his team there.[1]

In December 1925 the New York Americans, wearing star-spangled uniforms, debuted at Madison Square Garden, playing the Montreal Canadiens. The game, a charity fundraising event for a hospital, drew both hockey fans and society types from prominent clans, including the Roosevelt, Astor, Tiffany, Whitney, and Scribner families. "Society was out in force and the gorgeous gowns of the women blended a picture at which even an artist would have marveled," a spectator wrote. "The white line of men in evening dress around the edge of the rink served to create the impression of snow."[2]

The Montreal Canadiens skated onto the ice accompanied by the Governor General's Foot Guards Band decked out in crimson jackets, black trousers, and tall fur hats. The band from Ottawa paraded around the rink, "exhibiting various formations." Then, with a trumpet fanfare, the West Point Cadets' Band heralded the Americans' entry. After military-style drills, "with a fancy twist the cadets and the star-spangled players lined up opposite their rivals from the north." The bands played the national anthems of both countries.[3]

The New York Americans, dubbed the Amazin' Amerks by fans, lost their first game. Many other losses followed. Partying seemed to interest the players more than training. Dwyer housed his team in a small hotel he owned near Madison Square Garden. The jocks turned the place into a sort of frat house where bootleggers and broads supplied all their party needs. When they went clubbing, they were treated like royalty at the Big Apple's trendy speakeasies.[4]

Czar Dwyer missed his team's first game at Madison Square Garden because he was keeping a low profile. He had recently spent a few days in jail after being arrested for Volstead violations. This was not the right time for him to make a very visible public appearance. If he showed up at the Garden, the police might arrest him on additional charges, which would guarantee unflattering headlines and overshadow the game.

Due to the press coverage of Dwyer's arrest, the public knew a great deal about his rum ring. Big Bill made his headquarters in a bank building on Lexington Avenue in Manhattan; the ring had field offices in Brooklyn, Long Island, and New London. The syndicate built and maintained boats at marine garages on the Harlem River and the East River near the Hell Gate Bridge. Experienced boat builders as well as skilled sailors worked for the rum ring. According to a reliable source, the syndicate had eight hundred employees on its payroll.[5]

Dwyer's syndicate owned a fleet of vessels, including at least four schooners and 15 contact boats. The ring raked in millions supplying "the greater part of the liquor" smuggled into Gotham via New York harbor. Law enforcement didn't interfere with Dwyer's booze boats that delivered their illegal cargos to piers on the North and East rivers. Unloading liquor on the North River was "as easy as tomatoes," the Czar of Rum Row told a confidante.[6]

In addition to sending its mother ships abroad to buy whiskey, the Dwyer ring bought booze from liquor freighters on Rum Row. The czar's minions also hijacked booze cargos from other rumrunners. His syndicate "distributed wholesale quantities to 'middlemen' acting as bootleg jobbers," who sold it to retail outlets. Dwyer was so powerful that he collected $2 per case on "all liquor brought into New York City by rumrunners and bootleggers not members" of his ring.[7]

The star of Dwyer's Whiskito Fleet was *Klip,* a steel-clad powerboat that raced from Rum Row to shore in head-spinning time. The police patrol boat *Gypsy*, with a top speed of 34 mph, was the only enforcement vessel that could keep pace with the fastest booze boats in New York Harbor. Despite Dwyer's payoffs to officials, *Gypsy* sometimes chased *Klip*.[8]

Early in the morning on October 23, 1925, *Gypsy* was positioned at the Narrows off Rosebank, Staten Island. As the sun rose, the police patrol boat lurked in a dark hiding spot beside the shore. Suddenly *Gypsy's* skipper saw *Klip* shoot through the Narrows so fast it seemed to soar above the water. He took off after it. The motorboat roared away, with the patrol boat close behind. At top speed, the boats circled the Statue of Liberty, tore through the Narrows, raced around Fort Lafayette Island, and spurted through the Narrows again. They zigzagged across the bay, darting in and out of the morning boat traffic. *Klip* swung around Lady Liberty, with the patrol boat on its tail. The lawmen and the rumrunners exchanged gunfire. Bullets whistled across the water, barely missing commuters on the morning ferries.[9]

After a thrilling half-hour, the *Gypsy* skipper outmaneuvered *Klip*, trapping the powerboat in a recessed pocket in the shoreline. Seeing no way to escape, the rummy crew surrendered without a fight. The police found two hundred cases of scotch whiskey on *Klip*.[10] Even though the cargo was small, law enforcement had captured a real prize— the flagship of Dwyer's Whiskito Fleet.

U.S. customs officials learned that the steamship *Augusta* was at anchorage on the Hudson River above Edgewater, New Jersey, in July 1925. According to official records, *Augusta* engaged in coastwise trade, which meant that it was clearly out of place in waters plied by small craft, ferries, and river steamboats. Moreover, *Augusta's* location showed that the rumrunning ship had breached the Dry Navy's blockade of New York Harbor. It had either broken through or bribed its way through the "starvation and surveillance" perimeter.[11]

To keep *Augusta* under surveillance, the customs service dispatched a lone investigator who watched the ship from a distance. Subsequently, customs officials sent two inspectors to board the vessel and search it. They found mountains of coal but only a small quantity of whiskey, far too little for a mother ship. The crewmen confessed that the coal had hidden a cargo of liquor, but they claimed the booze had already been unloaded. The customs officials decided to keep searching, anyway. They ordered *Augusta* to move to the Statue of Liberty anchorage, where "expert searchers" began digging through the coal. Under coal in the bunkers, they found nearly four thousands cases and 50 kegs of liquor. Federal officials confiscated the booze along with the ship.[12]

The U.S. attorney's office needed time to prepare the case that would prove the Dwyer ring owned *Augusta's* liquor cargo. While the prosecutors put that case together, law enforcement moved to smash the syndicate. A large squad of Prohibition agents, deputy U.S. marshals, and New York City policemen set out on "the greatest roundup in the history of Prohibition." They carried arrest warrants for 43 men charged with multiple counts of conspiracy to violate the Volstead law. In less than an hour, they nabbed 20 of the wanted men, including Dwyer, several of his henchmen, a corrupt Coast Guard commander, and four Guardsmen.[13]

While searching the syndicate offices, lawmen found the key to the rum ring's secret code, which was so simple a schoolboy could've created it. The unsophisticated code substituted "sick" for "south," "easy" for "east," "nicely" for "north," and "well" for "west." The name of a ship was disguised by spelling it backwards. "Boy" referred to Montauk Point, "girl" Block Island, and "twins" Rum Row.[14]

The lawmen also found the key to the light signals used by the dishonest Coast Guards on Dwyer's payroll. The corrupt Guards utilized lights to tell the shore runners whether to sail or stay put. For example, if the signal light on a CG patrol boat flashed three times, the skippers on Dwyer's contact boats could safely transport their liquor from Rum Row to the docks.[15]

Czar Dwyer didn't put up a fight when lawmen took him into custody. At his arraignment, he smiled brightly and exuded cheery confidence. He wore gangster finery and flashy diamonds, including a glittery ring with gems that formed a swastika (a symbol of magical good luck before the Nazi era). Dwyer's attorney told the court that the allegations against his client were "pure romance." He said he would easily disprove the state's "ridiculous charges" when the case went to trial.[16]

U.S. Attorney Buckner stated that his staff was building a strong case against Dwyer, based primarily on the syndicate's own records. During the dragnet, the lawmen had confiscated stacks of records, including crucial financial documents. In addition, Buckner subpoenaed the telegraph companies to give him copies of all telegrams and cables sent or received by Dwyer's office in the two months preceding the roundup. Based on the paper trail, Buckner concluded that Dwyer's syndicate had smuggled more than $40 million worth of liquor into New York in less than three years.[17]

Buckner asserted that "the ring's business was as highly organized as that of any efficient manufacturer or merchant." Like a corporation, the Dwyer syndicate divided its operations into departments, such as purchasing, distribution, and intelligence. When a booze boat landed, the distribution department had men and trucks waiting to quickly unload the liquor cargo. Operatives called "roadmen" facilitated the swift transfer from the waterfront to the warehouse. The roadmen cleared the driving route, so the syndicate's truck convoy encountered no traffic tie-ups, hijackers, or honest lawmen. Corrupt police officers sometimes worked as roadmen, using their authority to detour traffic and close roads to ordinary drivers. Paperwork seized from "the ring's disbursing officer" showed a payment of $4,400 to ensure that the route would be clear for one night's convoy.[18]

Dwyer's rum ring maintained "a secret service" with undercover agents who mimicked the methods of government spies. The syndicate's secret agents ferreted out information from lawmen and also shadowed Prohibition administrators in New York and Washington, D.C. The ring paid a dishonest Prohibition agent to serve as a "liaison officer" because he could talk to government officials without arousing any suspicion. He acted as a go-between, conveying messages from Dwyer to public officials on the take.[19]

To facilitate shipments of liquor from foreign ports, the Dwyer ring had purchasing agents in London, Montreal, and St. Pierre. The syndicate kept an airplane pilot on standby at Long Island. When called upon, he flew his airplane out to sea, made contact with the mother ships, and directed them "to the positions they were to take at various times for unloading their cargo."[20]

U.S. Attorney Buckner decried the "bribery, corruption, perjury, and prostitution of government officials" that allowed Dwyer to defy the Dry Law. The Czar of Rum Row handed out princely bribes, even to low-ranking uniformed cops and Coast Guardsmen.

He routinely paid Coast Guard crews from $1,000 to $8,400 for allowing his rum boats to land liquor at a specific time and place. "These men had their price, but it was high," Buckner said. "The thirty pieces of silver that bought Judas is pocket change today."[21]

Dwyer didn't limit his largess to cash. He and his top lieutenants became friends with the Guards they corrupted. "Frequently, members of the Coast Guard were wined, feasted and entertained in royal fashion at some of the best restaurants, theatres and gilded night palaces in the city," Buckner said. "On one occasion…. Guardsmen were taken to a well-known hotel in the city. There they found that in addition to other forms of entertainment girls had been furnished by the rum ring for each of them. The party was given in a suite of rooms, and … it was lavish, to say the least."[22]

Due to the widespread violation of the Volstead law, Guardsmen found it easy to disregard Prohibition. In restaurants, hotels, and speakeasies, Guards witnessed "violations of the Prohibition law without apparent fear of interference," Buckner said. Thus, it was "but a small step for them to yield to the temptation to look the other way when the rum ship of their host and friend goes by and then receive sometimes as high as a year's salary for their purely passive services."[23]

Despite the corruption, Buckner stated that most Guardsmen were honest. He lauded "the loyal members of the Coast Guard who daily risk their lives for duty" while "they witness their weaker brothers" enjoying luxuries purchased with bribe money from the liquor lords.[24]

The Czar's Trial

Dwyer's trial got off to a slow start in July 1926. The Czar of Rum Row had just fired his attorney, purportedly because the man demanded too much money. Hence, Dwyer opened by asking the judge to postpone his trial, giving him enough time to find new counsel. U.S. Attorney Buckner objected, saying that Dwyer wanted a delay so he could go to Cincinnati to attend opening day at his racetrack there. The judge refused to postpone the trial.[25]

Finding citizens to fill the jury box proved to be time-consuming. The potential jurors knew they would have to sit in an uncomfortable chair in a hot courtroom without air conditioning. The trial would probably drag on for three or four sweltering weeks. Moreover, New Yorkers generally disliked the Dry Law and didn't want to waste their time serving on the jury in a Volstead trial. One potential juror spoke for many New Yorkers when he declared, "[I]n the first place I am against Prohibition, and in the second place I am against its enforcement."[26]

After the process of finding jurors was finished, the trial began in earnest. Buckner had appointed one his young assistants as lead prosecutor. Nevertheless, the U.S. attorney played a major role in presenting the state's case against Dwyer and his codefendants.

The prosecution's first witness was a rumrunning skipper who worked for the Dwyer ring. He testified that he had served in the U.S. Navy, where he learned to sail. After being honorably discharged, he sailed contact boats for Dwyer, delivering liquor to piers on the North and East rivers. On a typical run, his boat carried up to 750 cases. He usually received his orders directly from Dwyer via telephone. Before leaving the waterfront, he also received a handwritten note in code, specifying how many cases to take from the mother ship. Although he sometimes carried champagne or sauterne, he mostly delivered whiskey.

For each load the skipper brought to shore, Dwyer paid him $200 plus a case of liquor, which he shared with his crew. He had made roughly two hundred rumrunning trips, and law enforcement had seized only five of his cargos. Police arrested him only once; Dwyer furnished his bail and a lawyer, who arranged for the charges to be dropped.[27]

Under oath the skipper stated that uniformed New York City police had usually been present when he unloaded his illegal cargo at piers on the North or East River. He also said that railway police and New Jersey lawmen helped unload liquor at the Erie Railroad pier in Weehawken "on one or two occasions." Once during a phone conversation with Dwyer before heading out to the mother ship, the skipper worried aloud that patrol boats, especially the fast *Gypsy*, might pursue him. "They will not be anywhere near you tonight," the czar assured him.[28]

Defense attorneys impeached the skipper's credibility by producing his service records from the U.S. Navy. The documents showed that he had enlisted twice and deserted twice. He had been court-martialed, dishonorably discharged, and sentenced to a military prison. The shadow over the skipper deepened when evidence revealed that he had been a double agent, paid by the federal government to supply information about Dwyer while working for the rum ring. A defense attorney called the skipper "a moral monstrosity" and said he had never known "a perjurer of such proportions to take the stand."[29]

Although the skipper claimed that the Navy records were inaccurate, the court held him on a charge of perjury. The judge told the jury that the seaman's lies about his military service must be separated from his testimony about the rum ring. The skipper had lied about his service record, but that did not automatically mean he was lying about Dwyer.[30]

The state called a surprise witness, Paul Crim, a fugitive from justice and former Coast Guardsman who had worked for the rum ring. The indictment against Dwyer had named Crim as a co-conspirator, but he had disappeared and evaded arrest. He testified that Dwyer had arranged for him to hide out, first in New York and later in Canada. When a government agent found him at the Mount Royal racetrack in Montreal, he agreed to testify against the Czar of Rum Row.[31]

Crim admitted taking bribes from Dwyer, whom he had met shortly after joining the Coast Guard. Dwyer, through his high-ranking contacts in Washington, arranged for Crim to serve on the patrol boat *CG-203* in New York. The czar, with Crim's help, bribed the *CG-203* crew to allow the ring's rumrunning vessels to operate unhindered. When Crim complained to Dwyer that he wasn't being paid enough, the czar said he could make more if *CG-203* actually carried alcohol. Crim convinced the *CG-203* captain to smuggle liquor, and the patrol boat delivered booze on two occasions, landing seven hundred cases of scotch on one trip. Crim, who was paid $700 for that trip, decided to work full-time for the syndicate. He became Dwyer's personal chauffeur and also worked on the shore crew that unloaded liquor cargos.[32]

Other former Coast Guards, including a petty officer, corroborated Crim's testimony about aiding the rum ring. A prosecution witness said he had captained one of the Dwyer's contact boats but quit because he wasn't making enough money. He decided to join the Coast Guard and, with the czar's help, received an appointment as a warrant officer in Cape May, New Jersey. Later Dwyer asked the warrant officer if he wanted a transfer to New York and promised to discuss it with "the big boss in Washington." When the officer asked Dwyer if he had all the CG brass on the ring's payroll, the czar said "not all, only some." He added that several officers never asked for money but took "presents for their wives." A few were "just good sports," he said.[33]

The prosecution called U.S. Customs officials to testify about the seizure of the mother ship *Augusta* on the Hudson River. A case of scotch whiskey found on *Augusta* was submitted as evidence. A government chemist testified that she had tested samples of the confiscated scotch and found that it contained nearly 40 percent alcohol by volume. A defense attorney suggested that the jurors should take the evidence to the jury room for a taste test. The judge smiled but didn't authorize any tasting.[34]

After two weeks of testimony, the attorneys presented their final arguments. Defense counsel declared that the state's case rested on the testimony of "scoundrels," perjurers, and witnesses on the government payroll. U.S. Attorney Buckner made the summation for the prosecution. He emphasized the importance of the documents confiscated from the ring's offices because the papers corroborated the testimony given by the state's witnesses.[35]

Buckner was so persuasive that he impressed even Dwyer. After the jury left the courtroom, the czar spoke to the U.S. attorney, voicing his respect. "You know, while you were speaking, I thought to myself, I really should be convicted," Dwyer said.[36]

After deliberating for several hours, the jurors found Dwyer guilty on a single count of conspiring to violate the Volstead law. They also convicted one of his codefendants, identified as the syndicate's "pay-off man," on the same charge. They acquitted the other accused men, including the former Coast Guard captain who allegedly smuggled liquor on patrol boat *CG-203*.[37]

Despite the mixed verdict, U.S. Attorney Buckner said, "I consider it a complete victory." He shook hands with Dwyer and asked the czar if he had received "a square deal." With a faint smile, the liquor lord said, "Positively."[38]

The trial judge declared that the evidence of Dwyer's guilt was overwhelming. "The facts cry out to heaven of wholesale violation of the law in every way. There is no shadow of doubt of the existence of the conspiracy alleged," he said. Although the judge seemed to be outraged, he sentenced Dwyer to only two years in federal prison and levied a fine of $10,000—a paltry sum for a liquor lord.[39]

The U.S. Circuit Court of Appeals upheld Dwyer's conviction, and the U.S. Supreme Court refused to review the case. With his appeals exhausted, the czar surrendered to the feds, bought train tickets for himself and a guard, and traveled by rail to the prison in Atlanta. "I wish I had never seen a case of whiskey," he said. "I spent years in daily fear of my life, always expecting to be arrested, always dealing with crooks and double-crossers, and now look at me. My wife is heartbroken and I am worse than broke." He claimed he had never been a millionaire "but just a figurehead for a bunch of rich guys."[40]

Rolling the Dice

After serving barely one year, Dwyer was paroled. The Prison Commission agreed to release him because he had health problems that required surgery. After returning to New York from what he called his "short vacation," he pursued both legal and illegal ventures. He didn't return to rumrunning, but gangland sources said he was a partner in the Phoenix Cereal Beverage Company, Manhattan's largest illegal brewery.[41]

Dwyer's legal enterprises revolved around sports and gambling. He owned the Brooklyn Dodgers football club, ice hockey teams in Pittsburgh and New York, and a stud farm in Lakewood, New Jersey. He served on the New York Hockey Club Board of Directors and the National Hockey League Board of Governors. He promoted sports gambling, built the Tropical Park racetrack in Florida, and headed the Gables Racing Association of Miami.[42]

Although Dwyer hobnobbed with high society and appeared to be rich, his finances were shaky. Tax liens and debt dogged him. His sports teams didn't produce profits, and he sold the Brooklyn football club at a loss. By 1935 he was in danger of losing the New York Americans. The players weren't being paid on a regular basis, and the bank was returning Dwyer's checks stamped N.S.F. A former hockey player lent him $20,000 to save the Amazin' Amerks, but he quickly lost the money in a crap game. At the last minute, a friend came to his rescue with money to open training camp for the new season. The Amerks enjoyed a winning season and made the playoffs. Nevertheless, Dwyer simply couldn't raise enough money to keep the team solvent. The National Hockey League took control of the franchise.[43]

While Dwyer's hockey ventures were imploding, the horsey set was flocking to his Florida racetrack. Therefore, he looked to the Sunshine State for his financial salvation. He made grandiose plans for a venue with gambling and glamorous floor shows produced by a famous impresario. He spent $250,000 building the Palm Island Casino in Biscayne Bay on land he purchased from Mrs. Al Capone, who was managing the family finances while Scarface served time at Alcatraz.[44]

The casino had a glittery metallic, ultra-modern façade, and a visitor described the interior décor as "breathtaking." Dwyer announced he would open his casino on New Year's Eve 1934, but his plans were derailed by gangland murders. "Gunmen's bullets—their smoke had an unmistakably New York smell—rudely slew one local gambler," a reporter wrote. A few days later, gunshots killed another Miami gambler. "It began to look like an epidemic of imported lead-poisoning."

Floridians were justifiably alarmed. Officials quickly empaneled a special grand jury to investigate what seemed to be a war between gambling interests. Based on the grand jury's findings, authorities refused to issue a gaming license to any new casino, including Dwyer's. Once again, Big Bill had taken a huge gamble and lost. A casino without a gaming license was a money pit. His glittery white elephant sold at auction for only $4,000.[45]

During his last years, Dwyer spent a lot of time dodging the tax collector. The Internal Revenue Service accused him of tax fraud, and a federal court ruled that he owed nearly $3.8 million in unpaid taxes. Authorities expressed doubt about collecting the judgment. Over the years Dwyer had lived beyond his means and had lost a great deal of money in risky ventures. The feds planned to confiscate his assets, but his personal wealth appeared to be limited.[46]

In December 1946, the high-rolling Czar of Rum Row died broke at age 63.[47]

The Prime Minister's Lost File

After prosecuting Dwyer, the U.S. attorney's office in New York focused on the rum ring headed by brothers Edward and Frank Costello. The siblings, who grew up in East Harlem's Little Italy, were petty criminals before Prohibition began. In 1918 Frank Costello served time for carrying a concealed weapon, and prison rehabilitated him in one respect: he decided that he would never again carry a gun. He vowed to shun violence and use his mind to make his fortune in gangland. The Volstead Era provided the perfect opportunity for him to move up to the big time as a criminal entrepreneur.

With Frank at the helm, the Costello brothers built their own rum ring. *Vincent A. White*, their largest mother ship, carried up to 20,000 cases of liquor. After law enforcement cracked down on the Dwyer syndicate, the Costello brothers exploited the czar's predicament to expand their own operations. "With the disappearance of the Dwyer ring the business of rumrunning ... had a much wider field, and old employees of Dwyer found speedy work with the Costellos," a crime reporter wrote.[48]

The Costello syndicate imported liquor from St. Pierre et Miquelon, landed it on Long Island, and moved it by truck to Manhattan. One night, pirates on a vessel disguised as a Coast Guard cutter hijacked a Costello boat. The caper worked so smoothly that Frank decided to follow suite. He ordered his hirelings to turn several Costello vessels into phony CG cutters; for an authentic look, the crews on those boats wore Guard uniforms. This worked until Guardsmen discovered the ruse; when a real CG cutter passed one of Costello's fakes, the rumrunners didn't wave at the Guards in the traditional manner. The real Guardsmen captured the bogus cutter and arrested the phony crew. The skipper on the fake cutter "was soon telling all he knew to the authorities."[49]

In November 1926 the grand jury indicted the Costello brothers, four Coast Guardsmen, and 27 other men for conspiring to violate the Volstead and tariff laws. Prosecutors expected a number of the accused men, "all of them very little pawns" in the scheme, to become state's witnesses in return for leniency.[50]

Eighteen of the indicted men went on trial in January 1927. For its first witness, the state called a man who had worked as the supercargo on two Costello ships: *Integral* and *Vincent A. White*. Lured by the promise of easy money, he had given up his successful mechanical dentistry practice to join the liquor smugglers. He worked for the Costello brothers until he had a dispute with them about his wages; he claimed they had cheated him out of several hundred dollars, but they refused to pay up. Because he possessed valuable information, he contacted the Prohibition office and became a paid undercover agent.[51]

The former supercargo explained how the rum ring used the serial numbers on dollar bills to make sales. The "home office" gave him a list of the serial numbers on bills held by the contact boat skippers. When a contact boat pulled alongside the mother ship, the supercargo and the skipper matched the serial numbers with the bills.[52]

On one occasion the supercargo planned to take a launch to meet *Vincent A. White* on Rum Row, but the mother ship didn't show up because it was lost at sea. He went to Curtiss Field near Mineola, Long Island, and hired a pilot take him up in a seaplane to hunt for the ship. He didn't find it on his first flight but located it on the second trip, and the pilot put him aboard the liquor freighter. When he paid for the service, he gave the flier a case of liquor as a bonus.[53]

The state's second witness was a former Coast Guardsman who had served on *CG-126*. The CG patrol boat often went out to Rum Row and escorted Costello's liquor-laden contact boats to shore, keeping hijackers and the Dry Navy at bay. The rumrunners paid the *CG-126* crewmen based on the size of the liquor cargo—usually one dollar per case. When circumstances kept the rumrunners from landing liquor, the Guards went home with flat wallets.[54]

One night contact boats were positioned beside a Costello mother ship, loading cases of whiskey, when a Coast Guard destroyer sailed into sight. The *CG-126* crew flashed a warning to the rumrunners and the contact boats darted away. After the *CG-126* captain communicated with the destroyer commander, the destroyer sailed away and the contact boats returned to finish loading. *CG-126* actually joined the rumrunning fleet for at least one night. To make extra money, the Guards took three hundred cases of whiskey onboard from a Costello mother ship and landed them at Fort Pond Bay near Montauk Point, Long Island.[55]

Losing track of the mother ships seemed to be a chronic problem for the Costello ring. One night the contact boats sailed out to pick up liquor from *Vincent A. White* but failed to find it because it had wandered far off course. The shore runners needed help, so the commander of *CG-126* agreed to look for the elusive liquor freighter. After the Guards located the errant vessel and put it back on course, the contact boats sped out to pick up their cargo.[56]

The former captain of *CG-126* took the witness stand for the prosecution. He confessed that he had taken both money and booze from the Costello syndicate. But his memory was fuzzy about some events because he drank heavily, even while on duty. His problem became so debilitating that a Costello henchman told him to lay off the sauce because drinking on the job "would spoil the whole game."[57]

The former CG captain claimed that he had been coerced into testifying against the defendants. Operatives working for the "chief undercover dry agent" in New York had kidnapped him and carried him aboard the cutter *Seneca*. Along with three other men, he was thrown into the brig and shackled in irons when the cutter put out to sea for a week on patrol.[58]

"The place was like a madhouse," he testified. "I was almost out of my head. We were shackled with double irons and kept in confinement the whole week. The hatches were battened down and the air was foul. They fed us rotten meat and gave us rotten water."[59]

After being held hostage for a week, he agreed to plead guilty to Volstead conspiracy and to testify against the Costello ring. On the witness stand, he confessed that he had accepted large sums of money from the rumrunners. He had also acted as a go-between, taking $1,000 from a Costello lieutenant and passing it along to the executive officer in charge of the Coast Guard base at New London, Connecticut.[60]

Another Coast Guard captain, who had commanded *CG-129*, also testified for the state. He had taken bribes to protect the Costello ships and to allow the ring's contact boats to land liquor at Fort Pond Bay. If a rumrunner didn't offer bribe money to the *CG-129* crew, he was likely to regret it. One stormy night off the coast of Long Island, Guards on *CG-129* sighted the schooner *Dawn,* which had not paid for protection. The *CG-129* crew captured *Dawn,* confiscated the schooner's liquor cargo, and transferred it to the cutter.[61]

CG-129 took *Dawn* in tow, but the storm complicated matters. High winds pushed *Dawn* aground near Montauk Point. The *CG-129* captain feared that his cutter would suffer a similar accident since tow lines linked the two vessels. He ordered his gunners to fire on *Dawn.* The schooner burst into flames and began to sink. The Guards cast loose the tow lines and sailed to the CG base on Block Island. Later, the captain sold the confiscated liquor for $3,000 and split the money with his crew.[62]

When another former Guardsman testified for the prosecution, his honesty caused the jurors to chuckle. On the Guard's very first day on *CG-126*, the patrol boat sailed out to pay a friendly visit to *Vincent A. White.* The rumrunners lowered a case of whiskey over the side of their ship, and the Guards happily accepted the gift.

"What happened next?" the attorney asked.

"I don't know what happened to the rest of the men; personally, I got drunk," the witness said.[63]

Before the judge sent the jurors out to deliberate, the prosecution agreed to dismiss the charges against two defendants; four defendants were removed from the case; the judge directed the jury to acquit Edward Costello; a mistrial was declared for a sick defendant, who would be tried at a later date.[64]

A defense attorney made a spirited summation for his clients. He called the state's witnesses "rats" and decried the shady methods used by the federal Prohibition agents. He described the Prohis' chief undercover agent as a "mysterious and invisible power" who hired "hijackers, pirates, crooks, and bribe takers" as informants. In a stage whisper, the attorney told the jurors, "The depraved character of the witnesses and the foul use of money in this case by the government make it an insult to your intelligence to have to pass judgment on it."[65]

After lengthy deliberations, the jury acquitted eight defendants and failed to reach a verdict on the others, including Frank Costello. Newsmen covering the trial attributed the lack of guilty verdicts to the jurors' disapproval of the Prohis' unethical, coercive methods. Summing up the case, a juror said "he would have remained in the jury room 'until Doomsday' before convicting anyone on the testimony" of the state's witnesses.[66]

Costello later admitted that he had bribed one juror because he wanted to ensure a hung jury. However, events showed that he had wasted his money. The jurors deadlocked six-six on their final vote; so Costello didn't need the obstructionist he had paid for.[67]

Since the jury returned no verdict for Frank Costello, the government could prosecute him again. Although observers expected a retrial, the case was repeatedly put on hold. When the government finally announced it would proceed with the retrial, prosecutors simply couldn't build a case against Costello. Witnesses and evidence couldn't be found. In fact, the case file had vanished without a trace.[68]

Years later, when an attorney asked Costello about the retrial, Frank replied, "The witnesses ain't in the telephone book these days, and the file kind of got lost."[69]

Building a rumrunning syndicate proved to be a solid foundation for Costello's future in organized crime. He became a powerful Mafia boss, respected in gangland as "the Prime Minister of the Underworld." Although the typical mobster died a violent death or rotted in prison, Frank Costello lived to the ripe old age of 83 and died of a heart attack.

12

The Radio Rum Ring

Both Volstead enforcers and news reporters tended to call every roundup of liquor traffickers "the biggest dry raid" in Prohibition history. On October 16, 1929, law enforcement staged the Arid Era's umpteenth biggest raid ever, but this one had a better claim than most to the superlative title. In a series of simultaneous raids the Prohibition Bureau targeted the Radio Rum Ring, a giant among liquor syndicates. Headquartered in New Jersey, the syndicate operated along the Atlantic Coast and relied heavily on radio communications.

The Radio Rum Ring owned a fleet of heavily-armed vessels that moved booze from foreign ports to the United States, most often landing the illicit cargo in New Jersey or New York. Both the mother ships and the contact boats were equipped with radio equipment to transmit messages. If the skipper of a contact boat spotted the Coast Guard, he could immediately warn his comrades. If conditions mandated a change in landing spots, headquarters could quickly transmit that information.

A team of Prohibition officials and federal agents spent months planning the simultaneous raids to decimate the Radio Rum Ring. A crucial member of the federal task force was Forrest Redfern, a radio inspector and cryptanalyst. The feds intercepted coded messages that passed between the syndicate's transmitting stations and its ships at sea. Redfern cracked the code, enabling the Prohis to decipher the messages, which revealed details about the ring's operations.[1]

Federal officials identified 34 major players in the Radio Rum Ring. Prior to the raids, secret indictments were filed against them in a New Jersey court. Heading the most-wanted list was syndicate boss Alexander Lillien. On the day of the raids, New Jersey's federal Prohibition administrator called the shots. His force of 130 raiders included special Prohibition agents, deputy U.S. marshals, and New Jersey state troopers. Coast Guardsmen stood by on patrol boats, ready for action on the waterfront.[2]

The lawmen divided into groups, each with a specific target in New York or New Jersey. One raiding party searched a Manhattan office building where the syndicate bosses did business. The "managing directors" couldn't be found, but the raiders seized valuable evidence and arrested a minor operative. Lawmen armed with subpoenas went to banks to collect the syndicate's financial records. Detachments of raiders swarmed into syndicate strongholds to arrest bootleggers and confiscate illegal booze.[3]

Raiders stormed the syndicate's field headquarters, an isolated estate on a bluff overlooking the bay in Atlantic Highlands, New Jersey. The scrawling Victorian mansion, once owned showman Oscar Hammerstein, was furnished like an exclusive men's club. The raiders found the house eerily empty, as if the occupants had evacuated to avoid an oncoming storm.[4]

The mansion's porches and balconies provided clear vantage points for armed guards to stand watch. On the front balcony, a lookout post had telescopes and a signal light for flashing code to ships at sea. Inside the house lawmen found an arsenal of weapons, including pistols, submachine guns, sawed-off shotguns, and tear gas. A labyrinth of tunnels and storage vaults lay beneath the mansion. On the estate grounds, machineguns on concrete emplacements stood ready to repel intruders.[5]

In the accounting office, the lawmen found ledgers and financial documents. The records showed that the rum ring had made a profit of roughly $2 million in the preceding six months, despite substantial expenses. In only one month the syndicate had spent $700,000 for "ships, merchandizing, and operating expenses." The overhead included 140 employees, 50 trucks, six steamships, and a fleet of speedboats. Sailors, gunmen, truck drivers, mechanics, warehousemen, office workers, salesmen, and wireless operators were on the ring's payroll. So were dozens of lawmen and government officials. In a typical week the graft payments totaled $30,000.[6]

In a cottage on the estate grounds, the raiders found a wireless transmitter. When they went up to the attic, they also found the radio operator, frantically sending messages. After they arrested the operator, federal radioman Redfern took over. He sent coded messages, trying to lure the ring's mother ships close to shore, so the Coast Guard could capture them. Despite his best efforts, none of the rumrunning skippers took the bait. They remained well outside the rum line, beyond the Coast Guard's reach.[7]

The raiders expected to find a huge stockpile of liquor in the mansion's underground storerooms, but a thorough search turned up only a few cases. When the raiders spied a freshly-dug hole near the house, they rushed over, expecting to find the mother lode. But the gaping hole awaited the delivery of an oil tank for the mansion's heating system. Still convinced that the booze was stashed somewhere underground, the lawmen dug holes in the tennis courts. This yielded nothing but dirt.[8]

The lawmen suspected that the vaults were empty because the syndicate had advance notice of the raids. This proved to be the correct assumption. To gather intelligence before the raids, federal Prohibition agents had checked into a boardinghouse near the estate and stayed for several weeks. Since Highlands was a summer resort town and tourist season was over, the Prohis stuck out like the proverbial sore thumb. Watchmen at the mansion spotted the Prohis staking out the estate and alerted their boss.[9]

After the Radio Rum Ring raids, New Jersey's federal Prohibition administrator talked to the press and boasted that the offensive had completely dried up his entire district. While the raiders didn't nab Alexander Lillien or the other bosses, they did arrest more than two dozen syndicate operatives. The administrator was especially pleased that his agents had captured two notorious bootleggers, Emanuel "Mannie" Kessler and Morris Sweetwood.[10]

Although the dry faction applauded the raids, they had little impact over the long term. Authorities released Kessler and Sweetwood, due to lack of evidence. The other arrestees were arraigned on Volstead charges, but all were decidedly minor cogs in the syndicate machinery. Only the wireless operator faced serious charges. He was accused of conspiracy to violate Volstead and also with operating an unlicensed radio transmitting station. According to news reports, he was the first person ever indicted on the latter charge, which was a federal offense.[11]

Jersey Shore, Twenties Style

After the sensational raids, Highlands' mayor complained about the press coverage, saying that it gave his town an undeserved "bad name." He worried that it would adversely impact the tourist trade, which kept the local economy afloat. He admitted that Highlands had hosted rumrunners in the early 1920s but insisted it was "ridiculous" to think that the town was the headquarters of a major rum ring.

"Bootleggers can't operate here today because of the change in bootlegging methods," he said.[12]

In Volstead's early years, speedboats made daily runs up the river to Highlands, carrying liquor cargos. The booze boats stopped at private docks and boathouses, where

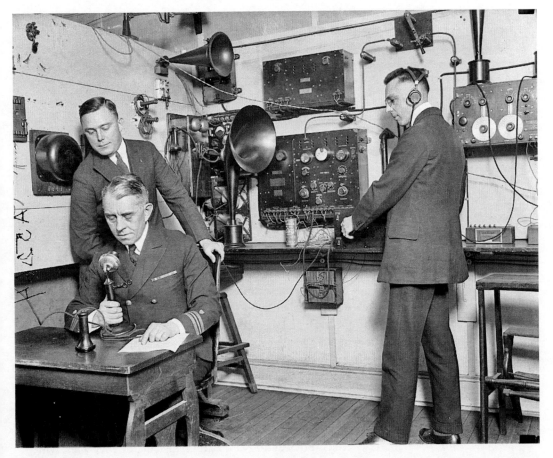

Officers at Coast Guard headquarters were learning to use radio equipment in 1923 (Library of Congress).

bootleggers waited to transfer the hooch to automobiles. On a typical day, rumrunners landed about 35,000 cases of liquor at Highlands. An observer said, "No one is making any bones about what is going on…. It is a lucrative day for everyone."[13]

Highlands' fishermen found rumrunning far more profitable than catching flounder or fluke. They sailed out to Rum Row, picked up booze, and sold it to bootleg gangs. They spent the windfall on luxuries for themselves and their loved ones. Women accustomed to making their own clothes suddenly sported store-bought dresses, fur coats, and glittery jewelry. Girls who worked in the riverfront sheds wore expensive coats to keep warm while shucking and stringing clams. Diamond rings adorned rough, scarred hands that opened countless clams in the sheds.

In the early 1920s the Highlands rumrunners made "not the least effort … to disguise their actions." As the swampers transferred hooch from the contact boats to the trucks, they talked and joked. Sometimes they sang or chanted to establish a rhythm for the physical work. They passed a bottle around to warm their insides. When a truck was fully loaded, it hit the road, escorted by one or two cars carrying armed guards to ward off hijackers. The majority of trucks went to Manhattan, although some headed to Newark, Jersey City, Philadelphia, Baltimore, or Washington, D.C.[14]

Highlands' mayor remembered those early Volstead years as being hectic and hazardous. "Why I've seen the stuff unloaded and carted away in open trucks in broad daylight," he recalled. "The bootleggers in those days had just started, and most of them never had any money before. So they used to run wild … getting drunk and shooting up the town. This was like a border town in those days, but it's not that way today," he said in 1929.[15]

The mayor claimed that the cowboys had deserted Highlands when the syndicates turned liquor trafficking into big business. "Why, eight years ago it was a common thing to have several gunfights in the streets in one night," he said. The rumrunners "were wild fellows then. But the men in it today, why, if you met them on the street, you would think they were Sunday school teachers. They aren't taking any chances."[16]

"Senseless" Signals

The October 1929 raids gave law enforcement valuable information about the Radio Rum Ring but failed to put it out of business. The ringleaders, including Lillien, escaped the dragnet. The syndicate's customers suffered little, if any, disruption in their booze supply. In Washington, Prohibition officials were frustrated but determined to put the Radio Rum Ring bosses in prison. Federal agents stayed on the case, looking for evidence that would smash the syndicate forever.

In 1930 federal radio inspectors intercepted signals from an unlicensed station in or near New York City. They recorded the "seemingly senseless combinations of letters and figures" because they suspected these were messages to ships at sea. The mysterious transmissions were passed along to federal cryptologists, who set to work on the code and cracked it in only a few weeks. The Radio Rum Ring had sent the messages, which exposed the syndicate's methods. Lookouts watched the Coast Guard patrol boats and gave information to the ring's radio operators, who sent radiograms telling the shore runners when to sail out to the mother ship, where to land their cargo, and so forth. Soon after the cryptologists broke the code, federal agents intercepted messages that enabled the Coast Guard to capture five contact boats.[17]

To further the investigation, federal agents went in search of the rum ring's illegal radio station. Using a portable radio compass, they took bearings at various points along the coast of New York and northern New Jersey. Based on that data, they believed the unlicensed station was located on or near Coney Island. After taking more bearings, they pinpointed a building on Avenue V in Brooklyn. When they saw a shortwave transmitting antenna of the Zeppelin type on the building, they knew they had found the place.[18]

Lawmen raided the unlicensed station and arrested the two men working there. The station was equipped with shortwave transmitters and receivers powered by a bank of storage batteries, rows of dry cells, and the electric-light main. (Although the two men had a government license to run an amateur station, they were using equipment not permitted for amateur use. They stood trial, were found guilty, and were sentenced to federal prison. Subsequently, one of them appealed his conviction, and the U.S. Circuit Court of Appeals ruled in his favor.)[19]

Based on evidence found at the unlicensed station, federal investigators knew that the Radio Rum Ring owned a network of illegal stations. Only days after the raid in Brooklyn, federal agents swooped down on the Albion Hotel, a fleabag on the waterfront in Highlands, New Jersey. The deserted hotel had a clubroom with a well-stocked bar, a slot machine, and card tables. More importantly, it had radio equipment for sending long-distance messages. Before the federal agents arrived, the radio operators had fled, leaving their maps and charts scattered about. A small heap of ashes indicated that they had burned paper, presumably a codebook, before their hasty exit. The agents suspected that the radiomen had been tipped off about the raid.[20]

In November 1930 the federal government stepped up its offensive against the Radio Rum Ring. The Coast Guard captured two speedboats, *Patricia* and *High Strung*, which were carrying booze for the syndicate. Prohibition agents raided a Manhattan warehouse and seized a large quantity of the ring's liquor. A federal grand jury issued sealed indictments against 50 men alleged to be principals in the syndicate; most were chronic Volstead violators well-known to police. Law officers began rounding up the suspects and soon had 22 of them in custody.[21]

Pallbearer's Gloves

Alexander Lillien reigned as lord of the manor at the Radio Rum Ring's estate in Atlantic Highlands. Although he had little formal education, he possessed intuitive business skills that could've brought him success in legal enterprises. He grew up in Elizabeth, New Jersey, where his father owned a produce store. As an adolescent, he worked for his father, delivering produce by horse-drawn wagon and later by truck. For a time, he also worked as an iceman, a muscle-building job in the days before modern refrigeration. The typical iceman had bulging biceps because he routinely lifted blocks of ice weighing one hundred pounds or more.[22]

When Prohibition began, liquor "wholesalers" did business at the Whiskey Curb in the Halsey Street-Branford Place section of Newark, New Jersey. Government permits allowed firms to buy and sell liquor in accordance with the legal exemptions to the Volstead law. If a wholesaler had a valid permit, the transactions were legal; but wholesalers often used counterfeit permits. Lillien began as a "curb broker" who negotiated prices with buyers. After a time he ventured into a more dangerous sector of the liquor traffic—hijacking. He led a small gang of men who posed as federal Prohibition agents, stopped bootleggers' trucks, and "confiscated" the booze. His connections at the Whiskey Curb made it easy for him to sell the purloined liquor.[23]

An ambitious young man, Lillien had a grand plan for the future. Acting as an agent for bootleg gangs, he traveled to Canada and set up deals with Canadian distillers and shippers. He earned a commission, but that was small potatoes compared to what he envisioned. He wanted to operate on a grand scale, mimicking a corporation. He persuaded businessmen to invest money in a syndicate that would sell illegal liquor but would function like a legal corporation. He found willing investors, including a man whose family had been in the liquor business for generations before Volstead.[24]

Lillien's syndicate grew quickly. Under his leadership, the ring bought mother ships, speedboats, trucks, garages, and private docks. The underworld grapevine reported that it also had "a secret harbor" two hundred miles from New York City. Mimicking a corporation, the ring set up departments for various functions, including management, sales, finance, transportation, personnel, and liaison (bribery). As Lillien enlarged his syndicate, he relied on the advice of "seasoned experts" who knew all the tricks of liquor trafficking.[25]

Lillien's fleet of mother ships included *Cask*, a four-masted schooner that held up to 20,000 cases. On a typical voyage, *Cask* picked up a cargo of aged whiskey in Glasgow, Scotland, and cleared for Le Havre, France. At Le Havre, the crew unloaded the cargo to comply with customs regulations and qualify for a tariff rebate. After dark, the crew secretly reloaded the whiskey. The liquor-laden ship sailed to Bermuda, where Lillien climbed aboard for the final leg of the trip to Rum Row. Although bootleg liquor was usually diluted, *Cask* reputedly "carried genuine, matured whiskey that for the most part passed uncorked" to buyers willing to pay top dollar.[26]

In April 1930, Lillien and 58 other men were indicted on charges related to the rum ring's operations in New Jersey. Investigators were still gathering evidence and had found recent deposits of nearly $1 million in syndicate bank accounts. The indicted men included ringleaders as well as low-ranking operatives who drove trucks. Among the defendants were two New Jersey lawmen, the Keansburg police chief and a motorcycle patrolman in Elizabeth.[27]

Thirty-seven of the indicted men went on trial in Newark in June 1931. In the prosecution's opening statement, the U.S. attorney promised to show that Lillien's syndicate operated on a "gigantic scale" and paid large sums of "graft money" to corrupt lawmen. To prove his case, he would rely heavily on evidence seized at the Highlands estate during the 1929 raids.[28]

The defense argued that evidence seized during those raids was not admissible because the lawmen had acted without a search warrant. According to the defense team, the raiders erred because they used bench warrants, which did not authorize them to search the mansion or the cottage.[29] (Stated simply, a bench warrant is issued for the arrest of a person who is named in the warrant. A search warrant directs law officers to hunt for and seize property that constitutes evidence of a crime.)

After the defense repeatedly objected to admitting evidence from the raids, the judge ruled on the matter. He stated that the best course would have been for the raiders to obtain a search warrant. Nevertheless, the "search was not unreasonable" but "was incident to the arrest" of alleged conspirators. The lawmen carried a bench warrant issued on a conspiracy indictment. They found men on the estate grounds and took them into the house, which was permissible and legal under the circumstances. Thus, the raiders' search of the Highlands mansion was constitutional.[30]

The prosecution called federal radio inspector Forrest Redfern to testify about the rum ring's communications. He stated that he had intercepted and decoded messages sent from a radio station with the call letters 4RD and 3RD. Using a radio direction finder, he traced the transmissions to the attic of a cottage on the Highlands estate. In the run-up to the 1929 raids, he intercepted hundreds of messages sent or received by that station.[31]

Reading aloud, Redfern shared his decoded versions of messages transmitted by four stations run by the Radio Rum Ring. He stated that two of the transmitters were located on *Shawnee* and *Lucky Strike,* mother ships owned by the syndicate. The terse radiograms were discreet, with few explicit references to liquor. A typical message gave the position of a Coast Guard vessel or specified the number of cases to load on a contact boat. The mother ships often sent shopping lists, telling a shore runner to bring food, cigarettes, soda pop, drinking water, and so forth.[32]

Although the radio messages were brief, some vividly conveyed the dangers of rum-running. One warned: "Be careful of hijackers impersonating patrol boat." Another said: "Boats were picked up by Coast Guard at dock." A longer one said: "L and speedboat just returned now. Both broke down last night, and speedboat was cut in two by patrol boat and went down, but men were picked up by patrol boat. So nothing doing tonight."[33]

A defense attorney objected to Redfern's testimony, saying there was no proof of a link between the intercepted radiograms and the men on trial. Another defense lawyer attacked Redfern's decoding as "guesswork." The judge let Redfern's testimony stand, saying that the jurors must assess the accuracy of his decoding.[34]

During an intense cross-examination, Redfern admitted that he had "assumed certain significant words in his decoding." In addition, he had inferred several words based on information he received from Coast Guard officials. The judge ordered Redfern to give a list of the suspect words to the court. They would be stricken from the transcript, and the judge would instruct the jury to evaluate the decoded messages without those words.[35]

The prosecution called a parade of Coast Guard officers who testified about picketing rumrunners in the waters around New Jersey and New York. They described their encounters with the Radio Rum Ring's ships, including *Shawnee* and *Lucky Strike.* Their testimony connected events at sea with Redfern's decoded messages. For example, a CG officer told about running down the motorboat *Toxaway* near Ambrose Lightship and picking up its crew. Redfern had intercepted a dispatch about this event shortly after it happened.[36]

A number of banking officials took the witness stand to testify for the state. They gave evidence about financial transactions and bank accounts belonging to several defendants, including Alexander Lillien. The vice president of a Newark bank linked credit slips and drafts to an account Lillien held under an alias. The banking records showed that the syndicate often sent large sums of money to a Canadian distillery.[37]

Staying on the money trail, the state presented records of large deposits in the personal bank accounts belonging to the defendants. One man, who claimed to be a truck driver, had deposited more than $572,000 in only five months. The judge admitted the bank records into evidence, despite defense objections that the state had not proved the money was earned by illegal liquor trafficking.[38]

For expert testimony about the rum ring's finances, the U.S. attorney called an accountant who had worked for Lillien. The liquor lord had told the accountant he was going out of business and needed a final accounting. Lillien supplied the bean counter with numbers representing income and expenses, primarily for equipment and salaries to low-level employees. He told the accountant to divide the profits among eight men, who were entitled to various percentages of the total. Prosecutors accused these eight of being the syndicate's top echelon.[39]

The state's exhibits included roughly four hundred invoices for liquor shipments. Each slip of paper specified the type and amount of liquor, the name of a truck driver, and the truck used to deliver the order. A handwriting expert compared the slips with writing specimens from the defendants and identified the writers.[40]

Before turning the case over to the jury, the judge removed half of the overt acts charged in the indictment, saying they were not supported by the evidence. On technical grounds, the majority of the defendants were dismissed from the case. The jurors would decide the fate of the remaining 17 defendants—Lillien plus his top lieutenants and assorted underlings.[41]

After hours of deliberation, the jurors told the judge they could not reach a verdict. He sent them back to the jury room to try again. When next the jurors returned to the courtroom, they delivered their verdict: not guilty for all defendants on all counts! Smiles, laughter, and applause erupted at the defense table. Although the prosecution had presented a mountain of evidence, the rumrunners walked out of the court as free men.[42]

After the acquittal, Lillien returned home to his headquarters at the Highlands estate. On March 23, 1933, he was alone in the mansion in the late afternoon. Even his bodyguard had gone out to run an errand. Without triggering any alarms, a gunman or gunmen slipped into the mansion. Three bullets, fired at close range, hit the liquor lord in the back of his head. Two bullets lodged in his brain; the other struck the nape of his neck. With blood oozing from his skull, he dropped to the floor.[43]

Near Lillien's corpse the killer dropped symbols of death—an ace of spades and a pair of pallbearer's gloves.[44]

Although the card and gloves seemed to be clues, crime reporters showed more interest in them than the police did. In keeping with the tradition of mob hits, law enforcement didn't look hard for the shooters. No one went to prison for murdering the ambitious young mastermind behind the Radio Rum Ring.

13

Pirates, Hijackers and Go-Thru Guys

On the high seas vicious hijackers preyed on liquor smugglers, stealing cargos and money. The pirates swarmed aboard rumrunning ships to overpower the crew and grab everything of value. Murder and kidnapping became commonplace. "The better class of rumrunners … quit the game and left the field open to murderous hijackers and cutthroats who stop at nothing," wrote a reporter in 1927.[1]

On rumrunning vessels the crewmen feared an invasion by armed strangers more than they feared the U.S. Coast Guard. "The hijacker is a dangerous man who spreads consternation among rumrunners," a newsman wrote. "It is doubtful if the combined forces of law and order are so much dreaded as one hijacker." The hijackers "have swift boats able to overtake any ordinary rum craft. They come up with shooting irons in hand and black masks affixed. They demand money or your life and shoot to kill."[2]

Because hijackers boarded ships in international waters, they didn't fear U.S. law enforcement. "Piracy is rampant among the liquor ships off New Jersey and Long Island," a Treasury agent said. "Of course, we can't do anything about it because the ships attacked are too far out." In investigating a case, this agent boarded a pirate ship and talked to the crew. "They were a desperate-looking lot of men. Some of them were young and athletic. Others were seasoned men. They looked ready for any kind of job."[3]

The auxiliary schooner *P.J. McLaughlin* was riding at anchor near Sea Bright, New Jersey, on a dark night. Shortly after midnight, the watchman spied the outline of a watercraft without lights; it seemed to be headed straight toward him. The watch alerted the captain, who called out a warning to the approaching ship, a steam trawler. Despite the warning, the trawler stayed on the same course. When the strange vessel pulled alongside *P.J. McLaughlin*, at least 20 armed pirates leapt aboard the mother ship. The invaders overpowered and locked up the rumrunning crew. Then they transferred the schooner's liquor cargo, more than 50,000 bottles, to their vessel and sailed away. Later, the pirate trawler was seen selling the stolen cargo off the coast of Philadelphia.[4]

What happened to *P.J. McLaughlin* was more or less a typical case of piracy. What happened to *Victor*, a known rumrunner, was an unsolved mystery. Customs officials found the schooner adrift, without its sails or rigging, near Barren Island, New York. No one was onboard, and the lifeboats were missing. In the cabin the tables were set for

The seagoing cutter *Seneca* made headlines when it seized famous mother ships along the New York–New Jersey shore (Library of Congress).

dinner; dishes of cooked food waited for the diners to arrive. The U.S. Coast Guard conducted a thorough search but didn't find *Victor*'s missing crew or the lifeboats.[5]

Mystery also surrounded the sinking of the steamer *John Dwight*, a decommissioned World War I Navy vessel owned by a rich yachtsman. While the ship was docked in Newport, Rhode Island, a new captain and crew took over. A few days later, *John Dwight* left Newport, anchored briefly in Buzzards Bay, and then put out to sea, headed for an undisclosed location. At the Gay Head lifeboat station near Vineyard Haven, Massachusetts, the keeper heard short siren blasts that sounded like a distress signal. Although thick fog limited visibility, a lookout spotted *John Dwight*. He heard an explosion, saw the steamer roll over, and watched it sink below the surface. Coast Guards hurried to the site and made an exhaustive search for the crew but found no one. Barrels of ale from a Montreal brewery bobbed in the water near the shipwreck.[6]

The next day, seven dead bodies wearing life preservers were fished out of Vineyard Sound. An eighth dead man was found in a small boat; it appeared that he had been rowing with improvised oars. All the corpses had been savagely slashed, mutilated, and disfigured, making identification almost impossible. *John Dwight* had sailed with a crew of 15 men, but investigators couldn't locate any survivors.[7]

Federal officials believed the shipwreck was related to the operations of a rum ring in New York City. They sent Navy divers to inspect the wreckage. The divers located the ship's mast and followed it down to the steamer. They found barrels of ale and cases of whiskey onboard but no evidence to explain the crew's disappearance. The case remained an unsolved mystery. Authorities didn't know if *John Dwight*'s crewmen had been killed by pirates or if they had fought among themselves. Either way, rumrunning could be fatal.[8]

The schooner *Eddie James* sailed from Nassau to New Jersey with a load of liquor and anchored near Highland Light. As the sun set one evening, five strangers in a launch drew alongside. The newcomers wanted to buy booze, so the *Eddie James* captain invited them onboard to discuss the matter. After climbing aboard, the strangers drew their pistols and opened fire, wounding the supercargo. The pirates stole the liquor cargo plus $8,000 in cash and took the supercargo hostage. *Eddie James* limped back to its home port—Halifax, Nova Scotia—minus its liquor and supercargo.[9]

Mulhouse, a French liquor freighter, also limped into port without its liquid gold. Investigators heard conflicting versions of what had happened onboard, and the truth proved to be elusive. Everybody agreed that *Mulhouse* had sailed out to sea with a large cargo of scotch whiskey and encountered the schooner *Patara* off Fire Island, New York. In the account published in many newspapers, a crewman on *Patara* shouted to the rumrunners, asking to buy champagne and whiskey.[10]

Two *Patara* men went onboard the mother ship to negotiate the sale. Suddenly, *Patara*'s entire crew swarmed aboard *Mulhouse*. Brandishing pistols and rifles, the intruders cornered their hosts and handcuffed them. Reports differed about exactly what happened next. According to one account, the *Mulhouse* crewmen were locked up below deck while the pirates stole the cargo. In another version, several boats appeared, seemingly from nowhere, and surrounded the mother ship. The intruders forced the *Mulhouse* crew to transfer the large liquor cargo to the other vessels—a chore that took several days. Then all the hijackers sailed away.[11]

French authorities investigated the *Mulhouse* incident, and U.S. federal agents joined the task force at the request of the French government. Despite extensive undercover work, the investigators failed to gather enough evidence to convict anyone in a court of law. Some observers concluded that the *Mulhouse* theft was a case of insurance fraud. In this scenario, a rum ring had purchased the liquor, insured it, and staged the hijacking. Then the ring sold the liquor and also collected the insurance money. In an alternate scenario, an American syndicate had robbed *Mulhouse* to show foreigners that the U.S. mobs wouldn't tolerate competition on Rum Row.[12]

Everyone on the British schooner *Patricia M. Beman* banished, probably after a gun battle. When a Coast Guard commander spotted the vessel near Fire Island, its sails were set and it was dragging anchor. He led a crew onboard for a routine check. The boarding party found no one on the ship, but the vessel was riddled with bullet holes and rifle cartridges that seemed to be evidence of a gunfight on deck. Strangely, there were no dead bodies or blood splatters. The Guards found many burlap sacks and empty wood cases but no liquor onboard. The schooner's records showed that it had recently offloaded a large amount of liquor worth $200,000.[13]

The CG commander theorized that freebooters had killed the crewmen and thrown their bodies into the ocean. Another scenario held that the crewmen had fought among themselves and tossed the losers overboard. Then the winners had taken the money and sailed away in a small boat. Yet another theory said that the crew had staged the gunfight, which explained the absence of blood and corpses. The crewmen had divided up the liquor money and gone ashore in a contact boat.[14]

Brothers Milo, Ariel, and Theodore Egger—nicknamed Mickey, Happy, and Ted—terrorized rumrunners in the Pacific Northwest. In one instance, they boarded *Kayak*, a boat riding at anchor in Peter's Cove waiting to take on a liquor cargo from another vessel. Brandishing their guns, the brothers overwhelmed *Kayak*'s crew. When the other vessel arrived, the Eggers opened fire on its two crewmen; after they shot one, the other wisely surrendered. The Eggers sailed away after transferring the whiskey to their own boat, which they had hidden nearby. In another incident, the Eggers hijacked a booze boat at D'Arcy Island, towed it across the strait, disabled the engine, and stole the liquor cargo.[15]

Because the Eggers hijacked boats with British registry, officials in London hired private detectives to search for the trio. After an extensive manhunt, law enforcement arrested Mickey and Happy in San Francisco. Canadian officials issued warrants charging them with piracy and planned to prosecute them in Vancouver. To start the extradition process, the two brothers were taken to federal court in San Francisco for a routine hearing.[16]

After the uneventful hearing, a deputy U.S. marshal escorted the duo out of the courtroom. As they went down a staircase, a man rushed at the marshal and threw ammonia in his face, blinding him. The sound of gunfire ricocheted in the stairwell. A bullet struck Happy Eggers. Mickey and the stranger ran out of the building and sped away in a waiting car, leaving Happy behind, struggling to stay alive. The hapless Happy died at the courthouse.[17]

Federal lawmen soon identified the ammonia-throwing stranger as Ted Eggers, who had come to San Francisco to help his brothers escape. Evidence suggested that he hadn't acted alone but had hatched the escape plot with at least one accomplice.[18]

Law enforcement launched a nationwide hunt for the Eggers. Officers nabbed Ted in Philadelphia and took him back to San Francisco. Ted's sister and a gangster were arrested as his accomplices. All three were arraigned on charges relating to the shootout at the federal courthouse. Ted was indicted for the attempted murder of a federal officer. With his two accomplices, he was also indicted for conspiracy to liberate a federal prisoner. When the case went to trial, Ted pled guilty to helping his brother Mickey escape and was sentenced to six months in jail. The court freed his codefendants, due to insufficient evidence.[19]

More than a year after the shootout at the courthouse, police arrested Mickey Eggers in Tacoma, Washington. Canadian authorities planned to prosecute him for hijacking two rum boats and holding four men hostage. He was also accused of shooting and seriously wounding a sailor during a hijacking. He fought extradition to Canada but lost. U.S. lawmen escorted him aboard the Coast Guard cutter *Arcata* for the trip to Victoria, British Columbia.[20]

To prove the charges against Mickey, Canadian officials planned to use the testimony of two Seattle men, but at the last minute the duo refused to go to Canada. At trial no witness positively identified Mickey as a hijacker. Mickey's family testified for the defense, giving him rock-solid alibis to show that he couldn't have been at the hijackings. The jury quickly acquitted him. Nevertheless, he was a habitual criminal who continued to follow his calling. Not long after his acquittal in Canada, he was arrested in Seattle, convicted on robbery charges, and sent to prison.[21]

Hijackings rarely led to a trial for murder. An exception was the case of *Beryl G*, a Canadian vessel that hauled liquor from British Columbia to Puget Sound. In Washington State's San Juan Islands a lighthouse keeper spotted *Beryl G* adrift near the rocky coast of Stuart Island. He told the island postmaster, and they went out to investigate. They found blood on the deck, on the cabin floor, in the companionway, and on clothing discarded near the bow. They saw spent shotgun shells and rifle cartridges as well as bullet holes in the hull and cabin door. The boat's two-man crew, a father and his teenaged son, had disappeared. The boat's anchor and liquor cargo had also vanished.[22]

Since the missing sailors were Canadians, Inspector Forbes Cruickshank of the British Columbia Provincial Police led the investigation. He found an amazing clue on *Beryl G*: a camera loaded with exposed film. When the film was developed, he had a clear photo of the registration number on the stern of a boat. That number was the first link in a chain of evidence leading to a gang of hijackers in Seattle, Washington.[23]

Two members of the gang went on trial for murder in Victoria, Canada. A third gang member struck a deal with the prosecution and testified against his comrades. He revealed that the hijackers had posed as revenue agents when they boarded *Beryl G*. He said he had heard gunshots on *Beryl G* but hadn't actually witnessed the father's murder. However, he had seen one of the defendants bludgeon the teenager to death. He had also seen both bodies thrown overboard, after they were cut into pieces and wrapped in the anchor chains.[24]

The jury found both defendants guilty, and the judged ordered them to be executed by hanging. In a later trial a third hijacker was also found guilty of murder; after the appeals process, he was sentenced to life in prison.[25]

Risk Reduction

Pirates, called "go-thru-guys" in Volstead slang, waited near Rum Row, watching the action around the liquor freighters. They sometimes intercepted a contact boat and robbed the crew at gunpoint. But more often they targeted mother ships that carried big payloads. When the go-thru-guys judged that a mother ship had sold all its liquor, they invaded the vessel and stole the cash. They usually bound and/or locked up the crew and smashed the engines or the wheel to ensure that the rumrunners couldn't chase them. In extreme instances, the go-thru-guys took hostages or killed the crewmen.

Due to the threat posed by armed pirates, rumrunners bought weapons for their boats and crews. Rumrunning pioneer Bill McCoy was more or less typical in this respect. He equipped his ship with an impressive arsenal, mostly weapons sold as war surplus by the U.S. government. His armory included Colt-Browning machineguns, Thompson submachine guns, Winchester rifles, and sawed-off shotguns. In addition, he armed each crew member with a Colt .45.[26] (Although rumrunning ships carried guns to fight off intruders, internecine gunfights were more common than invasions and crewmen sometimes killed one another in the heat of the moment.)

Rum rings devised various methods to limit the amount of cash onboard their mother ships and thereby reduce the risk of theft. As a safeguard, the rum ring's "home office" usually negotiated sales and demanded advance payment. One popular scheme used the serial numbers on dollar bills. Both the bills and the serial numbers were called "passports." Via courier or wireless, the ring's home office sent a list of serial numbers to the captain of the mother ship. When a contact boat came alongside, the skipper of the small vessel handed a dollar bill to the captain. If he found the bill's serial number on his list, he allowed the buyer to come aboard, confident that he wasn't dealing with pirates.[27]

Another method used a playing card cut into halves with a distinctive pattern, such as a diagonal zig-zag. The image or number on the card indicated the quantity to be purchased. For example, the ace of spades might represent four hundred cases or the three of hearts three hundred. In addition, invisible ink could be used to write information on the card. The buyer held one half of the playing card while the home office sent the other half to the mother ship's captain. The pieces were matched up when the buyer arrived to load his cargo. In a variation on the card scheme, a dollar bill was cut into halves.

In the rumrunning brotherhood, card or dollar halves were negotiable currency. They could be used to pay debts, secure loans, or wager in poker games. When radio became commonplace on rumrunning vessels, coded messages eliminated the need for card or dollar halves.

The major rum rings transported huge cargos on their liquor freighters and didn't sell to the buyer who wanted only a few cases. All or most of a freighter's load was contracted to buyers before it left the home port. The syndicates scheduled regular departures and arrivals for their ships and expected the skippers to stay on schedule. At any given time, 15 to 20 liquor freighters were in transit on the Atlantic Ocean, headed for Rum Row to replace ships that had to leave to replenish their stock. In some cases, a rum ring sent a supply vessel to restock the mother ships so they never had to leave Liquor Lane.[28]

Cutthroat competition was the norm in the illegal liquor traffic. The rum ring bosses aimed to eradicate competition from other syndicates and the independent rumrunners. If an independent captain positioned his vessel closer to shore and/or sold at lower prices than the rum ring's liquor freighters, he risked violent reprisal. One tough old captain didn't move when threatened by syndicate operatives, but he paid a high price. In the middle of the night, a syndicate ship fired a barrage at the old captain's schooner and set the vessel afire. The next morning the Coast Guard found the schooner's burned out hull but no survivors.[29]

When the syndicates took over the liquor traffic at sea, the public image of a rum-runner changed to reflect the new reality. The booze buccaneer was demoted from a romantic figure to a scruffy sailor who was just another cog in the mob machine. The big liquor freighters remained on Rum Row for weeks or months, and life became tedious for the crewmen. As the days dragged by, morale sank while tension mounted. The sailors felt restless and irritable. If the captain didn't maintain strict discipline, fistfights might break out. Sometimes the violence escalated to a gunfight and a bullet ended a sailor's life. If the captain allowed the crew to sample too much of the liquid cargo, discipline might break down entirely. Mutinies became an occupational hazard on Liquor Lane.

The greediest syndicate bosses took a shortcut to bigger rumrunning profits. They anchored old ships outside the rum line and converted them into floating distilleries. Men operated stills onboard the ships, turning out raw spirits that could be colored and flavored to resemble aged whiskey. The ersatz whiskey was packaged in bottles with fake labels and counterfeit tax stamps. Cutting corners reduced overhead to a minimum. Although the floating stills produced inferior spirits, the cheap liquor could be sold for top dollar as aged, imported whiskey.

14

Right Off the Boat
Rumrunning in Florida

Daring, expert sailors played the rumrunning game with gusto and skill in the Sunshine State. While mobs ran the rum rings in America's big cities, Florida's typical rumrunner didn't belong to an urban gang. He was an adventurous lone wolf or a veteran skipper who commanded a small crew. Florida's rumrunners seemed to be bulletproof, and their exploits made exciting tales. Most importantly to drinkers, they kept Miami and other Florida cities supplied with imported liquor right off the boat.

In Prohibition's early years the Coast Guard relied on a single vessel, *Vidette,* to patrol the waters around Miami. A pleasure yacht converted to a rum chaser, *Vidette* couldn't match the speed of the booze boats. It plodded along at six knots per hour while the typical rum boat moved more than twice as fast. Moreover, *Vidette* was often out of commission and didn't leave the dock for extended periods of time. When it did go out on patrol, the crew usually had to bail water. Rumrunners left *Vidette* behind when they sailed their shallow-draft boats into the mangrove swamps. The speedboats ran over reefs and sandbars to disappear into coves where the CG couldn't go because *Vidette* drew too much water.[1]

In the late Twenties, Washington's Prohibition policymakers beefed up enforcement efforts in Florida. In January 1928 the Dry Navy had 31 vessels in the waters around Florida, and an additional 15 patrol boats would soon join the fleet. Washington's master plan called for enlarging the Florida force to more than 90 vessels. In addition to boats, the Dry Navy had two amphibian planes that were used for reconnaissance.[2] The bigger, more aggressive Dry Fleet complicated life for Florida's rumrunners but didn't put them out of business.

Both Coast Guards and rumrunners were heavily armed in Prohibition's latter years. Gun battles between rummers and Coasties turned South Florida into a tropical Wild West. Despite the gunplay, the rumrunners landed vast quantities of liquor in the Sunshine State, ensuring that anybody who wanted a drink could find one. "The Florida bootleggers are well financed and equipped and are served by men who are apparently determined to stick to the trade until jailed or killed," a newspaper reported.[3]

Wet Tourism

Florida's showcase city, Miami, was known as the state's wettest. Ironically, the Magic City began as a community dedicated to sobriety. Prior to Miami's incorporation in 1896, the city's founding families envisioned a town without "malt, vinous, or intoxicating liquors." When the founders contracted with railroad tycoon Henry M. Flagler to develop the area, they stipulated that a ban on liquor must be part of the deed to each lot. This clause prohibited landowners from "buying, selling, or manufacturing" alcoholic beverages. If a buyer violated that clause, the original anti-alcohol owners could reclaim the land.[4]

In 1900 the door to wetness swung open when an heir to one of the original landowners sold a lot without the prohibitory clause in the deed. The new owner set up a saloon on his property, and other bars soon opened. Naturally, Miami's dry activists rallied to stop this wet trend. The dry faction persuaded the city council to ban saloons in residential areas, limit business hours for bars, charge a hefty fee for a liquor license, and enforce the state ban on alcohol sales to Native Americans.[5]

In the early 1900s the dissension over liquor led to a series of local-option elections in Miami. The wets won the first two elections, but the dry activists had lots of fight left. The dry bloc convinced the city council to pass new, stricter laws regulating the location of saloons, their facades, and their clientele. Miami's prohibitionists also worked hard to recruit new dry voters. In 1913 the arid forces narrowly won a local-option election that banned liquor in Dade County.[6]

Alas, the booze ban greatly disappointed the dry bloc. Far from giving up liquor, drinkers bought illegal hooch, and the clandestine liquor traffic boomed. Bootleggers, rumrunners, and moonshiners found a ready market for their products. Although the police made arrests, they "barely scratched the surface" of the bootleg trade, according to a Miami newspaper, which decried the "revolting state of affairs."[7]

Miami's dry leaders, discouraged by the failure of local-option laws, expected national Prohibition to create the arid paradise of their dreams in the 1920s. But they soon realized that the Volstead law wasn't being enforced in the Magic City and probably never would be. Less than a month after Volstead took effect, a newsman wrote, "Miami is agog with tales of smuggling…. Civil and state authorities are not against the smuggling, and they agree with the people that the nation should be wet."[8]

Bootlegging was "a solidly established, flourishing business—outside of the law, to be sure, but a fixture doing very well," wrote a Floridian in 1922. Bootleggers and the price of liquor were no longer the main topics of conversation in Miami because they weren't newsworthy. "Why talk about something as commonplace as bread and butter?" the Floridian asked. Bootleggers were easy to find, and liquor prices were more or less standardized. A Miami resident could place an order for "imported liquor" with a friendly bootlegger; a boat from Bimini or another nearby island would deliver it in a day or two.[9]

"Drinking is both safer and cheaper in Florida than anywhere else in these dry states," a Floridian wrote. Bootleg booze was often contaminated, but Floridians felt they were drinking safe products because their liquor usually came from a foreign distillery via an offshore island. The typical Sunshine State resident never tasted bathtub gin. "The citizen of Florida does not have to pawn the family flivver to buy the makings of a party. Neither does he have to drink synthetic gin or synthetic anything else," boasted a proud Floridian. "He does not have to wonder if the next bottle will be seasoned with wood alcohol."[10]

As word of Miami's wetness spread across the United States of Volstead, tourists found good hooch at reasonable prices as alluring as sandy beaches. Visitors flocked to the Magic City to slake their thirst. In Miami's business community, the prevailing attitude favored just about anything that boosted tourism. Zealous enforcement of the dry law would have a negative impact on "tourist travel," warned a local newspaper. A British tourist noted that wines and spirits were sometimes served at official city functions in Miami. "Prohibition in Florida has quite definitely collapsed," he said.[11]

Miami's thirsty visitors could drink potent potables at speakeasies, casinos, hotels, and blind pigs. At many hotels, bellboys delivered booze to the guest rooms. "As you are being taken to your room in the elevator, the bellhop gives you the 'once over.' Even before you are well out of the elevator, he is soliciting your liquor orders," wrote a visitor. "Competition is so keen in Miami ... that the prices are less than half what they are in New York City."[12]

Bellhops weren't the only Floridians selling bootleg booze. A visitor who wanted to buy land took a bus ride to look at a new real estate development. "The bus driver asked me if I could use a bottle," he wrote. "A woman next to me on the bus wanted to sell me some liquor, and even the real estate salesman, after he had done his best to sell me a lot, turned around and asked, 'Well, can I interest you in some liquor?'"[13]

Wet tourism led to sporadic, seasonal Volstead enforcement in the Sunshine State. "Prohibition Survey of Florida," a report published in 1931, looked at jurisdictions across the state. "Numerous sheriffs, mayors, and other public officials ... espouse the cause of Prohibition and believe in vigorous enforcement thereof—at least during the drowsy summer months when the tourist army has departed," the report stated. When the hordes of visitors arrived for the winter, Volstead enforcement took a holiday.[14]

"Prohibition Survey of Florida" noted that enforcement was especially lax in Dade, Duval, Hillsborough, and Palm Beach counties. According to the report, Tampa's police department was "wholly unsympathetic with Prohibition enforcement" and West Palm Beach's sheriff was "totally unreliable" in matters related to Volstead. With few exceptions, Florida's local lawmen sat on the sidelines waiting for the understaffed federal Prohibition Unit to deal with the illegal liquor traffic.[15]

The Nutt Case

South Florida was a wide-open gateway for rumrunners smuggling liquor into the United States. When Washington's Prohibition policymakers decided to close that gate, they chose Colonel Levi Nutt to head a special task force to dry up Miami. In March 1922 Nutt and a squad of 40 federal agents stormed into the Magic City.[16]

The federal agents quickly arranged introductions to "operators" who moved large cargos of liquor from the islands to Florida. "We were startled by the revelations," Nutt said. "Our investigators were directed to operators with the same frankness that a stranger receives directions from a corner policeman. Operators discussed transactions like bankers. Indeed, several of them gave bankers as references." The liquor traffickers were prepared to take orders for specific brands of booze and deliver the goods in Florida within 24 hours. If the buyer wanted to ship the liquor north, the traffickers could arrange that, too.[17]

Nutt learned that Florida rumrunners bought liquor for an average of $18 a case in Bimini, Nassau, or Gun Cay. The hooch sold for double that price in Miami and up to $100 per case in northern cities. The liquor could be shipped out of Florida via truck or railcar. In either case, the hooch was usually hidden under a load of fish or produce. Crates of oranges, tomatoes, or another crop could be stacked around the burlocks, and the trafficker could sell everything when the shipment reached its destination.[18]

On March 20, 1922, Nutt's squad sallied forth to dry up Miami, starting with predawn raids on inns and roadhouses on the outskirts of town. The Prohis seized small quantities of liquor from 25 places, including a chili parlor and a fishing dock. They also arrested 20 people allegedly involved in the illegal liquor traffic.[19]

The following day Nutt's agents caught a big fish; they arrested a vice president of the Miami National Bank. The feds alleged that he had conspired with a gang of rumrunners to violate the Volstead law. The vice president stated that he had received money from the rummers and had given a receipt for it, as he would in any business transaction. He declared that he had no special knowledge of the rumrunners' business and merely happened to handle their money because he was available when they needed a bank officer.[20]

Nutt extended his crime fighting to illegal punch-board games, because players could win bottles of booze. "So brazen was the law violated in the City of Miami that … the principal prizes of punch boards, operated in prominent cigar stands, were bottles of liquor," Nutt wrote in a report. "Our investigators not only made winnings of Gordon gin, Johnny Walker scotch, and Bushmill rye, but carried away the punch boards as souvenirs."[21]

Only days after Nutt's crime-fighting crusade got off to a rousing start, the momentum fizzled. "Prohibition Raids Prove Failure" proclaimed a Miami newspaper. Although the Prohis had staged numerous raids, they had made few arrests and had failed to find big stashes of liquor. Almost everybody, including the rumrunners, knew the feds were in town, so the smart rummers were taking a vacation. The few liquor traffickers caught off-guard didn't read the newspaper. Even before Nutt's special squad had arrived in Miami, the Associated Press sent out a dispatch about the Prohis' upcoming crusade, and many newspapers printed the wire service report.[22]

The special squad's raids had no lasting impact on Miami's liquor traffic. Only a handful of the arrestees were convicted in court. The bank vice president was released because he was a stakeholder, "not a principal in the plot." The Prohis had rounded up low-rent hoods but failed to nab the "big fellows in the liquor game." To add insult to injury, Miami officials accused some of Nutt's agents of misconduct and malfeasance. A newspaper said the special squad left Florida "before it was laughed out of the state, but not before the snickers were audible."[23]

Despite the embarrassment, Colonel Nutt's reputation suffered no lasting damage. He went on to have a long career as a federal lawman, primarily in narcotics enforcement.

A Wild Goose Chase

Duncan "Red" Shannon cut a dashing figure as he skimmed across the waters in *Goose*, his sleek, gleaming white speedboat. He loved both the adventure and the money that came with rumrunning. He routinely outran the Coast Guard to deliver booze to Miami's popular hotels and watering holes. Even after he was indicted on Volstead charges, he continued to smuggle liquor. His exploits were the stuff of rumrunning legend, repeated in tales told by the habitués of smoky dives on the waterfront.

Shannon became a hero to the rumrunning crowd when he pulled a daring prank to defy Lincoln Andrews, the Treasury Department official who supervised Prohibition enforcement. During a fact-finding tour in the Southeast, Andrews stopped in Miami, where he planned to go on patrol on a Coast Guard cutter. Andrews went aboard a small CG boat that would take him to the cutter outside the harbor entrance. As the boat moved along the Miami Channel, Shannon happened to be returning from the Bahamas with a cargo of liquor.

Speeding down the channel on *Goose*, Shannon spotted Andrews on the deck of the CG boat. A cautious rummer would've changed course and headed for open waters. But that wasn't Shannon's style. He circled around the CG vessel, thumbed his nose at Andrews, and triumphantly held up hams of liquor. Before the Guardsmen could shoot, he sped out of range of their small arms' fire.[24] His audacious defiance made him a hero to some people, a despicable showoff to others.

A rumrunner waits on his boat, which ran aground during a tropical storm in Daytona, Florida (State Archives of Florida).

On the afternoon of February 25, 1926, Shannon left Gun Cay, headed to Miami, with a load of liquor and two crewmen aboard *Goose*. Although he was under federal indictment for smuggling, he hadn't stopped plying his trade. He planned to cruise into port in the semi-darkness and mingle with the boats in the harbor while he waited for the right time to deliver his contraband to the dock at the Flamingo Hotel.[25]

When *Goose* left Gun Cay, an undercover agent who tracked rumrunners sent word of Shannon's departure to the Coast Guard at Fort Lauderdale. Ensign Philip Shaw was ordered to intercept Shannon and seize the booze boat. Shaw, with a crew of four Guards, immediately headed south to Biscayne Bay in *K-1445*, a captured booze boat converted to CG rum chaser.[26]

As the Guardsmen on *K-1445* neared Star Island, they saw a boat with a red running light under the MacArthur Causeway Bridge. They were certain they had spotted Shannon's *Goose*. Shaw ordered his crew to load their guns and to keep *K-1445* astern of the booze boat. After following *Goose* for a time, *K-1445* sped up to get closer. On Shannon's boat, a rummer began throwing hams of liquor overboard.[27]

Shannon turned *Goose* hard left and fled southward. The Guard vessel turned, too, trying to keep *Goose* on an inside course. People attending a tea dance at the Flamingo Hotel heard the boats' rumbling motors and rushed outside to watch the chase. When Shannon's booze boat disappeared behind the hull of an anchored yacht, Shaw ordered his crew to head across the yacht's bow. *Goose* roared down the yacht's starboard side, headed for *K-1445* and a high-speed collision. *K-1445* swung hard right to parallel the booze boat's course in the opposite direction. The two vessels missed a collision by inches![28]

Shaw yelled to Shannon, commanding him to heave to. Shannon ignored him. Shaw fired two shots across the rum boat's bow. Shannon's *Goose* roared off into the semi-darkness, gaining speed as the crew jettisoned more burlocks. The Guards lost sight of their quarry.[29]

Suddenly the Guards on *K-1445* spotted *Goose* racing along the Star Island shore. Shannon swung his boat around, speeding toward a deliberate collision with *K-1445*. The Guard vessel turned sharply right; *Goose* struck a heavy glancing blow, crushing *K-1445*'s guardrail and heeling the vessel over to port. The Guardsmen held on, struggling to stay onboard while their boat reeled from the impact.[30]

When *K-1445* stabilized, Shaw ordered his crew to shoot at Shannon's boat. Three Guards fired their guns, more or less in unison. Shaw fired his own gun, aiming at *Goose*'s engine room, trying to disable the motors. At least one bullet hit the rumrunner at *Goose*'s wheel; he grabbed his back and fell across a stack of burlocks. Shaw ordered the Guards to cease firing. The two vessels floated toward one another. On *Goose*, two men stood with their arms raised over their heads. The Guard crew lashed the boats together and took them to the dock at the Flamingo Hotel.[31]

When Shaw turned his attention to the bleeding, unconscious rumrunner, he instantly recognized Shannon. The two had known each other as youngsters and had crewed together on a schooner owned by Shaw's father.[32]

Men from the hotel brought a mattress and placed Shannon on it, until he could be moved to a nearby hospital. At the hospital, the rummer learned that his death was imminent. "It's all in the game," he said, sounding resigned to his fate. Like every rumrunner, he knew that he was gambling with his life when he carried a cargo of booze.[33]

A Coast Guard commander, who had often chased Shannon's boat, sounded sad when he heard of the rumrunner's death. He showed his respect for his rival, saying, "Red Shannon played the game squarely and on his nerve."[34]

Because so many people at the hotel had seen the chase, a maelstrom of controversy swirled around the shooting. Witnesses claimed that the Guardsmen had opened fire while Shannon's crew was trying to surrender. A Miami newspaper quoted an eyewitness who said, "The Coast Guard fired after the men had raised their hands." Another paper reported that the rumrunners "had their hands above their heads in token surrender when Guardsmen fired on them." A journalist called the shooting an "ambush by Coast Guardsmen" and said the bullets "narrowly missed crowds that surged down to the Flamingo docks."[35]

At a coroner's inquest, six eyewitnesses testified that Shannon had been shot even though he was holding his hands above his head. Those witnesses included businessman Carl Fisher, owner of the Flamingo Hotel. The civil coroner's jury charged the Guardsmen on *V-1445* with manslaughter, and a justice of the peace issued warrants for their arrest.[36]

At Fort Lauderdale Coast Guard base, the Guardsmen expressed disbelief and outrage. The CG brass stood by the Guards, claiming that the men had rightly done their duty. Military officials argued that the servicemen could not be charged in a civilian court. When a civilian constable went to the base to serve the manslaughter warrants, a Guardsman shot at him. Although the shooter later apologized for his itchy trigger finger, the gunplay added fuel to the firestorm. The flames grew even hotter when a Dade County grand jury investigated Shannon's death and upped the stakes, charging the Guardsmen with second-degree murder.[37]

Disputes over legal technicalities delayed the Guards' murder trial for nearly two years. The case was finally heard by a jury in federal court in Miami. The court excluded residents of Dade, Broward, and Monroe counties from the jury due to "anti–Coast Guard prejudice" in those areas. An assistant U.S. attorney general defended the Guardsmen, while the Dade County solicitor led the prosecution. To re-create the deadly chase, the lawyers used models of the boats, moving them around the courtroom floor to illustrate what had happened.[38]

The defense emphasized the Guards' duty to enforce the law and their right to use lethal force when necessary. The prosecution focused on whether the Guardsmen shot Shannon after he raised his hands in surrender. The prosecution's case was weakened when hotelier Fisher modified his earlier statements. He said that he was somewhat nearsighted and didn't remember if the rumrunners raised their hands before or after the shooting started. The prosecution argued that the Coast Guard had no right to shoot when the crime was only a misdemeanor; but the judge said, "Such is not the law."[39]

The jury found the Guardsmen not guilty on February 24, 1928, one day before the second anniversary of the shooting.[40]

Miami Mayhem

Only a few months after the death of Red Shannon, another shootout made news because civilians had to dodge bullets. Coast Guards on patrol boat *CG-297* and a rumrunner exchanged gunfire on the Miami River near a café and an apartment building on Southeast Fourth Street. Civilians "ran terror stricken from their rooms and dinner tables as volley after volley of shots ... showered about them," a newspaper reported. The gunfire endangered 50 persons as Guardsmen "pumped hot lead after the 'rummy' as fast as they could pull their triggers." Newspaper headlines declared "Diners Flee Shots in Rum Chase" and "Rain of Bullets Strikes Terror among Women."[41] (No men were scared?)

Despite the danger of stray bullets, onlookers rushed to the riverbank, where they had a clear view of the pilot steering the rum boat. He lay prone on the floor and raised his head up enough to see where he was going. With the Coast Guard in hot pursuit, the rum boat darted under the Miami Avenue drawbridge, which brought *CG-297* to a halt because it was too tall to pass under the closed bridge. While *CG-297* waited for the bridge to open, some of the Guards commandeered a private boat to continue the chase up the river.[42]

Despite the Guards' valiant effort, the rumrunner outran both the private boat and *CG-297*. Unable to catch its prey, *CG-297* turned and headed downriver, as if retreating from the battlefield. The onlookers on the waterfront taunted the Coasties with "catcalls, boos, and hisses" as they sailed by. "The crowd hooted the Guardsmen and cheered the vanished smuggler," a reporter wrote.[43]

Only days after the gunplay, a Dade County grand jury heard eyewitnesses testify about the affray. Subsequently, the jury filed an official report on the "serious menace" caused by the Coast Guard's artillery. The report said, "We denounce as a reckless, needless and uncivilized practice the methods used by Coast Guardsmen in Biscayne Bay and the Miami River." The Guards' use of lethal force endangered lives and prejudiced the public against them. The report recommended that CG policy be changed, so Guardsmen could shoot only in self-defense on the bay and the river.[44]

In Washington, U.S. Senator Duncan Fletcher (D-FL) and Representative W.J. Sears (D-FL) deplored the "indiscriminate firing" by Guards on *CG-297*, which had endangered everyone on the waterfront. To quiet the uproar, the Coast Guard ordered the commanding officer at Fort Lauderdale to conduct a thorough investigation of the *CG-297* gun battle.[45]

Based on the investigation, officials in Washington completely exonerated the crew of *CG-297*. The official report said the Guardsmen had simply done their duty. Although eyewitnesses claimed to see and hear many gunshots, the CG investigators concluded that only five shots were fired during the chase. Moreover, the official report declared, "No shots went wild or struck other than the place they were intended" to hit. A Miami newspaper said Washington's verdict on the incident "has met with pronounced disapproval by many citizens."[46]

When the combatants used machineguns on the river, the gun battles became even more dangerous for Miami residents. A gunfight on the Miami River in April 1929 showed the random damage a machinegun could do. As a CG patrol boat chased a rum boat upriver, the Guards opened fire with a machinegun. The Guardsmen failed to capture the booze boat, but the rummy crew abandoned it, with its sizeable cargo of burlocks, near a bridge across Southeast Second Avenue.[47]

The rumrunning boat had only one bullet hole, but stray shots had hit buildings

During Prohibition *Seneca* was armed with a battery of rifles and guns, including three pounders and six pounders (Library of Congress).

onshore as well as a houseboat on the river. One bullet pierced a cabin wall in the houseboat, ricocheted, passed within inches of an occupant, and struck another wall. A night watchman on a tugboat said he had felt bullets whizzing by, almost hitting him. A stray bullet was found on the chapel floor at a funeral home more than a block from the river. The Miami police stated that more than two hundred bullets had been fired from the CG machinegun.[48]

At first, the commander of the Fort Lauderdale CG base denied that the patrol boat crew had fired any shots. He later corrected this, saying that the Guardsmen "had done some shooting" and the CG would conduct a full investigation. Subsequently, authorities in Washington demanded the resignation of the CG boatswain who had ordered the gunfire. The official report declared that the boatswain had "used poor judgment in ordering the use of a machinegun in the Miami River, flanked as it is by dwellings, apartment houses, yachts, and houseboats.... The river at this point is very narrow and the use of firearms at this particular point is a menace to innocent people."[49]

Miami's mayor said the gun battles between the Guards and the rumrunners were "worse than a disease."[50] Miami residents divided into two camps on the gun issue, based on their views about Prohibition. Some saw the dangerous gun battles as another reason why Volstead should be repealed. Others vehemently argued that the Coast Guards were only doing their duty and Miami needed more, not less, dry law enforcement. If that meant gunfights, so be it.[51]

15

The Gulf Stream Pirate
Two Different Men

In the summer of 1927 the Coast Guard began to wage a more aggressive war against Florida's rumrunners. In addition to transferring more rum chasers to Florida, the CG opened new bases at Fernandina and St. Petersburg to supplement the existing ones at Miami, Key West, and Fort Lauderdale. "This move means a real liquor war and what I mean is war!" declared a top government official.[1]

The CG intensified its efforts to capture veteran rumrunners like James Horace Alderman, known as the "Gulf Stream Pirate." Alderman had a long history as an outlaw and smuggler. In his youth he learned to sail and fish. An excellent tarpon fisherman, he worked as a gillie or guide for tourists, including celebrities like Teddy Roosevelt and Zane Gray. He also used his sailing skills for sinister purposes. He trafficked in illegal immigrants, mostly Chinese nationals who had made their way to Cuba. He landed his illicit passengers in Florida at isolated spots in the Ten Thousand Islands. The rumor mill said that he sometimes threw the Chinese overboard after they had paid him. When Prohibition began, the Gulf Stream Pirate added liquor smuggling to human trafficking. An undercover customs agent persuaded Alderman to give him a job, which led to the smuggler's arrest and conviction on rumrunning charges. After serving a short prison term, he returned to smuggling.[2]

On the night of August 6, 1927, Alderman headed for Bimini on *V-13997*, with Robert Weech as his only crewman. He planned to make a routine run, buying liquor in Bimini and hauling it to Florida. Due to engine problems, the trip took several hours longer than normal. Early on August 7, Alderman reached Bimini, anchored his boat, and purchased his liquid cargo. Because the trip had taken so long, he had to make a choice: sail in the daylight or twiddle his thumbs until sunset. After loading his liquor on *V-13997*, the Gulf Stream Pirate headed back to Florida at midday, without waiting for cover of darkness.[3]

Boatswain Sidney Sanderlin commanded the six-bitter *CG-249*, which was stationed in Fort Lauderdale. Around noontime on August 7, *CG-249* headed for Bimini with a crew of seven Guards and a civilian passenger, Secret Service agent Robert Webster. Substantial amounts of counterfeit U.S. currency had shown up in Bimini and Florida. Law enforcement suspected that rumrunners were passing the bogus bills, and the Secret Service had assigned Webster to investigate.[4]

Before reaching Bimini, Boatswain Sanderlin spotted *V-13997*, which he identified as a booze boat headed for Florida. Sanderlin sent tracer fire across the rummy's bow, but *V-13997* didn't stop. After the Guards fired additional warning shots, Alderman stopped his boat.[5] (The participants later gave conflicting accounts of what occurred after Alderman stopped. They didn't agree on the sequence of events and had differing recollections about almost everything. The account in this book is based on court documents, newspaper articles, and the Coast Guard's official report.)

V-13997 hove to, *CG-249* pulled alongside, and the Guards lashed the two vessels together. Sanderlin boarded the rum boat, where he found Alderman and Weech, plus a cargo of liquor. Weech claimed it was his very first rumrunning trip. He said he had paid for the liquor and would give it to Sanderlin if the boatswain let him go. Sanderlin refused the bribe.

After arresting both Alderman and Weech, Sanderlin frisked them for weapons but found none. The boatswain took the rumrunners aboard *CG-249*, where he went to the pilothouse to report via radio to the base at Fort Lauderdale. He left his prisoners standing just outside the pilothouse. Guardsman Victor Lamby, a motor machinist's mate, "was standing abreast of the forecastle hatch on the port side," looking at the pilothouse.[6]

When Sanderlin turned his back on his prisoners, Alderman held up a gun as if it had materialized out of thin air. But it wasn't magic. Several automatic pistols lay on the pilothouse table, and he had picked one up. With deadly accuracy, Alderman shot the boatswain at close range, killing him instantly. Machinist mate Lamby immediately reacted to the coldblooded murder, running to get a gun from *CG-249*'s weapons cache. Alderman aimed at Lamby and pulled the trigger. A bullet pierced the machinist mate's back, lodging near his spine; he dropped to the lower engine room platform.[7]

Brandishing his gun, Alderman lined up the other Guards and agent Webster on the deck. He quickly returned to the pilothouse, grabbed another gun from the table, and fired a bullet into the deck. Then he aimed both pistols at his hostages. A Guardsman picked up a wrench from the deck and heaved it at Alderman. The wrench missed its target, and the Guard dived overboard to avoid a counterattack. Alderman threatened to shoot his hostages, saying, "I will use your own ammunition on you." However, he didn't immediately follow through on this threat.[8]

Alderman ordered his assistant, Weech, to wreck all the gas lines on *CG-249*. Weech went below and found Lamby, the injured machinist mate, in the engine room. Weech ordered Lamby to tear out the gas lines, but the wounded man said his legs were paralyzed. Weech kicked and beat Lamby. Summoning all his strength, the machinist mate somehow reached up to the tool board and handed a wrench to the rumrunner. Working quickly, Weech tore out the gas lines between the vacuum tanks and carburetors. When gasoline began pouring into the compartment, he went on deck to report to his boss. Alderman ordered him to set fire to *CG-249* and leave the wounded Lamby below to burn to death.[9]

A Guardsman spoke up, warning that an explosion on the cutter would also wreck *V-13997*, because the two vessels were lashed together. Alderman handed a gun to Weech and ordered him to watch the hostages. Then Alderman went into the *V-13997* engine room to start the motor, intending to untie the vessels and put some distance between them. Returning to the deck, he ordered Weech to torch *CG-249*. Before Weech could do so, the *V-13997* engine backfired and stalled. Alderman told Weech to fix the problem.[10]

Weech went below to work on the engine but couldn't fix it. The motor rumbled, then coughed, and balked. Alderman looked away from his hostages, glancing down the hatch to see what Weech was doing. The hostages seized the moment.[11]

A Guard grabbed Alderman's left arm while agent Webster reached for the other arm. Alderman fired both his guns, hitting two men. The Secret Service agent fell to the deck, mortally wounded. The other bullet injured a Guardsman, who tumbled overboard but was able to swim and stay afloat. A Guard stabbed Alderman with a long ice pick, while another wrenched the gun from his left hand. A third man grabbed a steel boat scraper and hit Alderman solidly on the head, knocking him unconscious.[12]

A Guardsman rushed to the engine room to deal with Weech, while other Guards rescued their comrades who had gone overboard. In the engine room, the two men tussled until Weech broke free. As Weech headed for the deck, the Guardsman grabbed Weech's leg and held on. Dragging the Coastie, Weech struggled up to the deck, where another Guard hit him on the head and rolled him overboard.[13]

The Guardsmen paused for a few moments, watching Weech in the water. Then they reacted as they were trained to do: they rescued him. When they had him back on the boat, they shackled him in double irons. When Alderman showed signs of regaining consciousness, they shackled him to the gun mounted on the deck.[14]

The Guards returned to *CG-249* and radioed for help. They could see ugly evidence of the fight on the cutter. Puddles of blood were coagulating on the deck. The pilothouse, with blood splatters and human viscera, resembled a slaughterhouse. The cutter drifted with its distress flag flying until the rescuers arrived.

Alderman was taken to a hospital, so his wounds could be treated. When he recovered, he was held in the Broward County jail, until the authorities heard alarming rumors. According to one source, local residents planned to storm the jail and lynch the Gulf Stream Pirate. However, another source said that 50 armed men, presumably rumrunners, had come to Broward to help him escape. To ensure public safety, a police vehicle transported Alderman from the jail to a docked Coast Guard vessel. A squad of Guardsmen, a U.S. marshal, and police officers "with revolvers in hand" saw him safely aboard the boat. The CG vessel, escorted by an airplane and another boat, moved him to a prison in Jacksonville. He was later transferred to the Dade County jail in Miami.[15]

Alderman had killed three men: Boatswain Sanderlin, machinist mate Lamby, and agent Webster. At the Coast Guard base in Fort Lauderdale, the CG convened a board of inquiry to investigate. Most of the *CG-249* crewmen gave their accounts of the incident. Alderman did not appear in person to defend himself. The board found that Alderman had intended to kill all the hostages and to burn *CG-249*.[16]

A grand jury indicted Alderman for murder, and he stood trial in federal court in Miami. He was charged with killing two men: the boatswain and the machinist mate. (If the jury acquitted Alderman in this trial, prosecutors would have another shot at him; he could still be indicted for killing the Secret Service agent.)

The federal government assembled a strong team of prosecutors led by an assistant U.S. attorney general. Weech, hoping for leniency, turned against his boss and cooperated with the prosecutors. At trial, the prosecution called more than 30 witnesses, including the Guards who had survived the nightmare at sea. In a surprise move, Alderman took the witness stand to defend himself. He claimed that he had acted in self-defense because he believed the Guards were trying to hijack his liquor. He pointed out that they were not dressed in their uniforms but wore ordinary t-shirts and dungarees. Moreover, *CG-249* was not readily identifiable as a Coast Guard vessel.[17]

Alderman said he had feared for his life because Sanderlin threatened to kill him. "After getting on the Coast Guard boat, he told me to go into the pilothouse," Alderman testified. The boatswain mentioned three rumrunners who had recently been killed by law enforcement. "Sanderlin says, 'Now, damn you. I got you. I'm going to fix you just the same as the rest of the rumrunners. Put you right with them.'"

The boatswain and the machinist mate huddled together, talking softly. Alderman believed they were plotting to kill him. When the machinist mate made a sudden move, Alderman thought he was reaching for a pistol on the table. Alderman reacted swiftly, grabbing a gun and shooting.[18]

After deliberating for several hours, the jury returned a verdict of guilty as charged, without recommendation of mercy. The judge sentenced the Gulf Stream Pirate to death by hanging. Weech fared much better. He pled guilty to minor charges and was sentenced to a short term in the federal penitentiary in Atlanta.[19]

Alderman petitioned the U.S. Circuit Court of Appeals at New Orleans to overturn his conviction. His counsel argued that the trial judge had erred by letting the jurors hear inadmissible evidence and by rejecting Alderman's request for special instructions to the jury. The appellate court found that the trial judge had committed "no reversible error." Alderman then appealed to the U.S. Supreme Court, which refused to hear his case.[20]

While Alderman was incarcerated, he "found Jesus Christ" and professed his faith. He claimed to be a totally new man. He read the Bible, led prayer meetings in the jail-house, and converted other prisoners to Christianity. The press reported his amazing conversion. For the most part, the public accepted his tale of rehabilitation and trans-formation. Thousands of people signed petitions urging leniency for him. A pastor from Miami went to Washington to plead for a pardon or a commutation of his sentence. Eleven of the 12 jurors who had convicted him signed a petition asking the Department of Justice to review his case. Even the judge who had sentenced him to death publicly recommended commutation.[21]

In a desperate ploy to save Alderman from the gallows, his partisans appealed directly to the White House, asking President Hoover to commute his death sentence to life imprisonment. Hoover, who had pledged to strictly enforce Prohibition, declined to help the Gulf Stream Pirate.[22]

Alderman's attorney acknowledged that his client's fate was sealed. The Gulf Stream Pirate said simply, "Hoover let me down, but God is with me still."[23]

A federal judge signed Alderman's death warrant and decided that the Gulf Stream Pirate would be executed in Fort Lauderdale, based on the old practice of hanging buccaneers in the port where they were first brought ashore. The judge's plan called for erecting the gallows in Fort Lauderdale at either the county jail or the county courthouse. Local officials objected to this because a public hanging would mar the town's image as a wholesome tourist resort. Moreover, Alderman had been convicted in a federal court, so hanging him on federal property would be more appropriate. The judge agreed to move the execution to the seaplane hangar at the Coast Guard base in Fort Lauderdale. The sheriff of Palm Beach County would serve as the hangman.[24]

In preparation for his execution, Alderman asked the court for permission to invite guests to give him moral support. "It's my personal hanging, and I want to invite my friends to it," he said. His request was denied, but the judge made one concession: Alderman could invite a spiritual advisor. The judge specified that the only other witnesses would be a deputy U.S. marshal, the Broward County sheriff, a physician, and essential legal or medical personnel. The judge forbade "anyone connected with the hanging to make public any information concerning it." Newsmen decried this as restricting freedom of the press, but the judge didn't back down.[25]

On August 16, 1929, Alderman spent his final night at the Broward County Jail. He chatted with family members who came to visit him one last time. He read the Bible—sometimes silently to himself, sometimes aloud to the guards. At daybreak, lawmen escorted him from his cell to a waiting convoy of six automobiles. He paused to acknowledge the small crowd of his supporters gathered outside the jail. Then the guards put him in a car, and the convoy sped along until it stopped at the cavernous, metal seaplane hangar. Lawmen stood guard around the perimeter, and concertina wire kept the curious away from the hangar.[26]

With squared shoulders and steady legs, the Gulf Stream Pirate walked to the gallows. At his own request, he wore starched white pants and a white shirt. He paused at the bottom of the gallows, then climbed the steps to the platform. As the hangman slipped the noose over his head, he began singing a hymn. When the trap door dropped open, a crackling snap rang through the hangar. Alderman's voice trailed off. But the hangman's knot didn't break his neck. He dangled from the rope, slowly strangling to death. After 12 agonizing minutes the doctor finally pronounced him dead.[27]

Despite the gag order, a few reporters managed to find reliable sources and publish accounts of the execution. One crafty publisher finagled his reporter a temp job driving the hearse for the undertaker who would embalm Alderman's body. The reporter attended the hanging and drove the corpse to the funeral home. However, the publisher decided not to print his scoop, due to the gag order. (The hearse driver/reporter's eyewitness account was finally published in 1960.)[28]

The Gulf Stream Pirate's body was taken to a Miami funeral home, where roughly two thousand people came to gawk at his coffin. "The chapel became an impromptu debating hall," according to a newspaper. "The sentiment of some favored Alderman," but "others had not forgotten the three government men" he heartlessly murdered.[29]

A large crowd, estimated to be seven thousand people, attended Alderman's funeral at the Alliance Tabernacle in Miami. The service continued for hours, as speakers prayed, read Scripture, and eulogized the Gulf Stream Pirate. Afterwards, his body was laid to rest in an unmarked grave in a South Miami cemetery.[30]

Alderman's memoirs, written while in prison, focused on his faith and salvation. The violent outlaw declared that he had become a gentle, loving Christian. "I have left a record of two different men," he wrote.[31]

16

The West Coast Connection
Canada to California

Rumrunners on the West Coast kept the region well supplied with liquor from Canada, Mexico, and the South Pacific. The lion's share of the booze went to California, although the liquor smugglers also served Washington and Oregon. The West Coast's busiest Rum Row flourished near the Farallon Islands, supplying liquor to San Francisco, Oakland, and nearby towns. Dry activists wielded a great deal of power in Los Angeles, but they couldn't stop the illegal liquor traffic. Mobsters from the East moved in to keep the booze flowing in the City of Angels. San Diego's proximity to Mexico guaranteed the city a vast reservoir of liquor from south of the border, delivered via land and sea.

In 1921 "more than one hundred vessels were plying along the western coast engaged in the sole occupation of liquor smuggling," according to customs service officials.[1] Seagoing liquor freighters with large cargos dominated the traffic. Many of the shipments originated in Vancouver, British Columbia, where hard times in the logging, fishing, and mining sectors had caused an economic depression.

Rumrunning was "a real bonanza to Vancouver" and "one of the most fabulous money-making businesses ever dreamed of." The liquor traffic brought U.S. dollars to Vancouver and provided jobs for sailors, boat builders, stevedores, and others. Seamen joined the rumrunning brotherhood because it paid well and "had all the excitement and thrills of a war without the risk." The rumrunning Canadians didn't think of themselves as outlaws. "We considered ourselves public philanthropists! We supplied good liquor to poor thirsty Americans who were poisoning themselves with rotten moonshine," said one Canadian captain.[2]

"Here in Vancouver, whiskey is no outlaw," a newsman reported. The Canadian liquor industry "laughs at the American law," he wrote. In Cold Harbor, he saw "halibut boats that have forsaken an honest calling, pleasure craft used exclusively as law violators, fast trim boats that can sail circles around the ancient obsolete American patrol boats." As part of his investigation, the reporter let it be known that he wanted to buy a shipload of whiskey. A friendly bartender introduced him to a warehouse manager who was willing to sell him a liquor cargo for export.[3]

The biggest liquor exporters on Canada's West Coast were the Consolidated Exporters Corporation and Henry Reifel's United Distillers. Consolidated was a consortium of Canadian brewers, distillers, and liquor merchants. Informed sources stated that U.S.

liquor lords invested heavily in the corporation and played a major role in management. Consolidated operated as many as 14 mother ships along the U.S. coast, according to Prohibition officials.[4]

In a typical operation, motorboats landed booze from Consolidated's liquor freighters at a ranch near Pescadero in San Mateo County, California. Syndicate operatives used "an intricate system of signaling lights" to communicate with the crews on the contact boats. To fend off thieves, the ranch had an arsenal of lethal weapons, including machineguns.[5]

Henry Reifel's United Distillers rivaled Consolidated Exporters as the most important source of Canadian liquor on the West Coast. Henry's father, a German emigrant, worked for beer makers in the United States before moving to British Columbia, where he supervised operations at a sizeable brewery. After a time, he bought a share of the brewery and guided the business through major expansions. As a young man Henry followed in his father's footsteps, working for breweries and bottling companies. When he gained sufficient expertise, he joined his father in the liquor business. By the mid–1920s the Reifel family owned distilleries, breweries, and export firms that sold potent potables to a multitude of customers, including rumrunners.[6]

In California's port cities, newspapers treated the rumrunning mother ships as if they were a legitimate part of the shipping industry. Papers reported when the booze boats arrived, where they dropped anchor, how much whiskey they carried, and when they sailed away. Likewise, Golden State newspapers often noted when a California liquor lord went to Canada to buy booze.

In a more or less typical article in June 1926, an Oakland paper reported that mother ships *Malahat, Marion Douglas*, and *Federalship* were riding at anchor on San Francisco's Rum Row. *Principio* and *Strathona* were expected to arrive shortly, bringing more inventory from Vancouver. Rum Row would have roughly 100,000 cases of liquor available for the upcoming Fourth of July festivities.[7]

For the most part, the liquor freighters didn't disrupt commercial shipping or navigation. However, contact boats anchoring near the mother ships repeatedly damaged the Pacific cable that ran into San Francisco. The cable in the shallow water around Noon Day Rock proved to be especially vulnerable. Feeder boats casting anchor there severed the underwater line more than once, causing serious disruptions in the cable service.[8]

In only a few months in 1924, the Commercial Cable Company repaired three separate breaks caused by shore runners using the cable as a catch for their anchors. The cable company sued the owners of *Prince Albert* to recover $90,000 spent repairing damage caused when the mother ship hooked onto the cable and cut it as the anchor was hauled up.[9]

Rumrunners who smuggled booze from British Columbia to California often claimed to be shipping freight to Latin America. To comply with Canada's export regulations, they found it expedient to clear their liquor cargos for a Latin American port. Ensenada, Mexico, and San Blas, Colombia, were very popular destinations for mother ships, although neither town had the infrastructure for international trade. Ensenada had an anchorage but no railway terminal. San Blas had a very shallow harbor, and the nearest railhead was 50 miles away. Yet shipping manifests showed that merchants in these villages routinely imported enough whiskey to fill dozens of railcars.[10]

(0-3-328-15)(10-20-34-10:30A)(12-1000) FARALLON ISLANDS

B-34146A.C

West Coast rumrunners anchored their mother ships near the Farallon Islands for easy access to San Francisco (National Archives and Records Administration).

Changes in Canada's export laws and transit tax prompted Vancouver's whiskey wholesalers to adopt new procedures in the mid–1920s. Consolidated Exporters began shipping Canadian liquor to Tahiti and from there to California, but this cost time and money. To reduce overhead, Consolidated opened a distillery on Tahiti, producing spirits for the U.S. market. Other cost-cutting tactics were buying liquor in Mexico and distilling alcohol onboard ships at sea. Coast Guard officers reported that the liquor smuggled ashore in southern California consisted "principally of cheap Mexican alcohol mixed with a concoction brewed aboard the rum ships."[11]

"A Continuous Conspiracy"

In the early 1920s, the federal government didn't have the resources to stop rum-running on the West Coast. The major vessels in the Dry Navy's Pacific Fleet were *Golden Gate, Shawnee, Swift, Vaughan,* and *Tamaroa.* None of them had the proper equipment or the speed needed to enforce Volstead. The fastest thing about *Swift* was its name. *Vaughan* was an older vessel that had seen duty as a sub chaser in World War I.

Tamaroa was a slow tugboat dubbed "the sea cow." On one occasion, *Tamaroa* found a "nest" of five mother ships lurking near the San Clemente Islands. The cutter "chased first one and then another" but couldn't muster enough speed to capture any of them.[12]

San Francisco's rumrunners, like Prohibition pirates elsewhere, used radio communications to stay a step ahead of the Coasties. Amateur radio stations onshore warned the mother ships when the CG cutters went out on patrol. "Innocent messages like 'Grandmother died today' or 'I am going to the ballgame' fill the air every time the *Shawnee* gets ready to pull out," said a CG officer. "That is why we are rarely able to find anything. They know we are going out before we start, and they just steam out of sight until the coast is clear."[13]

To beef up Volstead enforcement on the Pacific Ocean, the Coast Guard transferred two fast cutters from the East Coast to San Francisco in 1922. Although this was a step in the right direction, it didn't go nearly far enough. The rumrunners still had little to fear because the CG fleet could patrol only a tiny portion of California's long coastline.[14]

In April 1924 the CG announced a major offensive against West Coast rumrunners. "Spurred by mammoth booze-running activities" on the Pacific Ocean, CG officials stated that they were mobilizing all available resources for a new "anti-booze navy." The grand plan called for the CG to recruit more sailors, purchase new armaments, and retrofit Navy torpedo boats mothballed at San Diego.[15]

By May 1925 the CG had stationed ten new, fast cutters in San Francisco. The older, slower cutters were deployed to patrol Southern California. The rumrunners took advantage of this by anchoring five mother ships between San Diego and Santa Rosa Island. The ships attracted swarms of contact boats that landed liquor worth millions of dollars. To combat this traffic, the Coast Guard relied on "two cutters of ancient vintage, the *Tamaroa* and the *Vaughan*," which could "make possibly thirteen knots an hour with the aid of a ten-knot breeze." The contact boats raced across the water at 20 knots an hour, leaving the cutters far behind. The Guards admitted "that rum-runners with fast vessels equipped with radio were operating almost at will around the Santa Barbara Islands."[16]

Plans for the West Coast buildup included transferring four sub chasers from the Atlantic Ocean to the Pacific in autumn 1925. Federal officials announced that "new and 'airtight' Prohibition regulations" would go into effect in California on September 1, 1925. The Prohis expected the rumrunners to land large quantities of liquor before the crackdown started. "We know positively that at least six rum vessels are being used by the liquor rings in their desperate effort to make a 'cleanup' while they can," a top official said. During the summer *Principio* and *Malahat* hovered off the California coast, and the Prohis anticipated the arrival of more mother ships before September.[17]

The Dry Navy's West Coast buildup produced both fiascos and victories. Early in the offensive, Guardsmen were criticized for shooting at the wrong vessels. On one occasion a CG cutter repeatedly fired at a boat near the Golden Gate because the Coasties believed it carried booze. But the boat's frightened occupants weren't rumrunners. They worked for the Army Corps of Engineers and were trying to inspect dredging operations. Shortly after this incident, the CG cutter *Shawnee* fired shots across the bow of a ship that proved to be a U.S. Navy submarine on maneuvers. Fortunately, the sub sustained no damage.[18]

The Big Trade

The Canadian steamer *Quadra* was a sailing workhorse that saw service as a light-house tender, a rescue ship, an ore carrier, and a government patrol boat. During Prohibition *Quadra* became a liquor freighter that moved very expensive cargos of alcohol from British Columbia to the U.S. West Coast.[19]

In autumn 1924, the twin-screw steamer sailed from Vancouver with a liquor cargo, officially bound for Ensenada, Mexico. *Quadra* sold a portion of the booze to shore runners in the Straits of Juan de Fuca and off the coast of Oregon. In California, *Quadra* joined two other liquor freighters, *Malahat* and *Coal Harbor*, on Rum Row between the Farallon Islands and the Golden Gate. Contact boats, after picking up liquor from the mother ships, landed their cargos at Oakland Creek in San Francisco.[20]

When the Guards on the cutter *Shawnee* spotted *Quadra*, the mother ship was positioned several miles north of the Farallon Islands. At that time *Quadra* wasn't selling liquor but was taking on additional inventory from *C-55*, a small boat that transferred cargo from one liquor freighter to another. *Shawnee* sailed to the west of *Quadra*, planning to intercept it when it headed farther out to sea. As the CG cutter approached, *C-55* cast off and raced toward shore, trying to escape with its remaining burlocks. *Shawnee* zeroed in on the small boat and fired a warning shot; the rumrunners surrendered without a fight.[21]

Onboard *Quadra*, a crewman quickly raised the Union Jack as evidence of the ship's British registry. Strangely, the mother ship didn't sail away. Under normal circumstances, *Quadra* might have outrun *Shawnee*, but the liquor freighter was adrift with no power. The vessel had used all its fuel, and refueling attempts had failed.[22] Outrunning *Shawnee* wasn't an option.

The Guardsmen boarded *Quadra* but received no cooperation from the captain, who demanded a lawyer and refused to give his name or show his manifest. *Shawnee's* commander decided to tow *Quadra* into the harbor. He allowed *C-55* to travel under its own power but kept the cutter's one-pound gun trained on the shore runner to ensure that the skipper didn't attempt an escape. When the vessels reached San Francisco, law enforcement arrested *Quadra's* captain and crew for failure to comply with the Volstead law and the British-American rum treaty.[23]

News of *Quadra's* capture spread quickly, and the denizens of the waterfront came to gawk at the infamous mother ship. The waterfront buzzed with rumors. *Quadra* was in danger of sinking due to a serious leak. Pirates were plotting to hijack *Quadra*, sail it out to sea, and steal the liquor cargo. Coast Guards deployed to protect the mother ship had purloined bottles of booze and become "beastly drunk." And so the grapevine hummed.[24]

Quadra's owner of record was the Canadian Mexican Shipping Company, a division of Consolidated Exporters. The owners loudly accused the Coast Guard of illegally seizing their property. Company officials argued that the vessel had been captured near Noon Day Rock, which meant that it was floating in international waters, substantially more than an hour's steaming time from the California coast. *Quadra's* captain estimated that his ship's position had been at least one hour and 45 minutes from port.[25]

Quadra's capture aroused strong feelings in both Canada and the United States.

Canadians, fed up with trying to navigate around the Volstead law, were enraged. In their view, American authorities were interfering with Canada's shipping industry. They demanded the immediate release of the liquor freighter and the crew. Moreover, they wanted Washington to issue a contrite, diplomatic apology for the whole episode. But Washington had no intention of apologizing. *Quadra* routinely violated the U.S. dry law, and the Coast Guards were justifiably proud of catching the chronic offender.

A grand jury in San Francisco investigated the incident. After weeks of reviewing the evidence, the jury indicted dozens of men, including *Quadra*'s crew and the board of directors of Consolidated Exporters. The major charges were violating the National Prohibition Act, carrying on "a continuous conspiracy," contravening the Tariff Act of 1922, and failing to comply with the terms of the new British-American rum treaty.[26]

Consolidated Exporters' board of directors included both Canadians and U.S. citizens who had moved to Canada after the passage of the Volstead Act. Legal experts expected the defendants residing in Canada to remain there, beyond the reach of U.S. law. However, before the trial began, U.S. authorities located and arrested two of the directors who were in California on business.[27]

U.S. lawmen also arrested a well-known Canadian attorney, Frederick Anderson. He worked for the law firm representing Consolidated Exporters and had come to San Francisco for meetings about the *Quadra* case. After federal agents rousted Anderson out of bed at the Fairmont Hotel and took him to jail, he publicly protested his arrest. "My mission was to do whatever I could, through the American and British consul, toward obtaining the release of the ship and her cargo for our clients," he said. "I have not the slightest idea why I was arrested." He declared it was outrageous to arrest an attorney simply because his client was accused of a crime.[28]

Anderson quickly made bail and hired his own lawyer. His new mouthpiece claimed that U.S. lawmen had "insulted Anderson, searched his person, seized his private papers and the contents of his pockets, refused to permit him to telephone for counsel ... hustled him to the county jail, and threw him into a cell." Anderson's lawyer fumed over "this flagrant and astounding violation of the constitutional right of every individual to be safe from such brutal search and degrading arrest without a charge or warrant."[29]

From the Canadian point of view, Anderson was an attorney doing his job in a normal, professional manner. But U.S. authorities believed he was more than a lawyer for Consolidated Exporters; they thought he was a leading co-conspirator who should be on trial with his accomplices.

The British Columbia Bar Association asked the San Francisco Bar Association to investigate Anderson's arrest because the federal agents had acted without a warrant. The British Bar Association also got into the act, demanding that London withdraw from the new British-American rum treaty. Although the treaty was intended to facilitate Volstead enforcement on the high seas, it was clearly creating international tension.[30]

In the midst of the furor, Anderson jumped bail and returned to Vancouver. His countrymen greeted him as a hero. A crowd cheered when he delivered an impassioned speech claiming the Americans had arrested him solely because he was Canadian. He declared, "I will not back down an inch. In the interest of other Canadians as well as myself, who might receive unjust treatment at the hands of American authorities as I did, I swear to you that I will stand by my guns!" It wasn't clear exactly how he would stand by his guns, but he promised he would return to San Francisco for the *Quadra* trial.[31]

Before the *Quadra* case went to trial, "a dramatic eleventh-hour surprise arrest" snared another ringleader. Federal Prohibition officers arrested Vincent Quartararo, "a man of wealth and prominence" in San Francisco. Prosecutors called him the "brains" of the rum ring and "the most active agent of the conspiracy onshore" in the United States. When Consolidated Exporters' liquor freighters were positioned off the California coast, he gave "orders and directions" to the captains. He was president of two businesses, the Bohemian Cocktail Company and the Royal Finance Corporation of San Francisco. His companies owned contact boats that worked in tandem with the Consolidated mother ships.[32]

At a preliminary hearing, defense counsel argued that the case should be dismissed because the Coast Guard had violated international law, specifically the British-American rum treaty, by seizing *Quadra*. Thus, the ship and its cargo must be returned to the owners. In addition, the defense questioned whether the court in California had jurisdiction in the case. The judge ruled that the seizure was "in strict accord with the treaty with Great Britain." The evidence against the defendants, including the ship and its cargo, could not "be suppressed or returned" before the jury heard the case. Given the facts surrounding *Quadra*'s capture, the California court had jurisdiction.[33]

When the *Quadra* trial started, Vincent Quartararo and 30 codefendants faced the jury. Another 30 defendants, including Canadian attorney Anderson, didn't show up so they were declared fugitives from justice.[34]

The prosecution created a sensation by bringing samples of *Quadra*'s cargo into the courtroom. "Jurors gasped" as "customs officers wheeled into court tank after tank of beer, barrel after barrel of whiskey and case after case of wines, cordials, champagnes and rums." An observer said the courtroom resembled an old-time saloon. The judge refused to let the court clerk take custody of the illegal liquor and ordered it returned to safe storage outside the courthouse.[35]

The prosecution's first witness was the *Shawnee* commander, who recounted how the Coast Guards had captured *Quadra* near the Farallon Islands. The defense asked the commander to identify some photographs. When he failed to recognize them as pictures of the Farallones, the defense seemed to score points with the jury.[36]

Quadra's position at the time of capture was crucial in determining the legality of the seizure. *Shawnee*'s commander testified that radio compass bearings placed the mother ship in U.S. territorial waters. The data showed that *Quadra* was 5.7 nautical miles from the Farallon Islands, and a motorboat could traverse the distance to shore in less than one hour. (Under the terms of the British-American treaty, the speed of the contact boat, not the mother ship, determined the location of the rum line.)[37]

In cross-examination the defense team attacked the CG commander's testimony by discrediting his service record. Defense counsel revealed that he had been court-martialed three times, raising serious questions about both his seamanship and his character. Given his proven incompetence, he wasn't trustworthy and his testimony couldn't be believed.[38]

The prosecution called rumrunners who admitted they had offloaded liquor from *Quadra* onto contact boats. The rummers confessed to making multiple trips to *Quadra*, picking up booze, and landing it at Russian Gulf in Mendocino County. One of the men stated that he had worked for ringleader Vincent Quartararo.[39]

The state's exhibits included a thick stack of dollar-bill halves confiscated from the rum ring. Quartararo had kept one half of each torn bill and entrusted the other to the master of a mother ship. Before a contact boat went to Rum Row to pick up liquor, Quartararo wrote a notation on the bill and gave the skipper half to show the master. The matching halves proved that the shore runner was authorized to pick up hooch. A handwriting expert testified that Quartararo had made the notations on the bills.[40]

The defense attorneys focused on proving that the Coast Guard had illegally nabbed *Quadra* in international waters. Defense counsel called two of the mother ship's crewmen to the witness stand. They swore that their ship was positioned 13.6 miles off the Farallones, which meant it lay beyond the rum line.[41]

The defense called two surprise witnesses—Coast Guardsmen on the cutter *Shawnee*. The first had been an oiler aboard *Shawnee* when it seized *Quadra*. He stated that *Shawnee*'s crew hadn't taken soundings to determine *Quadra*'s position until 90 minutes after the capture. During that time, the cutter had towed the mother ship closer to shore. The second Guard agreed that the soundings were not taken until after *Quadra* was in tow. To counter this testimony, the state called a score of Guardsmen who had been onboard *Shawnee*. They stated that the soundings had been taken before *Quadra* was moved from its original position.[42]

After all the testimony, two prosecutors and five defense attorneys made closing statements. The lawyers for the minor defendants argued that their clients should be acquitted because the crewmen had played unimportant roles in the Volstead conspiracy. The sailors on *Quadra* were merely hirelings who had followed orders from the bosses.[43]

When the judge charged the jurors, he articulated the issue of guilt or innocence in simple terms and implied that they should separate the crewmen from the captain. "If you find that the crew of this vessel shipped aboard without knowledge that it was carrying contraband cargo, they should be acquitted," the judge said. "If the captain is found to have had knowledge that liquor was being unloaded from his vessel and delivered on the shores of the United States, he should be convicted."[44]

The jurors followed the judge's lead. They found *Quadra*'s officers and the ringleaders guilty but acquitted 19 men who had played minor roles in the conspiracy. The judge gave Vincent Quartararo the toughest punishment: two years at the federal prison in Leavenworth and a $10,000 fine.[45]

Five of the convicted men appealed, and the case reached the U.S. Supreme Court, which focused on the issue of jurisdiction. The appellants argued that the British-American rum treaty did not permit U.S. courts to prosecute British citizens sailing on a British ship, even if the vessel carried a liquor cargo. The U.S. Solicitor General countered that *Quadra*'s owners and officers had worked with paid agents in San Francisco, thereby placing the conspiracy within the jurisdiction of the federal court in California. He noted that the British government had never objected to having its subjects incarcerated and tried on liquor charges if they were seized onboard a mother ship.[46]

The Supreme Court ruled that the British-American rum treaty permitted U.S. courts to prosecute British subjects arrested on ships breaking the Prohibition law. The treaty gave neither express nor implied immunity to the crew on a mother ship. "The inference that both ship and those onboard are to be subjected to prosecution on incriminating evidence is fully justified." Therefore, the convicted men must serve their sentences. The U.S. federal government would retain possession of *Quadra* and its liquor cargo.[47]

Shortly before the *Quadra* trial began, another mother ship belonging to Consolidated Exporters, *Coal Harbor*, fell into U.S. hands. In February 1925 the CG cutter *Cahokia* chased and captured *Coal Harbor* near the Farallon Islands. The cutter towed the liquor freighter to a wharf in San Francisco.[48]

Coal Harbor's captain and crew were arrested and indicted for conspiring to break the dry law. Once again, the crucial issue was the legality of the Coast Guard's actions in seizing the liquor freighter. In federal court *Coal Harbor*'s first officer testified that the Guards had boarded the mother ship 45 miles offshore and towed it more than 20 miles before coming abreast of the Farallones.[49]

When *Cahokia*'s commander took the witness stand, he seemed unsure about *Coal Harbor*'s position relative to the rum line. Under oath, he stated that he hadn't taken radio bearings to determine *Coal Harbor*'s exact location. However, he estimated that the mother ship had been captured 10.5 miles from the shore, which placed it in U.S. waters.

Lawyers on both sides of the case seemed dissatisfied with the CG commander's testimony about *Coal Harbor*'s location. The prosecution recalled him to the stand to clarify some points. Under intense questioning, he confessed that he had taken bearings and later thrown the records away. He admitted that the soundings placed *Coal Harbor* outside U.S. territorial waters when the Guards boarded it. He took responsibility for the misdeed and denied that a superior officer had ordered him to destroy the records.[50]

Based on the new testimony, the attorneys for both sides agreed to stipulate that *Coal Harbor* was roughly 23 miles offshore at the time of capture. This meant that a contact boat must travel 23 miles in less than an hour to stay within the rum line as defined by the British-American treaty. The defense team argued that no contact boat on the West Coast could sail so fast, which meant that *Coal Harbor* had been seized beyond the rum line. The jurors agreed. They returned not-guilty verdicts for all the defendants.[51]

The prevaricating Coast Guard skipper faced both a court-martial and a civilian criminal trial for perjury. At his court-martial, he said, "I admit I acted in the wrong.... I felt it was my duty to do everything possible to obtain a conviction against the *Coal Harbor*." The military tribunal found that he had perjured himself and suspended him for two years without pay. After he appealed for mercy, his sentence was reduced to six months' suspension. A civilian federal court also convicted him on perjury charges and sentenced him to two years in prison. His motion for probation was initially denied but later granted.[52]

More than three years after the Coast Guard captured *Quadra*, the federal government still had possession of both *Quadra* and *Coal Harbor*. The not-guilty verdicts in the *Coal Harbor* case gave Consolidated Exporters good cause to demand that ship's return. In contrast, the federal government had a firm basis for holding onto *Quadra*. Washington hoped to improve relations with Ottawa and London by eliminating the tension over the two ships. Bargaining seemed to be the best course of action. Washington offered a compromise, which Consolidated Exporters accepted. Consolidated agreed to give up all claims to *Quadra*, relinquishing it to the U.S. government. In exchange, Washington returned *Coal Harbor*, along with its sizable liquor cargo, to Consolidated.[53]

The compromise clearly benefited Consolidated more than Washington. During the lengthy legal battles, *Quadra* had steadily deteriorated. Corrosion undermined the ship's structural integrity, and the rusty derelict sank at its moorings in California. The corroded remains were salvaged and sold at auction for only $1,625. *Quadra*'s liquor cargo, valued at a half a million dollars, had been kept in storage since the ship's capture. U.S. marshals transported it to the city dump, where a curious crowd assembled to watch them smash the bottles of forbidden liquid.[54]

More Than a Scrap of Paper

During World War I, British forces captured *Federalship*, an old German iron merchantman. In the postwar reparations the vessel was given to Belgium, and later it was sold to a Canadian firm. The new owner chartered it to the Canadian Mexican Shipping Company, part of the Consolidated Exporters cartel. Flying the Panamanian flag, *Federalship* plied the waters of the Pacific Ocean, carrying liquor from British Columbia to California. As a rule, it stayed far from shore, avoiding even an accidental incursion into U.S. territorial waters.[55]

In February 1927 *Federalship* left Vancouver loaded with liquor, purportedly bound for Buenaventura, Colombia. When the Coast Guard heard that the mother ship had sailed, the cutter *Algonquin* went to hunt for it. U.S. authorities believed that a fugitive from justice, wanted for killing a law officer, was aboard *Federalship*. This added a sense of urgency to capturing the mother ship. On a foggy night the Guards on *Algonquin* spied *Federalship* cruising off the coast of Oregon.[56]

The CG cutter trailed the black ship, following closely as it sailed southwest. Each night *Federalship* tried to shake the cutter by outrunning it, changing course, and/or doubling back. But *Algonquin* stayed close to the rum ship through fair weather and foul. *Federalship* followed its custom, staying far outside the rum line as it sailed south. Frustrated federal officials in San Francisco informed Washington of this and received orders to seize the black ship outside the 12-mile limit if the CG officers saw no other option.[57]

The Coast Guard cutter *Cahokia*, with orders "to seize or sink the smuggler," sailed out to help *Algonquin*. The CG vessels followed *Federalship* as it sailed far beyond U.S. territorial waters to a position roughly three hundred miles west of the Farallon Islands. One evening just before dark the Guards on *Cahokia* fired a warning shot across *Federalship*'s bow and ordered it to stop. The black ship continued on its way. *Cahokia* fired again. The rumrunners ignored the warning. The CG skippers conferred and, due to the limited visibility, decided to stop firing until daylight.[58]

All night the CG cutters stayed close to the mother ship to be sure it didn't slip away. At dawn *Algonquin*, which had more firepower than *Cahokia*, steamed ahead of *Federalship* and raised the international code flag "King," a signal for the rumrunner to stop. Shouting through a megaphone, the rummy captain declared he would not stop. "How do I know you're not a lot of bloody pirates?" he yelled.[59]

The cutters *Cahokia* and *Algonquin* (the latter depicted here) captured the infamous liquor freighter *Federalship* (Naval History and Heritage Command).

Proceeding with caution, *Algonquin*'s skipper radioed to headquarters in San Francisco to ask for orders. He was told to shoot at *Federalship*'s stern, taking careful aim not to hit anyone onboard. The Guards loaded service rounds in *Algonquin*'s six-pounder and fired a blast over the mother ship. The rummy captain didn't respond. *Algonquin* sent a one-pound shell zooming across *Federalship*'s bow, followed by a round that ripped off part of a mast. The Guards swung their three-pound guns into action. A shell wrecked a hatch door on the mother ship. Another three-pounder smashed the starboard rail. The Guards continued to fire rounds until the rumrunner wisely hove to.[60]

Guardsmen from *Cahokia* boarded *Federalship* and ordered the captain to sail his vessel to San Francisco. When he refused, a prize crew from *Cahokia* took charge. *Cahokia* and *Algonquin* towed the mother ship to Hunter's Point in San Francisco Bay. Lawmen searched the ship, looking for contraband. They didn't find the fugitive from justice, but *Federalship* held a cargo of 12,500 cases of high-quality liquor with a street value of $1 million. The lawmen seized an arsenal of rifles, revolvers, and ammo along with documents and evidence of *Federalship*'s smuggling activities. A squad of Coast Guards protected the mother ship's expensive inventory while it rode at anchor in the bay.[61]

Federal authorities called a grand jury into special session in San Francisco to hear evidence about *Federalship*. The jurors returned indictments against the rumrunning captain and crew as well as executives and agents who worked for Consolidated Exporters. After the rumrunners were arrested, they were detained at Bootleggers' College, a converted army barracks used to house Volstead violators.[62]

At trial, the defense argued that the U.S. Coast Guard had committed an act of war by seizing a ship flying the Panamanian flag in international waters. *Federalship* had purposefully stayed beyond the rum line, and the CG had captured it outside U.S. territorial waters. In fact, *Federalship*'s captain claimed that his ship had never been within 60 miles of the U.S. coast. He accused the Guards of illegally boarding a freighter on the high seas—"a peaceful merchantman" that had not violated the Volstead law.[63]

The U.S. attorney conceded that the Coast Guard had captured the mother ship in international waters. But he cited mitigating circumstances that legalized the seizure. Under Panamanian law, *Federalship* had forfeited its registry because it engaged in "habitual smuggling, illicit commerce, or piracy." Therefore, it was actually a ship without a country, a renegade pirate sailing with fraudulent papers. The Coast Guard had every right to seize an outlaw pirate ship.[64]

After hearing both sides of the case, federal judge George Bourquin ruled that the Coast Guard had seized *Federalship* in violation of international law based on the treaty relationship between nations. He called the seizure "sheer aggression and trespass," similar to that associated with the War of 1812. He said that contracts of law set forth in treaties must be "scrupulously observed, held inviolate, and in good faith precisely performed." He warned that such treaties must not be degraded to "mere scraps of paper."[65]

After Bourquin's ruling, Panama's government asked the U.S. State Department to release *Federalship*, but officials in Washington couldn't agree on what to do. The Department of Justice recommended relinquishing the ship, based on the court's ruling that it had been unlawfully seized. But the Treasury Department wanted to keep it because Panama's own law stated "that vessels engaged in smuggling into the territory of a friendly power should not have the protection of the Panamanian flag." Since the cabinet officials disagreed, the case went back to federal court, which ruled that *Federalship* must be released.[66]

After the ruling, two Coast Guard cutters were dispatched to escort the mother ship back to the place where it had been captured. The rumor mill said that *Federalship*'s costly liquor cargo had mysteriously disappeared while in port. High-ranking federal officials empathically denied this. Moreover, they ordered the Guards on escort duty "to see that not so much as one bottle was dropped from the liquor-laden ship" on its outward journey. The U.S. government even gave Consolidated Exporters a check for $413.50 to cover the cost of perishable food lost due to the illegal seizure.[67]

As the CG cutters escorted the mother ship out of San Francisco, *Federalship*'s captain stood on the bridge, "grinning like the Cheshire cat" while he puffed on a cigar. The CG boats trailed helplessly behind the black ship as it sailed to freedom, symbolically thumbing its nose at Prohibition. A writer described the event in a bit of repartee between a boy named Rollo and his father:

> Oh, see the big ship, Rollo, it is going out to sea.
> *But what are the two little boats doing behind it, Papa?*
> They are chasers, my son. Chasers always follow rum.
> *Why does this one need two chasers, Papa?*
> Because it leaves such a bad taste in Uncle Sam's mouth, Rollo.[68]

Federalship, still plastered with unbroken U.S. government seals, returned to Vancouver. The crew broke the seals, inventoried the liquor cargo, and repacked it. Then *Federalship* sailed to Tahiti, picked up more hooch, and headed to the West Coast to sell it. The Coast Guard observed the mother ship lurking off the coast of California, safely outside the rum line.[69]

During its long rumrunning career, *Federalship* sailed under four different names and five flags. In 1928 Consolidated Exporters changed the vessel's name to *L'Aquila* and registered it as a British ship. The name change fooled no one, and the Coast Guard kept the liquor freighter under surveillance. In November 1928 the cutters *Cahokia* and *Tamaroa* followed *L'Aquila* as it sailed off the coast of Southern California, purportedly on its way to Shanghai. *Tamaroa* intercepted the rumrunner near the Santa Barbara Islands. After firing shots that damaged the freighter's hull, the Guards captured it as a "pirate ship."[70]

The following day Washington ordered the CG to release *L'Aquila* and make no attempt to recapture it. Seizing *L'Aquila* would be a hollow victory if it caused more international tension over the Volstead law. Under Washington's new orders, Coast Guard cutters were deployed to prevent contact boats from reaching *L'Aquila*, but they could not capture the mother ship.[71]

17

Malahat
The Phantom of the Pacific

Malahat, the most profitable mother ship in the West, was called the "Phantom of the Pacific" because the Coast Guard had trouble finding it. Built in British Columbia during World War I, *Malahat* was a rugged yet graceful five-mast, auxiliary-engine schooner nearly 255 feet in length. Due to a shortage of steel during the war, *Malahat* was constructed of timbers hewn from giant fir trees on Vancouver Island. Hardwood treenails called trunnels were used in lieu of metal fasteners. Before joining the rum fleet, the windjammer carried timber and coal from the Pacific Northwest to Australia and South America.[1]

Liquor freighters usually had Spartan living quarters, but *Malahat* outclassed the typical black ship. The plush captain's quarters had a sitting room with large built-in cupboards, bookshelves, and a liquor cabinet. Handsome mahogany panels trimmed with oak covered the sitting room walls. To offset the dark wood, the ceiling had a thick coat of bright white enamel paint that reflected light. The captain worked at an impressive oak desk, and red velvet curtains graced the portholes. The captain's sleeping quarters had a built-in double bed; for extra privacy, velvet curtains hanging from a brass rod could be closed around the bed. An *en suite* bathroom completed the captain's quarters. Five staterooms housed the other officers.[2]

The typical mother ship had a short criminal career lasting only a few years, but *Malahat*'s smuggling life spanned almost the entire Arid Era. Exactly when *Malahat* started rumrunning is unclear, but newspapers reported that the Canadian Mexican Shipping Company, part of the Consolidated Exporters group, purchased the schooner in 1923. In 1929 *Malahat*'s ownership passed to the General Navigation Company, which appeared to be a transfer from one shipper to another within the Consolidated Exporters syndicate.[3]

Malahat routinely smuggled large, expensive payloads well above the average for a liquor freighter. When loaded to capacity, it carried an astounding 100,000 cases: 60,000 in the hold plus 40,000 on deck. On one of its first rumrunning trips, the floating warehouse sold $2 million worth of whiskey while anchored near Half Moon Bay, south of San Francisco.[4]

Malahat sold most of its hooch to Californians, but Alaskans also thirsted for good whiskey. Sometimes the mother ship left British Columbia, headed north to Alaska, anchored off Cape Flattery, and offloaded thousands of cases onto a fish packer, which doubled as a rumrunner. Then *Malahat* carried its remaining cargo south to an isolated landing spot off the California coast, where shore runners picked up their loads.[5]

The shore runners delivered booze to coastal towns in the Golden State, but once or twice a week, a speedy motorboat took a load of whiskey inshore all the way to Sacramento, where it was unloaded at a private dock on the river. It was a long trip, so the shore boat left *Malahat* just before dark, in order to finish the delivery before sunrise.[6]

To avoid capture, *Malahat* routinely stayed outside the rum line, waiting for the shore runners. In order to prevent the transfer of liquor to contact boats, the CG cutters picketed the Phantom. "Our sailors were always in the cross-trees, watching to see if it was a buyer's vessel approaching or one of the intervening Coast Guard ships," said a *Malahat* officer. If a CG cutter approached while a contact boat was being loaded, the rumrunners would quickly put the liquor back on *Malahat*. If the shore runner already had its cargo, it "would nip off and elude the Coast Guards."[7]

Malahat used coded telegrams to communicate with the syndicate bosses in Vancouver. To elude the Coast Guard, the mother ship changed position often and kept Vancouver informed via wireless. When Washington pressured Ottawa to rein in *Malahat*, the Canadian government revoked the ship's wireless license. Predictably, that had little impact on the Vancouver syndicate. The ring hired an amateur short-wave radio operator to design and install short-wave radio transmitters on all its mother ships.[8]

Malahat had remarkable rumrunning success in the mid–Twenties, making regular roundtrips between British Columbia and California. In February 1924 it sailed out of Vancouver with a large liquor cargo cleared for Nicaragua. The liquor freighter rode at anchor off the coast of Southern California, sold the booze to contact boats, and marked Nicaragua off its itinerary. In May the liquor-laden *Malahat* left British Columbia again, this time cleared for Buenaventura, Colombia.[9] Of course, no one really expected it to travel farther than the Golden State.

After a summer of rumrunning voyages, the Phantom of the Pacific rode at anchor on San Francisco's Rum Row in autumn 1924. In November, it returned to Vancouver to pick up a $2.5 million cargo. Official records showed that the hooch was going to South America, but it was really destined for the holiday trade in California. The costly inventory had nearly 33,000 cases of whiskey and one thousand barrels of beer. The stock also included rum, wine, brandy, and whiskey in bulk. The potent potables had high price tags in California because *Malahat's* owner had paid the Canadian tariff and passed that cost along to consumers.[10]

Golden State drinkers were willing to pay almost any price because the supply of top-quality imported liquor had fallen quite low. Absent from Rum Row were three mother ships that had been reliable sources of booze in the past. Law enforcement had seized *Quadra*; *Principio* had been delayed by problems in Vancouver; *Prince Albert* was staying away from Rum Row due to its legal troubles over the Pacific cable.[11]

Californians expected *Malahat* to arrive before Santa Claus did. However, only a few days before Christmas, Liquor Lane still awaited the Phantom of the Pacific. It was a no-show due to complications on the voyage south. After the mother ship sailed across the international border, U.S. patrol boats spotted it and gave chase. To evade the Dry Navy, *Malahat* reversed direction and headed back north at top speed. The Phantom escaped capture, but the chase pushed the vessel to its limits, causing engine trouble. The mother ship didn't put into port for repairs, so the Coast Guard didn't know its exact whereabouts. The rumor mill said that *Malahat*'s cargo was being offloaded onto smaller vessels, which would take the booze to California.[12]

For more than a month, the Coast Guard had no verified sightings of *Malahat*. During the same period, the syndicate bosses claimed they had received no messages from the ship. Shortly before Christmas, an unconfirmed sighting placed the Phantom near the Farallon Islands, but the CG cutters couldn't find it. On Christmas Day the Coasties finally found the wayward ship idling off the coast of Monterey. The Guards' surveillance prevented the rumrunners from selling liquor, so the Phantom of the Pacific moved on.[13]

Shortly before New Year's Eve, *Malahat* was seen hovering off the coast near San Simeon. Observers believed it was waiting for contact boats. On New Year's Day 1925 heavy storms battered the coast of California. Waterfront sources reported that *Malahat* and another rumrunner, *Saucy Lass*, had sunk in the choppy seas. The crews of both ships had perished. According to underworld gossip, *Malahat* had been headed to an isolated spot where a newly-formed rum ring planned to take delivery of its liquid cargo.[14]

The shipwreck reports proved to be false. Defying the odds, both *Malahat* and *Saucy Lass* survived the horrific storm. But the bad weather didn't abate. Dense fog shrouded the California coast; the sound of foghorns bellowed across the waters; limited visibility made navigation tricky. In the harsh January weather, the CG sent cutters to hunt for *Malahat* and *Strathona*, another mother ship believed to be lurking offshore. The CG announced that the cutters would seize the liquor freighters whether they were inside or outside the rum line. Moreover, the CG skippers had orders to use force and gunfire if necessary.[15]

In late January, a San Francisco newspaper reported that *Malahat* was "unloading somewhere off the American coast." The Coast Guard's intelligence seemed to be as vague as the paper's. Although the CG brass made capturing the Phantom a top priority, the cutters repeatedly returned empty-handed to base. The slippery *Malahat* somehow disposed of its liquor cargo, despite the bad weather, and returned to Canada to pick up a new load.[16]

In February 1925 *Malahat* sailed down the West Coast and set up shop outside the rum line off San Francisco's Golden Gate. U.S. agents in Vancouver had notified the Coast Guard of *Malahat*'s departure, so the cutter *Tamaroa* sailed out to meet the mother ship. Like good-natured competitors, the two crews exchanged friendly greetings. Then the waiting game began. When would the contact boats leave the shore? Both the rummers and the Guards would spring into action when the mosquito boats raced out to *Malahat*. But the CG cutter stuck so close to the mother ship that the shore runners stayed away.[17]

When the cutter *Tamaroa* returned to base in San Francisco, *Cahokia* took over the surveillance. *Malahat* kept *Cahokia* at bay by staying a safe distance outside the rum line. Showing less caution, *Coal Harbor* ventured close to shore near the Farallon Islands. After the Guardsmen spotted *Coal Harbor*, they kept watch, waiting for it to move into position for offloading booze onto contact boats. *Cahokia* was poised to pounce on the liquor freighter when the time was right.[18]

On a dark, wintry night *Coal Harbor*, running without lights, headed toward the coast at Bolinas Bay, north of the Golden Gate. *Cahokia* followed. *Coal Harbor* increased its speed and took a zigzag course but couldn't get up enough steam to outrun the cutter. When *Cahokia* caught up, the CG captain ordered *Coal Harbor* to stop. The rummy skipper ignored the command. The Guards threw ropes onboard the mother ship; the rummers hurled them back. The Guardsmen weren't deterred. With *Cahokia* alongside *Coal Harbor*, a few surefooted Guards jumped aboard the mother ship. The rumrunning skipper sped away, kidnapping the CG boarding party and leaving the cutter behind. *Cahokia* poured on the steam until it caught up with *Coal Harbor*. Daring Guards with ropes leapt onto the booze boat and lashed the two vessels together.[19]

As the CG cutter towed *Coal Harbor* toward port, *Malahat*'s skipper taunted the Coasties by sailing inside the rum line. He knew he was safe because *Cahokia* had a vessel in tow and couldn't get up enough speed to chase him. The *Malahat* crewmen shouted at the Guards and accused them of seizing *Coal Harbor* beyond the rum line.[20]

After the capture of *Coal Harbor*, Prohibition policy makers decided to ramp up enforcement in Northern California. Washington tripled the number of Coast Guard vessels assigned to the sector. The CG intensified its patrols near the Golden Gate, making it riskier for the contact boats to pick up liquor. This prompted the mother ships to move farther south where the Dry Navy had few enforcement vessels. Observers saw *Malahat* off San Pedro, doing a brisk business. Contact boats carried the liquor to shore, where bootleggers loaded it into cars for the drive to nearby Los Angeles or distant San Francisco.[21]

After *Malahat* left San Pedro, "shipping circles experienced anxiety" as to the ship's whereabouts. The Phantom, purportedly headed for a seaport in Central America, didn't reach its destination.[22] No one actually expected it to put into port in Central America, but there was cause for concern because *Malahat* failed to return to British Columbia on schedule. The ship might have serious mechanical problems or even be shipwrecked. When the tardy Phantom finally sailed into its home port, the anxiety evaporated.

In August 1925 *Malahat* arrived in San Francisco from Victoria, British Columbia, carrying a large cargo of booze. Three months later, *Malahat* returned home and picked up an expensive supply of liquor for the winter holiday trade. A few days before Thanksgiving, Prohibition agents captured a contact boat after a gun battle near the pier at Playa del Rey outside Los Angeles. The Prohis stated that the shore runner was carrying liquor from *Malahat*.[23]

In February 1926 *Malahat* was riding at anchor on the coast side of San Mateo County, south of San Francisco. "Semi-official" sources reported that it had sold more than four thousand cases of whiskey in only two weeks. Two months later *Malahat* and another mother ship were bobbing around in rough seas just outside the rum line off San Francisco. The Phantom of the Pacific had 50,000 cases of scotch whiskey onboard, according to a press report.[24]

Mother ships hovering offshore in June 1926 had more than 100,000 cases of liquor to quench the Golden State's summer thirst. San Francisco's Whiskito Fleet was buying booze from *Malahat* and another chronic offender anchored in international waters. The steamer *Federalship* was servicing Southern California while another liquor freighter was selling to contact boats near the Monterey peninsula.[25]

Malahat's crew endured a hijacking during this June trip to California. One night pirates invaded the ship while most of the crewmen slept. The hijackers surprised the watchmen and wounded two sailors in a gunfight. After subduing the crew, the thieves carried away three thousand cases of liquor. Of course, *Malahat's* skipper made no official report of the theft, but the Prohis heard about it because the wounded sailors were taken ashore for medical treatment. A small boat, presumably a launch from *Malahat*, landed at Point Reyes where it was met by a "fast touring car." Two sailors, one on a stretcher and the other with a bandaged head, were moved from the boat to the car. The press reported that doctors couldn't save the man on the stretcher and he died from a gunshot wound.[26]

A few weeks after the hijacking, bad weather blew in while *Malahat* was anchored alongside other mother ships on San Francisco's Rum Row. The violent storm hammered Northern California. When the weather cleared, observers saw that Rum Row had disappeared. It was widely assumed that the mother ships had sunk during the storm, but the Coast Guard learned otherwise. Guards on *Vaughan* located three of the rum schooners, including *Malahat*, which had moved farther south. The mother ships were staying far beyond the rum line, trying to avoid both bad weather and the Dry Navy.[27]

In March 1927 *Malahat* picked up a cargo of liquor in Papeete, Tahiti, and cleared for Vancouver. The Phantom sailed for California, and the following month the Coast Guard sighted it far out at sea. Later that spring, it was up to its old tricks, riding at anchor outside the rum line off the California coast.[28]

In June 1927 *Malahat* anchored near the Golden Gate, and lawmen noticed "a sudden increase in rumrunning." At Yellow Jacket Bay in San Mateo County federal Prohibition agents seized large amounts of booze that came from *Malahat*. Relying on a tip from an informant, Prohibition agents captured a bootleg convoy of three cars and a truck on the road between Half Moon Bay and San Francisco. The Prohis also seized more than eight hundred cases of liquor, which had been landed on the beach at Half Moon Bay. They pointed to *Malahat* as the source of the booze.[29]

To combat the influx of illegal booze, the Coast Guard brass in San Francisco deployed all available cutters to look for the Phantom of the Pacific. CG officers believed *Malahat* had sailed south. They expected the skipper to anchor near the Santa Barbara Channel, which would allow feeder boats to deliver liquor to Ventura, Santa Barbara, and Los Angeles.[30] But the skipper had other plans.

The CG conducted a fruitless search for *Malahat* in the waters around Santa Barbara. After a week, the cutter *Cahokia* found the Phantom off the shore of Northern California, hundreds of miles from Santa Barbara. The CG commander in San Francisco estimated that the liquor freighter had eight thousand unsold cases onboard.[31]

Cahokia picketed *Malahat* to prevent the sale of the remaining alcohol cargo. Contact boats approached the mother ship but sped away when they spied the CG vessel. At night the cutter slowly circled *Malahat*, focusing its searchlights on the schooner and slowly edging it farther out to sea. *Cahokia* gradually forced *Malahat* far from shore to a position about six hundred miles west of Point Arena Lighthouse in Northern California.[32]

The Guards planned to play the waiting game and starve *Malahat's* crew into surrendering. Although the schooner had left port with ample supplies, the Guardsmen believed the rummers' provisions were getting low. The CG commander stated that *Cahokia* was provisioned for a full month so it could outlast *Malahat*. Furthermore, if the mother ship didn't surrender by the end of the month, another government vessel would take over the patrol duties.[33]

Despite the Coast Guard's close watch, the Phantom of the Pacific silently slipped away one night. The CG officers were angry and frustrated. They assumed *Malahat* had sailed north, headed for port in Vancouver. CG vessels went in pursuit but couldn't find the mother ship. Canadian revenue patrol boats joined the search. After disappearing for about a week, the Phantom sailed safely into Victoria, Canada, beyond the reach of the Dry Navy.[34]

In 1928 the Vancouver press reported that *Malahat* was for sale and would "probably never be associated with the liquor traffic again." This bit of news proved to be a red herring. After the schooner's purported retirement, the Coast Guard spotted *Malahat* near the coast of Mexico, south of San Diego, where a short Rum Row anchored off Point Santo Thomas (AKA San Ysidro Point) in Baja California. The vessels were positioned beside "a sandy shoal which ranged from fifteen to twenty fathoms deep—perfect for anchoring the heavily laden supply ships."[35]

In 1929 *Malahat* was stationed near Isla Guadalupe, a volcanic island off the west coast of the Baja peninsula. Tenders came alongside to deliver supplies as needed. Supersized liquor freighters kept the Phantom well stocked with distilled spirits from Tahiti or Europe. Liquor was transferred by "an intermediary vessel plying between the larger rum ships and the small powerboat runners." CG cutters picketed *Malahat* and the other mother ships to keep them far from shore.[36]

Until the end of Prohibition, the Phantom of the Pacific could usually be found near Baja California and rarely returned to its home port. When a freighter delivered booze in wood crates, *Malahat*'s crew repacked the bottles in burlocks for easy handling. The empty wood crates were burned as fuel for the boiler in *Malahat*'s desalination plant, which produced badly-needed fresh water. When *Malahat*'s crew transferred liquor to a tender or contact boat, the rummers worked fast, using winches and slings to lift the burlocks or barrels and swing them over the side.[37]

To keep *Malahat* well provisioned, vessels from Vancouver delivered canned food, medical supplies, diesel oil, and other necessities. The tender *Dixie* purchased fresh meats, vegetables, and dairy products onshore, usually at a ranch located a short distance from Whiskey Point, Mexico. To break the monotony of life aboard ship, the captain sometimes allowed *Malahat*'s crewmen to go ashore at Whiskey Point. This entailed obtaining a special pass for the crew from the police chief in Ensenada. In keeping with local custom, bribe money changed hands. Without the proper pass, the crewmen might be arrested as trespassers or kidnapped by bounty hunters.[38]

The ennui of being at sea for months sometimes caused unrest among the rum-running crew. On one occasion an officer on *Malahat* noted discontent among the sailors and reported it to the captain, who sent the second mate to investigate. Someone had been pilfering liquor from the cargo, and several sailors had been drinking. The liquor thief was soon identified. In a combative, drunken outburst, he defied the captain and boasted about his plans to shake things up. To foil a possible mutiny, the captain moved to lock up the thieving sailor. When the thief resisted, the captain subdued him, handcuffed him, and stuffed him into the rope locker. Some of the thief's buddies loudly demanded his release. But the captain knew how to handle them. He offered to improve conditions by hiring a new cook; their resistance melted. The captain sent the would-be mutineer back to Canada on the next ship headed to Vancouver.[39]

When *Malahat* stayed on Rum Row for long stretches, maintenance work had to be done without putting into port. In one instance, the crew dismantled the engines for a routine overhaul. While the engines were disabled, problems developed; the weather turned bad and *Tooya*, a ship delivering liquor from Europe, anchored too close to *Malahat*. Every big wave pushed *Tooya*'s iron bow against *Malahat*'s wood stern. But *Tooya*'s cantankerous skipper refused to move.[40]

Tooya's metal hull ground against the Phantom of the Pacific, threatening to hack a hole in the stern. The mother ship desperately needed to move away from *Tooya*. Working frantically, *Malahat*'s engineer managed to start an engine, and the schooner inched away from the danger. The next morning, *Malahat*'s captain was relieved to find no damage to his ship, except two missing lifeboats. It appeared that *Tooya*'s bow had been grinding against the lifeboats, which had protected the stern. Overnight the small boats had broken loose, and the wind had carried them away.[41]

In December 1930 *Malahat* extended a "professional courtesy" to the U.S. Coast Guard. In Mexican waters south of Ensenada, the booze boat *Chapel Point* caught fire and began to sink. The CG cutter *Montgomery*, in the area looking for smugglers, rescued *Chapel Point*'s crewmen. Since the rumrunners were in Mexican waters and the evidence against them was sinking, the Guards had no reason to detain their captive guests. When the CG skipper radioed headquarters, he was instructed to find *Malahat* and transfer the rumrunners to the schooner. After searching for several hours, *Montgomery* located the Phantom, and the rummy skipper agreed to take the seamen aboard.[42]

In October 1931, after 14 months at sea, *Malahat* returned to Vancouver for maintenance. In December the Phantom set sail, and on Christmas Day it was far from land, roughly 1,800 miles west of Mexico. West-to-east trade winds prevailed, so the schooner took advantage of the breeze, crossing the Tropic of Cancer in the morning, on its way to the Baja Rum Row south of San Diego. In honor of the season, a decorated Christmas tree was lashed securely to the foremast. Everyone on board seemed to be infused with the Christmas spirit. The sailors gathered to sing carols, accompanied by crewmen who played the accordion and bagpipes.[43]

The officers' mess served a holiday breakfast of fresh fruit, lamb chops, mint jelly, hash browns, and toast. For the officers' Christmas dinner, fancy menus were hand-painted by a talented artist/seaman. The feast included crab cocktail, oyster sauce, turkey, mince pie, champagne, and plum pudding with brandy sauce. The captain's wife, who was aboard ship, wrote, "The Christmas evening party after dinner—officers and crew together—was like a tonic: renewing friendships, bolstering trusts, and rehearsing promises of things to come."[44]

When *Malahat* reached the Baja Rum Row, it joined the liquor freighters already there: *Lillehorn* from Canada, *Nederiede* from Norway, *Limey* from Britain, *Valencia* from Tahiti, and a two-masted ship from Panama. The captain of a Coast Guard cutter recognized *Malahat* and steamed out to greet his familiar foe, dipping his flag to welcome the rumrunner home. Since the liquor freighters on Rum Row stayed outside U.S.

territorial waters, the Coast Guard could only keep an eye on them. The rumrunning crews made friends with the Coasties by slipping them free bottles of the good stuff.[45]

When a newsman interviewed the rumrunners and Guards in Baja California, he found a spirit of camaraderie and mutual respect. The foes helped one another during tough times. "There is a spirit of fellowship prevalent which extends so far as to have the cutters rush sick or injured men ashore for hospitalization," the reporter wrote. In addition, the rumrunners appreciated the safety afforded by the CG cutters. "They've driven hijackers off the ocean, which is a relief to us," a rummer said. The Coasties gave "almost motherly" attention to the crews on the rum ships because the rummers were "fine fellows."[46]

Malahat, Lillehorn, Mogul, and Valencia rode at anchor south of Ensenada, Mexico, in February 1932. Six months later, after a trip to pick up liquor, *Malahat* was stationed on Baja Rum Row with at least 100,000 cases packed in burlocks. "There was no clear deck space, the whole open waist of the *Malahat*, from poop to fo'c's'le, was filled with sacks of firewater level with the bulwarks," a visitor wrote. It would take months to sell all that inventory.[47]

At Christmastime 1932, *Malahat* was among the mother ships riding at anchor on the Baja Rum Row. The ships, which had already sold much of their holiday inventory, still held roughly 40,000 cases of hooch. The stock included bourbon, rye, scotch, vodka, champagne, and Chinese wines. A reporter who visited Rum Row was favorably impressed with the discipline aboard the liquor freighters. "You will find none of your rough-and-tumble gangster life aboard the rum ships," he wrote. "The crews are composed of law-abiding men who drink little. In fact, they are permitted only a pint of ale a day as long as they are aboard ship."[48]

When voters elected Franklin D. Roosevelt to the presidency, the repeal of Prohibition seemed certain. Congress set the repeal process in motion in 1933, and optimistic drinkers believed that relief would come soon. While Americans waited for the states to ratify the repeal amendment, *Malahat*'s owners ordered the captain to stay at anchor off the coast of Baja California until he sold the remainder of his liquor cargo, roughly 30,000 cases. In preparation for the voyage home, the crew refurbished the schooner— mending sails, repairing the rigging, overhauling the engines, and scraping seaweed and barnacles off the hull. Despite the hard work, a holiday mood prevailed. The captain took the crewmen ashore to a village where they procured "sexual favors." The officers attended a farewell party on another mother ship, where they drank many toasts, their glasses filled with costly liquor.[49]

By September 1933, *Malahat* had quit the rumrunning racket and headed back to Vancouver to start a new career. After being sold, the schooner returned to its roots when the new owner put it to work in British Columbia's timber industry.[50] Its glory days had passed, but the Phantom of the Pacific would always star in the legend of the West Coast rumrunners.

18

Golden Gate Rumrunners
The Tailor and the Mayor

In the Arid Era, San Francisco was widely known as the wettest spot on the West Coast. Alcoholic beverages were plentiful and cheap in the City by the Bay. Mother ships from around the world anchored outside the rum line, and speedy feeder boats carried the booze ashore. Many Napa Valley wineries ignored the Volstead law, and families with a wine-making tradition continued to make their own. Bootleggers hauled hooch into San Francisco via car, truck, ferry, and railroad. California's vast expanse meant that booze often had to be transported long distances, but the liquor traffickers met the challenge.

San Francisco officialdom showed little respect for the dry law. Mayor James Rolph defied Prohibition both publicly and privately. When the 1920 Democratic National Convention met in his city, he procured a railcar filled with "Bourbon whiskey, old, mellow, and full of pungent but delicate tangs—in brief, the best that money could buy." Any delegate who requested a bottle of bourbon received a free one, delivered to his hotel room by a bevy of young women. The bourbon had a "soothing pharmacological effect," said journalist H.L. Mencken. Unlike the Democrats' typical acrimonious conclave, the San Francisco convention went smoothly. The delegates engaged in friendly socializing and treated one another with great civility, according to Mencken.[1]

During the convention, Rolph invited a group of newsmen to his ranch to watch cockfights. While the poultry squawked, pecked, and mutilated one another, the men drank deeply of the mayor's superior hooch. His Honor "poured illegal but authentic liquor into us until I ... was ready for a two-week cure," a guest wrote.[2]

Mayor Rolph wasn't the only local official who defied Volstead. District Attorney Matthew Brady served as vice president of the California Association against the Prohibition Amendment. He publicly declared that state and local resources shouldn't be used to enforce the dry law. "Prohibition should be left up to the federals," he said. "They are responsible for the law. Now let them enforce it." The outspoken D.A. didn't hide the fact that he patronized speakeasies. On one occasion, he was caught at "a notorious bootlegging resort" when federal agents raided it.[3]

The San Francisco Board of Supervisors shared the general hostility toward Volstead. In 1926 the supervisors unanimously voted to oppose the use of local police in enforcing the dry law. Moreover, the board actually reprimanded two police captains for raiding blind pigs. According to a customs service report on Volstead enforcement, the San Francisco police were "of little help, due in main to a decided wet sentiment."[4]

When an explosion rocked a hotel on Kearney Street near the Hall of Justice, police hurried to the site but quickly lost interest. In the hotel basement they found two large stills, bar equipment, and ten thousand gallons of wine. After learning that the basement was leased to "persons unknown," they ended their investigation.[5] Such cursory investigations were typical in potential Volstead cases.

San Francisco's federal Prohibition office, which had a chronic shortage of funds and manpower, did little to disrupt the liquor traffic. To placate the city's small but vocal dry movement, the Prohis periodically raided a few of the most notorious speakeasies. The owners generally took the raids in stride and were soon back in business. One of the federal agents' favorite targets was Shanty Malone, who ran a 1920s–style sports bar. According to local lore, he was a fun-loving guy who occasionally arranged for the Prohis to raid his place, just to amuse his customers. Whenever law enforcement shut down his bar, he simply moved to a new location.[6]

On multiple occasions, federal Prohibition agents raided the Hotel d'Oloron, which was situated at the apex of a triangle formed by alleyways. Every time law enforcement padlocked the hotel, the proprietor hired a carpenter to cut a new door in the exterior.[7] After a few raids, the Hotel d'Oloron had enough doors to confuse any drunk looking for the exit.

Stay in Chicago!

For decades, San Francisco city officials informally decreed that vice would be a local industry. Officialdom tolerated so-called "victim-less crimes," like gambling and prostitution, but forbearance did not extend to strangers who came to town to "muscle in." Eastern mobsters who wanted to move out West found that "the more lucrative forms of crime were so highly organized and well protected that outsiders couldn't break into San Francisco."[8]

During Volstead's final years, big cities in the East and Midwest became a less hospitable milieu for mobsters. Social, economic, and political forces converged to make gangland more dangerous. Violent mob wars claimed many lives. Even if a gangster avoided jail and a one-way ride, he found it harder to make a fast buck. As the Great Depression cast a pall over the country, enterprising big-city mobsters moved to smaller cities in the West, hoping to find Easy Street.

When outside gangs tried to spread their tentacles into the City by the Bay, the police department met the problem head-on. In 1931 police chief William Quinn learned that eastern gangsters were coming to set up shop in San Francisco. He deployed cops to meet the strangers and firmly turn them away. "They will be met at ferry and railroad stations and turned back," he vowed. "Or, if they slip by the cordon of watching policemen, they will be clapped in jail."[9]

Despite Quinn's vigilance, "many mysterious gentlemen from Chicago who flourished large rolls of $100, $500 and even $1000 bills visited San Francisco" in the summer of 1931. "These emissaries dropped in by airplane and bought up all the big wholesale bottle and bootleggers' supply houses in Northern California," a newspaper reported. They raised the price of the bottles and labels, forcing the local alky cookers to pay more for supplies. Then they began to elbow the local bathtub gin producers out of the market.[10]

Chief Quinn formed a special gangster squad to keep the Chicago interlopers and other criminal newcomers "from securing a foothold in San Francisco." The squad proved to be very persuasive. "The Chicago representatives went so far as to make proposition to, and sit in meeting with, this squad with the net result that they decided to, and did, leave town," according to the Police Committee Report of the San Francisco Grand Jury. (The report didn't explain how the special squad managed to be so persuasive.)[11]

Chief Quinn was proud of his role in perpetuating the local monopoly on crime. San Francisco "stands out among the large cities of the West as one of the few where gangsters have been unable to gain a foothold," he said. "Organized crime does not exist here due to a small but efficient number of hardworking police officers. We watch the trains, the planes, and the boats. We have a welcoming committee awaiting all such gentlemen from other parts of the United States. We meet them, we entertain them, but they don't like our entertainment. They, therefore, seldom pay us a second visit."[12]

San Franciscans lauded Quinn for keeping crime local. The police department had come "to the aid of San Francisco's 'honest, hard-working bootleggers' and delivered them from the toils of the Eastern racketeers!" crowed a local newspaper. "Of course, the chief's primary idea was not to protect the local bootleggers but to keep Eastern mobsters out of San Francisco, but in accomplishing one he did the other."[13]

The Battle of Moss Landing

J. Herbert Madden didn't fit the stereotype of a rumrunner. He belonged to a prosperous, respected family in upscale Sausalito, a bayside suburb north of San Francisco. He was a pillar of the community, active in local civic affairs. In fact, voters elected him to the post of town trustee in 1922, and he became the mayor two years later.

When Madden's father died, the dutiful son took over the family's boatbuilding business. The firm specialized in fishing boats and tugs but also built expensive yachts. Madden suffered a devastating setback when a fire destroyed his manufacturing plant along with several boats. The business was underinsured, which caused serious financial problems. But Madden was resilient, ambitious, and resolute. He rebuilt his plant and took on new projects. Under his management, the shipyard built several of San Francisco's famous Bird-class sailboats, including Osprey, Curlew, and Kookaburra.[14]

Joseph Parente's pedigree differed from Madden's in almost every respect. As a young man, Parente became involved in crime, was convicted of forgery, and served time in San Quentin prison. When Prohibition began, he was a struggling ex-con working in a tailor's shop in San Francisco. But he had big ambitions. Like countless other hustlers, he set out to make his fortune selling illegal booze. With the help of his gangland connections, he formed a rum ring to smuggle Canadian liquor from British Columbia to California.[15]

Parente needed fast rumrunning boats and was willing to pay top dollar for them.

Madden needed customers, so he agreed to build boats for the rum ring. The ex-con and the pillar of the community were an odd couple; yet in many ways, they complemented one another. Madden had boating expertise, political clout, and social status; Parente had street smarts and underworld connections. They meshed so well that Madden became a major player in the Parente syndicate. Ironically, while the mayor engaged in liquor trafficking, he also worked for the Coast Guard, repairing rum chasers.[16]

The Parente syndicate landed shipments of liquor at isolated spots near Pebble Beach, Pacific Grove, and Carmel-by-the-Sea on the Monterey Peninsula. Many dry activists lived in the area, particularly in Pacific Grove, which had been founded by Methodists as a summer religious retreat. Due to the dry sentiment, the local lawmen tended to take the Volstead law seriously. From time to time, the backwater gendarmes actually arrested rumrunners from the big city.

Monterey County Sheriff William Oyer wasn't afraid to tangle with the gun-toting rumrunners. One night in June 1925, a tipster told Oyer that Parente contact boats were landing liquor at the wharf at the Pebble Beach Yacht Club. Oyer quickly assembled a posse. The lawmen drove to the wharf in cars and watched from distance. They saw cases of liquor stacked up on the beach and a shore crew busy at work, loading the booze onto trucks. A boat idled offshore, its silhouette visible in the darkness. Strangely, it was not a typical sleek, low-slung shore runner. To the posse, it looked like a Coast Guard picket boat or a vessel camouflaged to resemble one.[17]

The sheriff's posse hopped out of the cars and swarmed onto the beach, trying to trap the rumrunners. But the rummers were prepared for unwanted visitors; they drew their guns and blasted away. The lawmen returned fire. Dozens of bullets flew across the beach. The rumrunners dashed for cover, shooting as they ran. The posse managed to nab three swampers, but the others disappeared into the heavy brush along scenic Seventeen-Mile Drive. They left their cars and booze behind.[18]

Before sailing away, the rum boat blew its siren three times, presumably sending a signal to someone onshore or on another vessel. The sound of the siren was "unmistakably that of a government patrol boat." It appeared that corrupt Coasties were working with Parente's rumrunners. As the boat departed, the sheriff's posse shot at it, unleashing a barrage of automatic gunfire, puncturing the vessel's hull. Despite the damage, the craft sailed away.[19]

After the gunfight, the posse counted three hundred cases of liquor on the trucks and 75 more on the beach. The shore crew had also left behind seven automobiles. The sheriff confiscated all the booze and vehicles.[20]

The Parente syndicate suffered heavy losses that night, and it was obvious that the rum boats needed a safer landing spot. Parente arranged for his boats to unload their cargo at Moss Landing, on the bay north of Monterey. The first landing went smoothly; the shore crew spent two nights moving liquor from boats to a shack in a hayfield. No police showed up to interfere.[21]

On July 6, 1925, an informant told Monterey County lawmen that rumrunners were loading liquor on trucks in a hayfield at Moss Landing. Three deputy sheriffs, a special deputy, and a state policeman piled into a car and drove to the field. Before the lawmen even got out of their vehicle, they spotted a pilot car escorting a liquor truck away from the site. The lawmen hollered out the car windows, ordering the drivers to stop. Of course, the rumrunners didn't obey. The rummer riding shotgun in the pilot car fired at the lawmen. Bullets shattered the windshield, spraying glass over the officers, but no one was injured.

The lawmen immediately saw that they needed more manpower to capture the heavily-armed rumrunners. One officer went to the nearest police station for reinforcements. The other lawmen spread out in the hayfield, taking positions "at wide distances" around the perimeter.[22]

The officer who raced to the police station phoned Sheriff Oyer, who quickly formed a posse of police, deputy sheriffs, and civilians. Oyer and his posse drove to the hayfield and parked their cars. In the foggy darkness, they tramped through the tall grass, ready to do battle with the rumrunners. The rummers had prepared the hayfield for a gunfight with lawmen or hijackers. At strategic points, they had stacked bales of hay as barricades to shield them, in case they couldn't reach their cars when the shooting started. They were armed with pistols, automatic rifles, and machineguns.[23]

As Oyer's posse moved forward in the darkness, three gun-toting strangers popped up in front of them. The staccato rat-a-tat of machinegun fire rang out. Bullets seemed to come at the posse from all sides. The lawmen drew their guns and returned fire. Sheriff Oyer grabbed a gunman's coat and held on, but the shooter escaped by slipping out of his coat. Then he shot Oyer at close range, hitting the sheriff's knee, shattering the bone.[24]

Gunfire exploded in the darkness. A posseman took a bullet in his leg. The rumrunners hopped into their cars and sped across the hayfield. The first car drove through a fence at breakneck speed, knocking down a section, leaving a gaping hole for the others to pass through. The lawmen shot at the fleeing cars but failed to stop them.[25]

The uninjured officers divided into two groups. One group rushed their wounded comrades to the hospital in Salinas. The other searched the hayfield for evidence that might lead them to the escaped gunmen. The searchers stumbled on a Luger pistol and empty clips for machineguns, apparently left behind by the shooters. They also found a truck and a car near the scene of the shootout. Although the vehicles were clearly intended for hauling liquor, both were empty.[26]

As the lawmen combed the landing for evidence, they made a shocking, gruesome discovery. Beside the road, they found the lifeless body of a fallen comrade, the special sheriff's deputy. He had been struck down by machinegun bullets. His hand still clutched his gun, which had been fired five times, leaving a single bullet in the chamber.[27]

The sheriff's posse, aided by other lawmen, searched the area for the rumrunners who had fled. By dawn the lawmen had nabbed three rumrunners and taken them to local jails. But an unknown number of rummers had escaped. Officials deployed a squad of deputy sheriffs and "many armed citizens" to hunt for the outlaws still on the loose. At first, the searchers focused on the marshes along the waterfront. Then they moved inland along the roads leading away from the coast.[28]

Authorities issued shoot-to-kill orders in the jurisdictions near Moss Landing. In San Francisco the police shotgun squad was placed on alert, and detectives hunted for rumrunners who might have slipped into the city. The Coast Guard ordered a cutter to the Monterey Bay area to search along the shore.[29]

Based on information provided by the rumrunners in jail, law enforcement soon had a list of suspects. Joseph Parente, Mayor Madden, and "wealthy San Francisco club-man" William Adams were named as the leaders of the rum ring. Simon Bube and Paul Brokaw were identified as the shooters who had killed the special deputy. Authorities initiated a manhunt for Bube and Brokaw, who was known as "the rumrunning fashion plate" due to his stylish wardrobe.[30]

After arrest warrants were issued for Madden and Parente, the duo surrendered to law enforcement. A warrant was also issued for the wealthy clubman, and police soon took him into custody. Nearly three months after the shootout, law officers nabbed Brokaw, the fashionable rumrunner. They couldn't find the other suspect, Bube, so a $500 reward was offered for his capture, dead or alive.[31]

During the gun battle at Moss Landing, Bube had been shot in the thigh, probably by Sheriff Oyer. The rumrunner spent a week in a private hospital in Marin County, where he was treated for the gunshot wound. The hospital, which had a reputation for harboring fugitives from justice, didn't contact the police. Officers hunting for Bube went to the hospital but arrived too late; he had already been discharged.[32]

After leaving the hospital, Bube moved around, hiding in various places in Northern California. He rented a room in Redwood City, where he found work as a carpenter. When law enforcement heard he was in town, cops disguised as plumbers went to the construction site where he worked. The policemen caught Bube off-guard, drew their pistols, and handcuffed him.[33]

Bube and Brokaw were indicted for shooting the lawmen at the Battle of Moss Landing. (A third rumrunner was also indicted, but the court dismissed his case due to lack of evidence.) At the preliminary hearing, the star witness was a swamper who had driven a truck at Moss Landing. He said that Brokaw had been heavily armed with a pistol, a rifle, and a sawed-off shotgun. Bube had carried a machinegun and "swept the roads with machinegun fire" when the rumrunners first saw Sheriff Oyer's posse.[34]

Although this was only a preliminary hearing, the attorneys on both sides argued passionately. Their animosity toward one another seemed to know no bounds. The court-room resounded with accusations of misconduct, deceit, double-dealing, and witness-coaching. The prosecutor and a defense lawyer actually came to blows in the court-room—not once but twice! Court officers had to jump in to separate them. After the second scuffle, the judge warned the lawyers that they would be arrested if another fight broke out.[35]

Defense counsel argued that the special deputy had been killed by friendly fire, not by rumrunners' bullets. This scenario was certainly possible, but the lawyer offered no evidence to prove it. The court ordered Bube and Brokaw to stand trial for homicide.[36]

The murder trial lasted for three weeks, with more than two dozen witnesses taking the stand. The state's case relied heavily on rumrunners who had been granted concessions for helping the prosecution. A rummer testified that both defendants had been heavily armed at the Moss Landing shootout. He had seen Sheriff Oyer grappling with one of the rumrunners in the hayfield. Oyer seemed to have the upper hand, so Bube and another gunner "opened up on him." The witness did not name Brokaw as the second gunman.[37]

Adding a new twist to the tale of the shootout, a rumrunner testified that Sheriff Oyer had been paid a bribe to allow Parente's crew to land liquor that night. The witness said $200 had been given to Oyer's brother to pass along to the sheriff. Therefore, when the posse showed up, the rumrunners were surprised and mad because they thought Oyer had doubled-crossed them. Other witnesses disputed this testimony about the sheriff taking a bribe.[38]

A San Francisco gunsmith testified as an expert witness for the prosecution. He stated that the bullet taken from Sheriff Oyer's knee was fired from a Luger pistol, like the one found at Moss Landing after the shootout. Because the bullet that killed the special deputy was badly damaged, he couldn't positively classify it. However, he believed it also came from a Luger.[39]

The prosecution produced an incriminating document signed by Bube after his arrest. The prosecutor called it a "confession," but defense counsel vigorously disagreed. Bube's attorney stated that the so-called confession had been obtained by subterfuge when a Prohibition agent pretended to be a lawyer. Moreover, it was an equivocal confession at best: Bube admitted he had carried a gun at Moss Landing but swore he had never fired it.[40]

Despite the murky evidence, the prosecution asked for the death penalty for both defendants. After hearing the closing arguments, the jurors retired to deliberate. They cast dozens of ballots without reaching a verdict. Seeing no way to end the impasse, they told the judge they were hopelessly deadlocked. He reluctantly declared a mistrial.[41]

Because the evidence against Brokaw was weak, the state put his case on the backburner and opted for separate trials for the accused men. Therefore, Bube was the sole defendant at the second Moss Landing murder trial. His attorneys aggressively cross-examined the state's witnesses and strongly objected to the prosecution exhibits, particularly Bube's purported confession.[42]

The defense claimed that Bube had fired no shots in the gunfight at Moss Landing. Of course, the state argued otherwise. To show that Bube was in the thick of the battle, the prosecutor emphasized that he had needed medical care for a gunshot wound after the shootout. In response, the defense claimed that Bube accidently shot himself, but it didn't happen at Moss Landing.

As in the first trial, the jury deadlocked. The judge was clearly frustrated because he believed the evidence proved Bube's guilt beyond a reasonable doubt. However, the government had spent considerable money on two futile murder trials, and there was no guarantee that another would produce a guilty verdict. The judge reluctantly dismissed the homicide charge against Bube.[43]

The prosecutor dropped the murder charges against Brokaw. But the criminal court system wasn't finished with Bube and Brokaw. They were accused of participating in a rumrunning conspiracy and stood trial on Volstead charges. Bube pled guilty and was sentenced to 16 months in the federal prison at Leavenworth, Kansas. Although Brokaw pled not guilty, the jury convicted him. The court ordered him to pay a $5,000 fine and serve two years in federal prison.[44]

"Guilty Knowledge"

After the Battle of Moss Landing, Mayor Madden and 20 other men were indicted for conspiring to violate the Volstead law. The state alleged that this conspiracy had culminated in the shootout at Moss Landing, but the charges didn't include killing the special deputy. Madden was accused of being part of "a gigantic rum-smugglers' conspiracy" and having "guilty knowledge of the Moss Landing battle." His codefendants included "master mariners," a rancher, a farmer, an ex-con, a night watchman at a whaling station, a former Prohibition agent, and the owner of the docks at Moss Landing. Although Joe Parente was widely reputed to be the rum ring boss, he was not indicted in this case.[45]

After a long delay, Madden and eight codefendants went on trial for the Volstead conspiracy. Although 21 men had been indicted, the state dropped the cases against the defendants who agreed to cooperate with the prosecutor. Three defendants pled guilty, and four of the accused men had absconded.

Testifying for the prosecution, a night watchman at a seafood company said he knew the rumrunners who unloaded booze at Moss Landing. When asked to identify them, he pointed to Madden and several other defendants, saying they had paid him "to remain silent about certain liquor smuggling activities." Another state's witness said he had been hired to drive "a booze delivery car" on the night of the gun battle. He identified two of the defendants as the men who had hired him. Sheriff Oyer gave a detailed account of the Moss Landing gunfight, describing the men in his posse and the firearms they carried.[46]

A college student who worked at a bait shop testified that he knew several of the defendants. He had notified lawmen on two occasions when he learned that the rumrunners were unloading booze boats at Moss Landing. When he saw the rummers a third time, he didn't notify officials because he feared there would be trouble. The student's credibility was damaged when he mistakenly identified a deputy sheriff as a rumrunner he claimed to know.[47]

To prove that the defendants conferred often, the prosecution relied on a Pacific Telephone Company superintendent, who testified about their long-distance phone bills. The telephone records showed numerous calls made by various defendants from San Francisco to Sausalito, Salinas, Monterey, and Moss Landing.[48] (Long-distance phone calls required the assistance of an operator; they cost extra and were itemized on the customer's monthly bill. Long-distance calls were so expensive that making one was a special event for many consumers.)

The defense team challenged the veracity of the state's witnesses and criticized the methods used by federal agents. A defense attorney said the agents "had threatened the defendants and had used force and duress" to persuade witnesses to testify for the prosecution. The attorney claimed the agents "had presented false affidavits" and, in one instance, had threatened to take a defendant's wife and child away from him. The defense scored a victory when the judge barred the confession of a rumrunner who had been promised leniency by a federal agent.[49]

Madden's attorney argued that there was no evidence linking the mayor to the rumrunners at Moss Landing. However, a man testified that Madden had hired him to salvage the engine from a booze boat wrecked off the Monterey coast. Because Madden hadn't paid him for the work, the man had agreed to be a prosecution witness. Madden's lawyer argued that revenge was the man's motive for testifying, so he couldn't be believed. Similarly, an alky cooker testified that he had sold liquor to the Parente-Madden rum ring but had not been paid. Subsequently, he talked to federal authorities and agreed to testify at the conspiracy trial.[50]

The closing arguments took many hours as counsel, including a half-dozen defense attorneys, made the final pitches to the jury. The jurors returned guilty verdicts for seven defendants, including Madden. The judge sentenced the mayor to two years in federal prison, but his lawyer immediately filed notice that the conviction would be appealed.[51]

A Dose of Bad Medicine

Principio was an infamous mother ship often seen off the coast of Northern California. Only days before the Moss Landing shootout, Mayor Madden, Joseph Parente, and several accomplices were indicted on Volstead conspiracy charges related to *Principio*'s suspect voyages.[52]

Principio began its seafaring life as a German warship that saw service in the Great War. When peace returned, a fruit distributor bought the ship, sailed it to San Francisco, and added cold storage for shipping produce. When the fruit distributor had financial problems, a court ordered the sale of *Principio* to help pay the company's debts. Parente bought the vessel, probably with financial help from Consolidated Exporters, the rum-running conglomerate in British Columbia. After *Principio* was retrofitted for rumrunning, it made frequent trips to California.[53]

When Mayor Madden was indicted on the *Principio* rumrunning charges, he surrendered to authorities, pled not guilty, and posted bond. He denied knowing Parente or the other defendants. "It is more than possible that I have done work for the people charged here with me," he said, "but that work was centered in my shipbuilding plant in Sausalito, and I do not know them personally." He insisted that he had never willingly worked for liquor smugglers. "If any rum ships ever have been repaired in my shipyards at Sausalito, it was without my knowledge."[54]

Madden's declarations of innocence didn't satisfy his political rivals in Sausalito. Allegations that he was rumrunning led to a recall election to oust him in 1925. He won more than 55 percent of the vote and stayed in office. After being indicted in the Moss Landing case, the mayor ignored calls for his resignation. His supporters emphasized that he had not been found guilty of a crime and the presumption of innocence was a basic legal right.[55]

Federal prosecutors clearly hoped to crush Madden and Parente under a pile of legal charges. In September 1925 two sealed indictments were made public, revealing new Volstead charges against the duo and their accomplices in the rum ring. Among other crimes, Madden and Parente were accused of sailing a speedboat out to *Principio*, loading it with liquor from the mother ship, and taking the illegal cargo to San Francisco.[56]

When Madden, Parente, and their codefendants went on trial in the *Principio* case, they were represented by a battery of 13 attorneys, including a former United States senator. In contrast, Assistant U.S. District Attorney Eugene Bennett singlehandedly presented the state's case. Bennett was a young, inexperienced lawyer, who had joined the U.S. district attorney's staff only a few months earlier. The trial progressed slowly as the army of defense lawyers objected to almost everything.[57]

U.S. rum rings bought liquor from the Consolidated Exporters' warehouse in Vancouver (City of Vancouver Archives).

The defense attorneys tried to undermine the prosecution's evidence by claiming that the state had bribed witnesses and had also obtained evidence by coercion. Defense counsel alleged that a sailor who testified for the state had been paid a bribe and had been promised help in becoming a naturalized U.S. citizen. Another state's witness, a former rumrunner, admitted to being on the government's payroll. He said that he had previously worked for Parente, who paid him $1,000 for picking up liquor from *Principio*. He had landed his cargo in Oakland and San Francisco. When he quit rumrunning, he went to work as a special investigator for the government.[58]

A "confessed bootlegger" took the stand to testify about rumrunning for the Parente-Madden ring. He had sailed in contact boats to pick up liquor from the mother ships *Principio* and *Malahat*. Madden's attorney contended that this witness lied about his dealings with the mayor because the rum ring had cheated him out of money and he wanted revenge.[59]

The prosecution called a "surprise witness" who stated that the Parente-Madden rum ring had unloaded liquor on his dock at Inverness, north of San Francisco. The witness accused Madden of trying to intimidate him. He said that Madden and a defense lawyer had visited him and advised him not to testify. They warned him that he would be indicted on Volstead charges if he did so. On the witness stand, he did not fare well under questioning by the defense attorneys. He couldn't remember dates and gave vague answers. During cross-examination, he retracted some of his previous statements.[60]

The prosecution stated that Madden was part owner of *Principio;* but the mayor's attorney said he was simply a boat builder hired to retrofit the ship. Like other honest businessmen, he couldn't control what happened to his product after it left his plant. The defense called *Principio*'s skipper to testify about the vessel's ownership. He stated that Madden had attended meetings about the syndicate's plan to buy the mother ship but hadn't been involved in the actual purchase. He described Madden's role as that of "master ship-fitter." The skipper took his orders from Parente, who routinely referred to *Principio* as "my ship."[61]

Before turning the case over to the jurors, the judge instructed them to acquit two of the codefendants due to insufficient evidence. After deliberating, the jury returned not-guilty verdicts for a total of four defendants. Madden, Parente, and another defendant were found guilty. A few days later, the mayor's political rivals finally triumphed. California's attorney general declared that Madden's conviction disqualified him from serving as Sausalito's mayor and, therefore, the post was vacant.[62]

The court sentenced Madden and Parente to two years in federal prison and ordered each to pay a fine of $5,000. They appealed their convictions, but the United States Circuit Court of Appeals in San Francisco upheld the guilty verdicts. Madden then petitioned the lower federal court, asking to serve his sentence on probation, thereby avoiding prison. His petition, signed by numerous California politicos, argued that Madden deserved special treatment because he was "the least involved" of all the rumrunners convicted in the case. The judge was not impressed by the argument or the signatures. He rejected Madden's appeal, and the rumrunning mayor went to serve time at McNeil Island prison.[63]

Although Madden accepted his fate, Parente wasn't ready to concede defeat. Leaving no rock unturned, the liquor lord took his petition all the way to the U.S. Supreme Court, which refused to hear his case.[64]

Parente had exhausted his legal remedies, but he wasn't averse to illegal ones. He went on the lam, forfeited his bail, and didn't show up to start serving his prison term. According to the rumor mill, he had slipped out of San Francisco disguised as a sailor and was working as an oiler on a northbound steamer.[65]

Parente fled to Vancouver where he had friends and business associates. Normally, Vancouver was a safe haven for American rumrunners because Canada did not routinely extradite Americans in Volstead cases. However, when an especially notorious liquor smuggler slipped across the border, Washington requested and often received Canada's help. In Parente's case, Canadian authorities agreed to aid U.S. law enforcement. Canadian immigration officials promptly arrested him as an undesirable alien. He was taken to court, posted bail, and was freed, pending a deportation hearing before the immigration examining board.[66]

To speed up the legal process, prosecutors in San Francisco decided to charge Parente with an extraditable offense. A grand jury indicted him for perjury in connection with fraud, which qualified him for extradition. But Parente vanished. He didn't show up for his hearing before the Canadian immigration examining board. Nor did he appear in court in San Francisco to answer the perjury/fraud charge. Both Canadian and U.S. authorities hunted for him. The U.S. Coast Guard boarded liquor freighters to search for him, and federal agents searched for him in the Pacific Northwest. His San Francisco bail bondsman hired private detectives to find him.[67] He eluded everyone.

After nearly a year on the run, Parente was finally arrested by Canadian officials acting on information from U.S. agents who had spotted him in Vancouver. He agreed to return to the United States; Canadian lawmen escorted him to Blain, Washington, where he surrendered to American authorities. He was incarcerated at McNeil Island penitentiary in Washington. After a short stay there, the feds transported him to San Francisco to answer charges in court. He finally seemed to be tired of running. In the courtroom, he pled guilty to violating the dry law and was sentenced to four years in federal prison.[68]

In an interesting coincidence, on the day lawmen nabbed Parente in Vancouver, Madden returned home to Sausalito. After 15 months in prison, he had been released on parole. "I come home without any bitterness and without any complaints of ill treatment," he said. "They handed me out a dose of rather bad medicine, and I did not enjoy it a bit, but I do not think that my worst enemies can say that I have whined any, in spite of the fact that I cannot convince myself that I have ever done a criminal act."[69]

The ex-con proved that he still had friends in high places. Powerful politicos, including a U.S. senator, pressed the White House to exonerate the former mayor. In 1932 President Herbert Hoover granted Madden a pardon that restored his full citizenship rights. After registering to vote as a Republican, he waded into the thick of local politics. In 1936 Sausalito's forgiving residents voted for the ex-con, giving him another term as mayor.[70]

Madden devoted his time to business, community projects, local charities, and his church. He served as president of the Sausalito Chamber of Commerce and as a director of the Sausalito-Marin City Sanitary District. He prospered in the boating business and developed the Sausalito Yacht Harbor. When he died at age 86, a newspaper obituary described him as "a humorous, practical, industrious, and controversial man."[71] His political activism—not his rumrunning career—had earned him the "controversial" label. The obituary writer didn't even mention Madden's exploits during the Arid Era.

19

Repealing Prohibition
The End of the Great Drought

During the first decade of Prohibition, millions of Americans became disillusioned with the United States of Volstead. The dry law didn't produce the utopia promised by the Prohibitionists. On the contrary, it spawned crime and lawlessness on a scale the country had never seen before. It created a vast illegal liquor traffic, corrupted law enforcement, and led to unprecedented violence in American life. Yet there was no national consensus on what to do about it. Wets wanted to repeal Volstead. Dry activists wanted to keep it and beef up enforcement. Moderates searched for a middle ground; many wanted to modify Volstead to legalize beer and wine but not distilled spirits.

In general, Americans focused on moral and social issues when they debated the pros and cons of Prohibition. But the focus changed after the 1929 stock market crash. The Great Depression put the economic impact of Prohibition at the center of the debate. The liquor lords and mob bosses were living in luxury while ordinary Americans struggled to pay the rent. Legalizing the liquor industry would divert money from gangland into the legitimate economy. It would put law-abiding citizens to work in breweries, wineries, distilleries, bars, and liquor stores. Liquor taxes would bolster government revenues and reduce dependence on the income tax.

By 1932 polls showed that the public overwhelmingly supported repeal or modification of the dry law. In May 1932 cities across the United States held Beer for Taxation Parades. The biggest was in New York City, where two million spectators watched the parade of floats, bands, and marching units. The marchers carried banners: "Down with Bootleg," "Help the Taxpayer," "Vote as You Drink," and "End Business Stagnation with Beer Taxation." One marching unit carried a banner saying "We Want Beer," followed by another declaring "We Want Work, Too." A popular banner called for drastic action: "Open the Spigots, Drown the Bigots."[1]

The economy dominated the 1932 elections, but Prohibition was also a major issue. The Presidential election pitted Republican incumbent Herbert Hoover against Democrat Franklin Delano Roosevelt. Both parties debated the dry law at their national conventions and included a Prohibition plank in their platforms.

When the Republicans met, "the sentiment of the convention was overwhelmingly for repeal." However, President Hoover wanted to proceed cautiously, and the delegates followed his lead. They adopted a plank that would allow each state to hold a convention

This young woman is surrounded by signs and petitions demanding modification of the Volstead law (Library of Congress).

to determine the fate of Prohibition within that state's borders. The GOP would permit "states to deal with the problem as their citizens may determine, but subject always to the power of the federal government to protect those states where Prohibition may exist and safeguard our citizens everywhere from the return of the saloon and attendant abuses."[2]

The Democrats' platform didn't mince words. "We favor the repeal of the Eighteenth Amendment," it said. It also outlined a process for ratifying a new constitutional amendment to repeal Prohibition. Because the ratification process would take time, the Democrats promised "immediate modification of the Volstead Act to legalize ... beer and other beverages of such alcoholic content as is permissible under the Constitution." The Eighteenth Amendment banned "intoxicating liquors" but didn't define the term, so Congress had the power to revise the Volstead Act to legalize light beer and wine.[3]

After Roosevelt won the election, the Democrats took action to honor their promise to revoke the dry law. On January 9, 1933, the Senate Judiciary Committee approved the repeal resolution that would be submitted to the state ratifying conventions. After a little tweaking, both houses of Congress put their stamp of approval on the resolution.[4]

Under Volstead a legal beverage could have an alcohol content of no more than one-half of one percent. To keep the Democrats' promise to legalize low-alcohol beverages, Congress passed the Cullen-Harrison Act, which permitted the sale of beer and fermented fruit juices with an alcohol content of 3.2 percent or less. Roosevelt quickly signed the bill, and the new law went into effect on April 7, 1933.[5]

Also during April 1933, Michigan's state convention became the first to ratify the repeal amendment. Other states quickly followed suite. Even dry strongholds in the South and Midwest voted for repeal. On December 5, 1933, Utah's state convention

President Roosevelt signs the Cullen-Harrison Act to make beer legal beginning April 7, 1933 (Library of Congress).

approved the repeal amendment, satisfying the Constitutional requirement that three-fourths of the states ratify it.[6]

As soon as Utah's vote was certified, President Roosevelt issued the formal Repeal Proclamation. He lauded repeal as a positive step toward restoring "greater respect for law and order." He called on all citizens to cooperate with law enforcement in "the breakup and eventual destruction of the notoriously evil illicit liquor traffic." He urged Americans to forever banish "the menace of the bootlegger." He endorsed moderate drinking, saying, "I trust in the good sense of the American people that they will not bring upon themselves the curse of excessive use of intoxicating liquor to the detriment of health, morals, and social integrity."[7]

Major Frederick Silloway, a Prohibition Bureau official, summed up the feelings of many Americans. "I believed in Prohibition," he said. "I still believe in Prohibition. I'd like to see real Prohibition in this country—but I don't think that I ever will. It's against all human nature. It's against all the rights guaranteed in the Constitution. It's a legal, psychological, physical impossibility."[8]

The End of Rum Row

When Congress set the repeal process in motion, no one knew exactly when Prohibition would end, but everybody knew that Rum Row was headed for extinction. *Yukatrivol* had the distinction of being the last Canadian boat custom-built to be a Volstead rumrunner. In April 1933 the vessel left British Columbia on its maiden rumrunning trip, headed for San Francisco. The 62-footer sped across the water, powered by a 200-HP diesel engine plus three 450-HP Liberty gasoline motors.[9]

The mother ship *Malahat* ended its long, lucrative career as a liquor smuggler in late summer 1933. Rumrunners *Kagome*, *Lillehorn*, *Tapawinga*, *Principio* (AKA *Tooya*), and *Chief Skugaid* returned to their Canadian ports by December 1933. The booze boats *Shuchona*, *Algie*, *Audrey B*, *Hickey*, and *Zip* sailed to Canada in January 1934.[10]

The Great Drought ended. Rum Row faded away, but the tales of the rumrunners endured as a unique chapter in American history.

Glossary

airedale: A lookout, especially one who signaled rumrunners when the coast was clear.

alky cooker: A person who distilled alcohol in his home or apartment and sold it to a mob or bootlegger.

amenity boat: A boat that carried prostitutes out to Rum Row to service crewmen on the mother ships.

banana boats or **banana fleet**: Streamlined, low-slung boats designed for rumrunning.

Bimini boat: A boat built for smuggling liquor to Florida from Bimini or another nearby island; typically, a 25-foot boat that carried up to four hundred cases of liquor and traveled from Bimini to Florida in about two hours.

black ship: A large vessel used for rumrunning.

blind pig: An illegal saloon.

blockade: a formation of watercraft deployed to close a port, harbor, or section of coast to prevent liquor smugglers from entering or leaving.

blockade runner: A contact boat.

bootlegger: A land-based liquor trafficker.

booze buccaneer: A rumrunner.

bottle fisherman: A commercial fisherman who quit fishing and joined the ranks of the rumrunners.

buck and a quarter boat: The U.S. Coast Guard's 125-foot-long, heavily-armed patrol boat.

burlock: a large sack, usually burlap, filled with bottles of liquor surrounded by straw or another cushioning material.

Coasties: U.S. Coast Guard personnel.

contact boat: A small vessel, especially a speedboat, which picked up liquor from a mother ship and transported it to shore.

cutterized: Rumrunner slang for being picketed or followed by a Coast Guard cutter.

daughter boat: A contact boat.

deadline: The rum line, where the United States' territorial waters ended and international waters began.

distributor: A contact boat.

dock fixer: The person who supervised the unloading of illegal liquor and bribed officials to ensure that law enforcement didn't interfere.

dollar boat: U.S. Coast Guard's 100-foot long, steel-hulled, twin diesel watercraft.

Dry Fleet or **Dry Navy**: The vessels and personnel of the U.S. Coast Guard and other government entities that enforced Prohibition on the waterways.

feeder boat: A contact boat.

fifth: A standard bottle size for distilled spirits; five fifths equal a gallon.

fireboat: A fast boat carrying a cargo of firewater; a contact boat.

firemen: The crew on a fireboat.

firewater: Alcohol or intoxicating beverages.

four hundred boat: An improved, faster version of the Coast Guard six-bitter; added to the fleet in the last years of Prohibition and used primarily on Long Island Sound.

go-thru-guys: Hijackers.

gray ghost: A rumrunning vessel.

Guard or **Guardsman**: A member of the U.S. Coast Guard.

ham: A burlock.

hijack: To steal a cargo in transit; to illegally seize control of a vessel.

Hooligans' Navy: Rumrunners' nickname for the U.S. Coast Guard.

in-between boat: Contact boat.

intermediate: A medium-sized vessel that took liquor from a mother ship on the high seas and sailed near the rum line to transfer the booze to contact boats.

Isle of Champagne: The French island of St. Pierre.

Isle of Rum: The Bahamas.

Johnnie Walker's Navy: The rumrunning fleet, especially the vessels on Rum Row.

knock off a load: Hijack a cargo of liquor.

land shark: A bootlegger who picked up liquor from a boat on the beach or at the dock.

liquor freighter: A vessel carrying a large liquor cargo, especially a mother ship on Rum Row.

monk or **monkey**: A rumrunner's underling who did menial chores, such as loading liquor on the boat.

moonlighter: A bootlegger or rumrunner.

mosquito boats or **mosquito fleet**: motorboats used to smuggle liquor.

mother ship: A large watercraft carrying a cargo of liquor that would be sold to smaller vessels.

No Man's Land: Rum Row.

over the rail or **over the side**: Transferring liquor from one watercraft to another on the high seas without putting into port.

parent ship: Mother ship or liquor freighter.

passport: A dollar bill, or the serial numbers on it, given to a buyer purchasing liquor onshore to be picked up on Rum Row.

pilot car: An automobile leading a convoy of trucks or cars carrying illegal liquor.

polecat: Rumrunners' nickname for 75-foot Coast Guard cutter.

Prohibition pirate: A rumrunner.

Prohis: Nickname for Prohibition agents and the federal agency that enforced the Volstead law.

puller: A small contact boat, especially a row boat.

rum chaser: A Coast Guard ship or another law enforcement vessel that pursued rumrunners.

rum line: The border that separated U.S. territorial waters from international waters during Prohibition.

rum lugger: A contact boat.

rummer: A shortened form of "rumrunner."

rumrunner: A person who transports illegal liquor, especially on the waterways.

rum tramp: An old vessel used by liquor smugglers, especially one owned by a syndicate and anchored outside the rum line.

run goods: A cargo of illegal liquor.

running dark: Sailing without lights.

sand pounders: Coast Guard beach patrols.

Scotch Navy: A fleet of rumrunning vessels, especially the mother ships on Rum Row.

shore crew: The men who waited onshore to unload contact boats.

shore runner: A contact boat or the person who sailed it.

six-bitter: Seventy-five-foot Coast Guard cutter.

sunset fleet: A group of contact boats.

swamper: A manual laborer, particularly one who unloaded illegal liquor from a rum boat.

water shark: A contact boat skipper or crewman.

Whiskito Fleet: A group of fast booze boats, especially the contact boats that picked up liquor on Rum Row.

Chapter Notes

Chapter 1

1. "In the Lair of the Rum-runners," *New York Times,* July 27, 1930.

2. H.L. Mencken and George Jean Nathan, "Clinical Notes," *American Mercury* 1, no. 4 (January-April 1924): 451.

3. "Christmas Rum Meets Stiffer Blockade," *New York Times,* December 14, 1924.

4. Fraser Miles, *Slow Boat on Rum Row* (Madeira Park, Canada: Harbour Publishing, 1992), 98.

5. Ira L. Reeves, *Ol' Rum River: Revelations of a Prohibition Administrator* (Chicago: Thomas S. Rockwell Co., 1931), 285–286.

6. C.W. Hunt, *Booze, Boats and Billions: Smuggling Liquid Gold* (Toronto: McClelland and Stewart, 1988), 98.

7. *Ibid.,* 98–99.

8. J.P. Andrieux, *Prohibition and St. Pierre* (Lincoln, Canada: W.F. Rannie, 1983), 97.

9. "Ocean Liquor Traffic Gigantic, Haynes Says," *New York Times,* December 5, 1922.

10. Steven Hart, *American Dictators: Frank Hague, Nucky Johnson, and the Perfection of the Urban Political Machine* (New Brunswick: Rutgers University Press, 2013), 66–67, 70.

11. Stephen Schneider, *Iced: The Story of Organized Crime in Canada* (Mississauga, Canada: John Wiley and Sons, 2009), 194.

12. Jim Stone, *My Dad, the Rum Runner* (Waterloo, Canada: North Waterloo Academic Press, 2002), 111–112.

13. "Bases of Whiskey Smuggling Numerous," *Dallas Morning News* (Dallas, TX), February 3, 1925; "Six in Dry Navy Guilty of Smuggling Rum," *New York Times,* May 18, 1925; "Twelve Vessels in Action on East Coast," *News Herald* (Franklin, PA), December 5, 1924.

14. Malcolm F. Willoughby, *Rum War at Sea* (Washington, D.C.: United States Printing Office, 1964), 50–51; James A. Carter III, "Florida and Rumrunning during National Prohibition," *The Florida Historical Quarterly* 48, no. 1 (1969): 51.

15. "Hughes and Geddes Sign Liquor Treaty," *New York Times,* January 24, 1924.

Chapter 2

1. "Liquor Enriches Atlantic Islands," *New York Times,* July 11, 1923; Frederic F. Van de Water, *The Real McCoy* (New York: Doubleday, Doran, and Company, 1931), 10; Patricia Buchanan, "Miami's Bootleg Boom," *Tequesta* 1, no. 30 (1970): 18.

2. James Morrison, *Alcohol, Boat Chases, and Shoot-outs! Part 1: 1919–1924* (Charleston, SC: Royal Exchange Publications, 2008), 168; Van de Water, *Real McCoy,* 71.

3. Sally J. Ling, *Run the Rum In: South Florida during Prohibition* (Charleston, SC: The History Press, 2007), 42.

4. "Rumrunners Hold Fire Dance to Celebrate Big Profits," *Sheboygan Press Telegram* (Sheboygan, WI), November 14, 1921.

5. *Ibid.*

6. Carter, "Florida and Rumrunning during National Prohibition," 48.

7. *Ibid.,* 48–49.

8. Harold Waters, *Smugglers of Spirits: Prohibition and the Coast Guard Patrol* (New York: Hastings House, Publishers, 1971), 166.

9. "Bethel of Bimini, Bahama Rum King," *New York Times,* March 18, 1928.

10. "Bimini Rum Row Gone," *New York Times,* October 24, 1926.

11. "Whiskey Smugglers Outwit Uncle Sam, Play Tag with Boat," *Sheboygan Press Telegram* (Sheboygan, WI), October 22, 1921.

12. "Bahama Whisky 'Exports' to U.S. Continue to Rise," *New York Times,* August 26, 1928.

13. "In the Lair of the Rum-Runners," *New York Times,* July 27, 1930.

14. *Ibid.*; Hart, *American Dictators,* 61.

15. "A Smugglers' Boom in St. Pierre," *New York Times,* June 25, 1933.

16. Schneider, *Iced,* 194.

17. Andrieux, *Prohibition and St. Pierre,* 15–16.

18. "Rum Boom off Nova Scotia," *New York Times,* December 3, 1921.

19. "In the Lair of the Rum-Runners," *New York Times,* July 27, 1930.

20. Andrieux, *Prohibition and St. Pierre,* 36.

21. "A Smugglers' Boom in St. Pierre," *New York Times,* June 25, 1933.

22. "In the Lair of the Rum-Runners," *New York Times,* July 27, 1930.

23. "Rum Boom off Nova Scotia," *New York Times,* December 3, 1921; "A Smugglers' Boom in St. Pierre," *New York Times,* June 25, 1933.

24. "In the Lair of the Rum-Runners," *New York Times,* July 27, 1930; Andrieux, *Prohibition and St. Pierre,* 52, 54.

25. Andrieux, *Prohibition and St. Pierre,* 110.

26. *Ibid.,* 111–112.

27. *Ibid.,* 71–72.

28. Phelps Haviland Adams, "Right off the Boat," *North American Review* 230, no. 3 (1930): 285–290.

29. "Smuggling that Goes on across American Bor-

ders," *New York Times*, March 30, 1930; "French Islands Got $8,856,320 Whisky," *New York Times*, October 25, 1931.

Chapter 3

1. "New Dry and Wet Fleets Mobilize for War," *New York Times*, March 29, 1925.
2. "Get Four Rum Boats; Miss 35,000 Cases," *New York Times*, January 12, 1923; "Scoff at Rum Tale, But Fear Its Truth," *New York Times*, January 13, 1923.
3. Morrison, *Alcohol, Boat Chases, and Shootouts*, 114.
4. "Colossal Fortune," *Queensland Figaro* (Brisbane, Australia), September 13, 1923.
5. "Liquor Fleet Veers off Jersey Coast," *New York Times*, May 6, 1923.
6. *Ibid.*
7. Eric Mills, *Chesapeake Rumrunners of the Roaring Twenties* (Centreville, MD: Tidewater Publishers, 2000), 64, 65, 69–71.
8. "Armed Cutter Joins Guard on Rum Runners," *New York Times*, May 23, 1923.
9. "Liquor Fleet Edges Back to Old Stand," *New York Times*, May 9, 1923; "Dry Chief Visits Bootlegging Fleet off Ambrose Light," *New York Times*, April 20, 1923.
10. "Christmas Liquor Waits Twelve Miles Out," *New York Times*, December 7, 1923; "Bootleggers Begin Price-cutting War," *New York Times*, December 12, 1923.
11. "Liquor Smugglers Have a Good Day," *New York Times*, December 16, 1923.
12. "Weather Hits Liquor Vessels," *Call Leader* (Elwood, IN), January 25, 1924.
13. "$11,200,000 in Liquor Waits Twelve Miles Out," *New York Times*, March 7, 1924; "Twenty-eight Vessels in Rum Fleet, Scouts Learn," *Reading Times* (Reading, PA), March 7, 1924.
14. Willoughby, *Rum War at Sea*, 34, 46.
15. *Ibid.*, 36; "Dry Chief Visits Bootlegging Fleet Off Ambrose Light," *New York Times*, April 20, 1923.
16. Willoughby, *Rum War at Sea*, 36.
17. *Ibid.*, 39, 46.
18. *Congressional Digest* 6 (1926): 187; Willoughby, *Rum War at Sea*, 47.
19. Willoughby, *Rum War at Sea*, 47–48.
20. *Ibid.*, 57; Donald L. Canney, *U.S. Coast Guard and Revenue Cutters, 1790–1935* (Annapolis, MD: U.S. Naval Institute Press, 1995), 54; Eric S. Ensign, *Intelligence in the Rum War at Sea, 1920–1933* (Washington, DC: Joint Military Intelligence College, 2001), 9.
21. Ensign, *Intelligence*, 21; Donald L. Canney, *Rum War: The U.S. Coast Guard and Prohibition* (Washington, DC: The U.S. Coast Guard, 1989), 15; Willoughby, *Rum War at Sea*, 88.
22. Canney, *Rum War: The U.S. Coast Guard*, 15.
23. Willoughby, *Rum War at Sea*, 88; Canney, *Rum War: The U.S. Coast Guard*, 7.
24. Ensign, *Intelligence*, 34, 35, 61.
25. "New Dry and Wet Fleets Mobilize for War," *New York Times*, March 29, 1925.
26. *Ibid.*
27. Willoughby, *Rum War at Sea*, 90, 163.
28. "Fleet Sails to Wipe Out Rumrunners," *San Francisco Chronicle*, May 6, 1925; "Thirty-five Ships Put to Sea to Smash Rum Row," *New York Times*, May 6, 1925.
29. Canney, *Rum War: The U.S. Coast Guard*, 8; "Fleet Sails to Wipe out Rumrunners," *San Francisco Chronicle*, May 6, 1925; "Mobilize Dry Fleet for Big Liquor Drive," *New York Times*, May 5, 1925; "Thirty-five Ships Put to

Sea to Smash Rum Row," *New York Times*, May 6, 1925; "Start Rum Fleet Blockade off Coast," *New Castle News* (New Castle, PA), May 5, 1925.
30. "Mobilize Dry Fleet for Big Liquor Drive," *New York Times*, May 5, 1925; "Thirty-five Ships Put to Sea to Smash Rum Row," *New York Times*, May 6, 1925; "Coast Guard Wins 'Battle' of Rum Row," *San Francisco Chronicle*, May 17, 1925.
31. "Thirty-five Ships Put to Sea to Smash Rum Row," *New York Times*, May 6, 1925.
32. *Ibid.*
33. "Gale Hits Rum Row and Dry Besiegers," *New York Times*, May 7, 1925.
34. "Thirty-five Ships Put to Sea to Smash Rum Row," *New York Times*, May 6, 1925; "Blockaders Watch Four More Smugglers Arrive in Rum Row," *New York Times*, May 8, 1925; "Dry Navy Chief Says War Is Yet to Begin," *New York Times*, May 13, 1925.
35. "Smugglers Try Bribes and Threats," *New York Times*, May 9, 1925.
36. "Dry Navy Chief Says War Is Yet to Begin," *New York Times*, May 13, 1925.
37. "Extend Rum War to Border Sectors and Western Coast," *New York Times*, May 15, 1925.
38. "Champagne Evades Coast Guard Patrol," *New York Times*, May 10, 1925.
39. "Liquor Ships Retire Southward, Dogged by the Dry Fleet," *New York Times*, May 12, 1925; "Dry Navy Chief Says War Is Yet to Begin," *New York Times*, May 13, 1925.
40. "Dry Raiders Succeed on Land and Sea," *Reading Times* (Reading, PA), May 12, 1925.
41. "Champagne Evades Coast Guard Patrol," *New York Times*, May 10, 1925; "Dry Navy Chief Says War Is Yet to Begin," *New York Times*, May 13, 1925.
42. "Thirty-five Ships Put to Sea to Smash Rum Row," *New York Times*, May 6, 1925.
43. "Rum Row Vanished, Says Dry War Chief," *New York Times*, May 17, 1925; "Reports Nine Ships Now in Rum Fleet," *New York Times*, May 21, 1925.
44. Barry J. Grant, *When Rum Was King: The Story of the Prohibition Era in New Brunswick* (Frederickton, Canada: Fiddlehead Poetry Books, 2007), 14.
45. *Ibid.*, 13; "Liquor Ships Retire Southward," *New York Times*, May 12, 1925.
46. "New York's Rum Row Shifts to the Gulf," *New York Times*, July 16, 1925; "Rum Row Is Active at Southern Ports," *New York Times*, October 15, 1925; "New York Rum Ship on Way to San Francisco," *San Francisco Chronicle*, May 12, 1925.
47. "Offer Liquor Cheap Forty Miles off Coast," *New York Times*, May 22, 1925; "Forest Hills Raid Due to Dry League," *New York Times*, June 16, 1925.
48. "Rum Row Deserted, Fleet Chief Finds," *New York Times*, August 28, 1925.
49. *Ibid.*; Canney, *Rum War: The U.S. Coast Guard*, 8; "Coast Guard Plans Winter Dry Drive," *New York Times*, August 31, 1925.
50. "Biggest Prohibition Showdown in Years Faces Next Congress," *New Castle News* (New Castle, PA), August 8, 1925.
51. "One Enforcement Difficulty," *Ironwood Daily Globe* (Ironwood, MI), July 6, 1925; "Start Rum Fleet Blockade off Coast," *New Castle News* (New Castle, PA), May 5, 1925.
52. "Long Island Talks of Rising Rum Tide," *New York Times*, September 26, 1925.
53. "Seize Fake Cutter with Liquor Cargo," *New York Times*, December 17, 1925; "U.S. Coast Guard Annual Re-

port 1925," 12–13, Records of the U.S. Coast Guard, RG 26, National Archives, Washington, D.C.; Hunt, *Booze, Boats, and Billions*, 129.

54. Adams, "Right off the Boat," 290; David P. Mowry, *Listening to the Rumrunners* (Fort George G. Meade, MD: Center for Cryptologic History, National Security Agency, 1996), 18.

Chapter 4

1. Willoughby, *Rum War at Sea*, 65.
2. "Swift New Rum Squadron Ready for Spring Service," *New York Times*, March 29, 1925.
3. Marion Parker and Robert Tyrell, *Rumrunner: The Life and Times of Johnny Schnarr* (Victoria, Canada: Orca Book Publishers, 1992), 82–83, 100, 114, 157.
4. *Ibid.*, 123, 127–129.
5. *Ibid.*, 193–197.
6. Buchanan, "Miami's Bootleg Boom," 19.
7. Miles, *Slow Boat*, 182, 186, 195, 248; Parker and Tyrell, *Rumrunner*, 68–69, 173.
8. Hunt, *Booze, Boats, and Billions*, 99.
9. "Swift New Rum Squadron Ready for Spring Service," *New York Times*, March 29, 1925.
10. Daniel Okrent, *Last Call: The Rise and Fall of Prohibition* (New York: Scribner, 2010), 280.
11. "Watch Junk Boats to Keep out Liquor," *New York Times*, September 10, 1923.
12. *Ibid.*
13. "Haynes Sees End of Rum Running," *New York Times*, July 24, 1923.
14. Willoughby, *Rum War at Sea*, 62.
15. Ling, *Run the Rum In*, 78.
16. Willoughby, *Rum War at Sea*, 62.
17. "New Dry and Wet Fleets Mobilize for War," *New York Times*, March 29, 1925.
18. Willoughby, *Rum War at Sea*, 63.
19. *Ibid.*, 64, 66.
20. Ruth Greene, *Personality Ships of British Columbia* (West Vancouver, Canada: Marine Tapestry Publications, 1969), 101.
21. Willoughby, *Rum War at Sea*, 65.
22. Victor Bulloch, "The Rumrunning Era," *Update* (February 1972): 7.
23. "Bootleggers Defy Jersey Authorities," *New York Times*, December 13, 1924.
24. "Outwitting the Rum Runners," *Atlanta Constitution*, February 16, 1930.
25. *Ibid.*
26. Willoughby, *Rum War at Sea*, 65–66.
27. *Ibid.*, 113.
28. "Rum Runners Bid in Their Old Vessels," *Urbana Daily Courier* (Urbana, IL), March 7, 1930; Bullock, "The Rumrunning Era," 7.
29. Canney, *Rum War: The U.S. Coast Guard*, 6.
30. Carter, "Florida and Rumrunning during National Prohibition," 55.
31. *Congressional Digest* 6 (1926): 187.
32. Willoughby, *Rum War at Sea*, 88.
33. Carter, "Florida and Rumrunning during National Prohibition," 50.
34. "Coast Guard Lays Siege to Runners," *Boston Daily Globe*, September 26, 1927; "Submarine Used by Rumrunners, Seattle Learns," *San Francisco Chronicle*, January 12, 1922; "Clever Dodge," *World's News* (Sydney, Australia), May 28, 1930.
35. Ensign, *Intelligence*, 34.
36. "Sub Discharges Booze from Rum Ship, Is Claim," *Emporia Gazette* (Emporia, KS), January 19, 1925; "German-manned Rum U-boat Is Operating Off Jersey Coast," *Charleston Daily Mail* (Charleston, WV), January 19, 1925.
37. "Liquor-running Submarine Periscope Only a Porpoise Fin," *New York Times*, May 8, 1924.
38. "Outwitting the Rum Runners," *Atlanta Constitution*, February 16, 1930.
39. Willoughby, *Rum War at Sea*, 63.
40. C.W. Hunt, *Whiskey and Ice: The Saga of Ben Kerr, Canada's Most Daring Rumrunner* (Toronto: Dundurn Press, Ltd., 1995), 86; Harold B. Clifford, *The Boothbay Region, 1906 to 1960* (Freeport, ME: Bond Wheelwright Company, 1961), 198.
41. Willoughby, *Rum War at Sea*, 63.
42. *Ibid.*
43. "Seven Bootleg Ships Land Their Cargoes on Jersey Coast to Supply Holiday Trade," *New York Times*, November 21, 1923.
44. Jim Merritt, "New York's Rum Row: Bootlegging on Long Island," *New York Archives* 2, no. 3 (2003); www.nysarchivestrust.org/apt/magazine.
45. "Two Hundred Cases of Whiskey Drift Ashore, Vanish," *New York Times*, August 30, 1923.
46. Ellen NicKenzie Lawson, *Smugglers, Bootleggers, and Scofflaws: Prohibition and New York City* (Albany, NY: State University of New York Press, 2013), 21–22.
47. Clifford James Walker, *One Eye Closed, the Other Red: The California Bootlegging Years* (Barstow, CA: Back Door Publishing, 1999), 287.
48. Buchanan, "Miami's Bootleg Boom," 15.
49. David J. Seibold and Charles J. Adams III, *Shipwrecks and Legends 'round Cape May* (Reading, PA: Exeter House Books, 1987), 51–52.
50. "Beach Mobs Grab Lost Liquor Cargo," *New York Times*, July 25, 1924.
51. *Ibid.*
52. *Ibid.*

Chapter 5

1. "Federal Dry Agent Taken in Round-up as Liquor Ring Aid [*sic*]," *New York Times*, December 6, 1925.
2. Letter signed by W.H. Munter, Commander USCG, New London Patrol Area, May 11, 1926, "Records Relating to Seized Vessels 1926–1935," Records of the U.S. Coast Guard, RG 26, Box 49, National Archives, Washington, D.C.
3. Parker and Tyrell, *Rumrunner*, 116–117.
4. "Twenty Coast Guards Seized for Bribery," *New York Times*, January 9, 1932.
5. Jenny Wilson, "Battling Bootleggers, Rumrunners, and Secret Supplies of Hooch," *Courant* (Hartford, CT), April 25, 2014.
6. Maureen Ogle, *Key West: History of an Island of Dreams* (Gainesville: University Press of Florida, 2003), 136.
7. "Florida Sees Real Rum War," *Charleston Daily Mail* (Charleston, WV), September 18, 1927.
8. *Ibid.*
9. Hart, *American Dictators*, 68.
10. "Coast Guard Lays Siege to Runners," *Boston Daily Globe*, September 26, 1927.
11. "Coast Guards Held for Liquor Brawl," *New York Times*, December 31, 1929.
12. "Pilferage of Seized Booze Investigated," *Hutchinson News* (Hutchinson, KS), December 31, 1929.
13. "Coast Guards Held for Liquor Brawl," *New York Times*, December 31, 1929.

14. "Gang of Men Beats Two Coast Guardsmen," *New York Times*, January 5, 1930; "Crowd Terrifies Coast Guard's Wife," *New York Times*, January 7, 1930; "Coast Guards Plead Guilty to Rum Theft," *Scranton Republican* (Scranton, PA), January 7, 1930.

15. Ling, *Run the Rum In*, 66–67.

16. *Ibid.*, 68.

17. *Ibid.*

18. *Ibid.*

19. *Ibid.*

20. "Rum Runner Captured," *Evening Independent* (St. Petersburg, FL), April 5, 1932.

21. Waters, *Smugglers of Spirits*, 108–109.

22. "Florida Sees Real Rum War," *Charleston Daily Mail* (Charleston, WV), September 18, 1927.

23. *Ibid.*

24. *Ibid.*

25. *Ibid.*

26. "Coast Guard Spurns $70,000 Liquor Bribe," *New York Times*, July 25, 1923.

27. *Ibid.*

Chapter 6

1. "Says Paulding Hit S-4 on Rum Chase," *New York Times*, January 6, 1928.

2. "Baylis Calls Loss of S-4 Unavoidable," *New York Times*, January 10, 1928.

3. "S-4 Rolled Over, Sinking Bow First," *New York Times*, December 19, 1927.

4. "Baylis Calls Loss of S-4 Unavoidable," *New York Times*, January 10, 1928; "S-4 Rolled Over, Sinking Bow First," *New York Times*, December 19, 1927.

5. "Submarine S-4 Sinks with Forty Aboard in Deep Water off Provincetown," *New York Times*, December 18, 1927; "Baylis Calls Loss of S-4 Unavoidable," *New York Times*, January 10, 1928; "Six Men Found Alive in Torpedo Room of Sunken S-4," *New York Times*, December 19, 1927.

6. "U.S. Sub, Forty-three Aboard, Goes Down in Crash," *Decatur Review* (Decatur, IL), December 17, 1927.

7. "Submarine S-4 Sinks with Forty Aboard in Deep Water off Provincetown," *New York Times*, December 18, 1927.

8. "Numbed Watchers Stand By," *New York Times*, December 18, 1927; "Six Men Found Alive in Torpedo Room of Sunken S-4," *New York Times*, December 19, 1927.

9. "Hope to Save Men by Tilting the S-4," *New York Times*, December 19, 1927.

10. "Six Men Found Alive in Torpedo Room of Sunken S-4," *New York Times*, December 19, 1927.

11. *Ibid.*

12. "'Please Hurry,' Exhort Men Trapped in Submarine S-4," *Lowell Sun* (Lowell, MA), December 19, 1927.

13. "Six Men Found Alive in Torpedo Room of Sunken S-4," *New York Times*, December 19, 1927; "Last Oxygen Bottle Exhausted by Men in Sunken S-4," *New York Times*, December 20, 1927.

14. "'Please Hurry,' Exhort Men Trapped in Submarine S-4," *Lowell Sun* (Lowell, MA), December 19, 1927.

15. "Last Oxygen Bottle Exhausted by Men in Sunken S-4," *New York Times*, December 20, 1927.

16. *Ibid.*

17. "Hope Fades of Saving S-4 Crew as Sea Balks Divers," *New York Times*, December 21, 1927.

18. "Divers Get Air into Torpedo Room of S-4," *New York Times*, December 22, 1927.

19. *Ibid.*

20. "Rescuers Admit S-4 Men Are All Dead," *New York Times*, December 23, 1927.

21. "Divers Get Three Bodies from the S-4 Wreck," *New York Times*, January 5, 1928; "Four More Bodies Taken from S-4," *Chester Times* (Chester, PA), January 7, 1928.

22. "Says Paulding Hit S-4 on Rum Chase," *New York Times*, January 6, 1928; "Baylis Calls Loss of S-4 Unavoidable," *New York Times*, January 10, 1928.

23. "Says Paulding Hit S-4 on Rum Chase," *New York Times*, January 6, 1928.

24. "Blame for S-4 Loss Put Upon Both Ships by the Naval Court," *New York Times*, February 22, 1928.

25. *Ibid.*; "Army and Navy: Again, S-4," *Time*, March 5, 1928, 9; "Will Reopen Sub Probe," *Logansport Pharos Tribune* (Logansport, IN), February 22, 1928.

26. "National Affairs: S-4, Finis," *Time*, April 23, 1928, 11.

27. "Paulding Absolved in Sinking of S-4," *New York Times*, May 7, 1928.

28. "Army and Navy: Dead Raised," *Time*, March 26, 1928, 12–13; "S-4 Reveals Fight of Crew to Escape," *New York Times*, March 22, 1928.

29. "S-4 Will Be Sunk Again to Make Rescue Tests," *New York Times*, December 2, 1928; "S-4 Sunk for Test on Tragedy Day," *New York Times*, December 18, 1928; "S-4 Up in Forty-nine Hours after Test Sinking," *New York Times*, December 20, 1928.

30. "Assails Dry Law in S-4 Disaster," *New York Times*, December 27, 1927.

31. Willoughby, *Rum War at Sea*, 148–149.

32. Judith A. Babcock, "The Night the Coast Guard Opened Fire," *Yankee* 63, no. 12 (1999); www.ebscohost.com/c/articles/2562298.

33. "Three on Rum Boat Slain by Coast Guard in Chase; Three Vessels Captured," *New York Times*, December 30, 1929; Babcock, "The Night the Coast Guard Opened Fire," www.ebscohost.com/c/articles/2562298.

34. "Three on Rum Boat Slain by Coast Guard in Chase; Three Vessels Captured," *New York Times*, December 30, 1929; Babcock, "The Night the Coast Guard Opened Fire," www.ebscohost.com/c/articles/2562298.

35. Willoughby, *Rum War at Sea*, 149; "Three on Rum Boat Slain by Coast Guard in Chase; Three Vessels Captured," *New York Times*, December 30, 1929.

36. Willoughby, *Rum War at Sea*, 150; Babcock, "The Night the Coast Guard Opened Fire," www.ebscohost.com/c/articles/2562298.

37. Babcock, "The Night the Coast Guard Opened Fire," www.ebscohost.com/c/articles/2562298.

38. *Ibid.*

39. "Would Disarm Coast Guard," *New York Times*, December 31, 1929.

40. "Bostonians Tear up Coast Guard Bills," *New York Times*, January 3, 1930; "*Black Duck* Aftermath," *Time*, January 13, 1930, 13.

41. "Bostonians Tear up Coast Guard Bills," *New York Times*, January 3, 1930; "*Black Duck* Aftermath," *Time*, January 13, 1930, 13.

42. "Bostonians Tear up Coast Guard Bills," *New York Times*, January 3, 1930; "*Black Duck* Aftermath," *Time*, January 13, 1930, 13.

43. "Crowd Terrifies Coast Guard's Wife," *New York Times*, January 7, 1930; "Gang of Men Beats Two Coast Guardsmen," *New York Times*, January 5, 1930.

44. Willoughby, *Rum War at Sea*, 150; "Stop or Get Hurt, Billard Warns," *New York Times*, December 30, 1929; "*Black Duck* Aftermath," *Time*, January 13, 1930, 13.

45. Babcock, "The Night the Coast Guard Opened Fire," www.ebscohost.com/c/articles/2562298.

46. "Coast Guard Shots Hit Black Duck Aft," *New York Times*, January 4, 1930.

47. "Jury on Rum Killing Absolves Coast Guard," *New York Times*, January 15, 1930; "Upholds Coast Guard in *Black Duck* Killing," *New York Times*, January 17, 1930.

48. "*Black Duck* Guard Runs Amuck," *New York Times*, January 6, 1930; "Drunken Guard Menaces Crowd with Revolvers," *Olean Times* (Olean, NY), January 6, 1930.

49. "*Black Duck* Guard Runs Amuck," *New York Times*, January 6, 1930; "Drunken Guard Menaces Crowd with Revolvers," *Olean Times* (Olean, NY), January 6, 1930; "Customs Agent Will Lose Job," *Reno Evening Gazette* (Reno, NV), January 13, 1930.

50. "Dry Men Get *Black Duck*," *New York Times*, March 7, 1930.

51. "Exciting Motorboat Dash Is Staged," *Newport Mercury and Weekly News* (Newport, RI), April 11, 1930; "*Black Duck* Was Used by Coast Guardsmen," *Newport Mercury and Weekly News* (Newport, RI), September 5, 1930; "Man Badly Wounded; Three Others Captured," *Newport Mercury and Weekly News* (Newport, RI), August 29, 1930.

52. Merritt, "New York's Rum Row," www.nysarchivestrust.org/apt/magazine.

53. *Ibid.*

54. *Ibid.*

55. Andrieux, *Prohibition and St. Pierre*, 93.

56. Willoughby, *Rum War at Sea*, 128.

57. Andrieux, *Prohibition and St. Pierre*, 93–94.

58. "*I'm Alone* Skipper Describes Cruises," *New York Times*, December 30, 1934.

59. Willoughby, *Rum War at Sea*, 128.

60. "Held Here as Owner of the *I'm Alone*," *New York Times*, December 21, 1929.

61. Willoughby, *Rum War at Sea*, 128; Joseph Anthony Ricci, "'All Necessary Force': The Coast Guard and the Sinking of the Rum Runner *I'm Alone*," University of New Orleans Theses and Dissertations, Paper 1342, 18, http://scholarworks.uno.edu.

62. Ricci, "All Necessary Force," 18, 37–38, http://scholarworks.uno.edu.

63. *Ibid.*, 18.

64. Willoughby, *Rum War at Sea*, 129.

65. *Ibid.*, 129; Ricci, "All Necessary Force," 19, http://scholarworks.uno.edu.

66. Nancy Galey Skoglund, "The *I'm Alone* Case: A Tale from the Days of Prohibition," *University of Rochester Library Bulletin* 23 no. 3 (1968); rbscp.lib.rochester.edu/1004.

67. *Ibid.*

68. Ricci, "All Necessary Force," 21–22, http://scholarworks.uno.edu; Willoughby, *Rum War at Sea*, 129.

69. "Manacled Prisoners Land," *Dallas Morning News* (Dallas, TX), March 25, 1929; U.S. State Department, *I'm Alone Case*, Arbitration Series Two (Washington, DC: Government Printing Office, 1935), vol. 1, 37–39.

70. Willoughby, *Rum War at Sea*, 129–130; "Would Search *I'm Alone* for Drugs," *Dallas Morning News* (Dallas, TX), March 29, 1929.

71. "To Arbitrate on *I'm Alone*," *Dallas Morning News* (Dallas, TX), April 26, 1929; U.S. State Department, *I'm Alone Case*, vol. 4, 18–19, 23–32.

72. "Held Here as Owner of the *I'm Alone*," *New York Times*, December 21, 1929; "$15,000,000 Rum Ring Bared by Radio Raid," *New York Times*, September 28, 1930.

73. U.S. State Department, *I'm Alone Case*, vol. 6, 199–202; "Rum Ship American Owned," *New York Times*, January 28, 1931.

74. "*I'm Alone* Traced to Ownership Here," *New York Times*, December 29, 1934; Mowry, *Listening to the Rumrunners*, 21–22.

75. "*I'm Alone* Sinking in Gulf of Mexico Held Not Justified," *Dallas Morning News* (Dallas, TX), January 10, 1935; "*I'm Alone* Apology Given to Canada," *New York Times*, January 22, 1935.

76. Ricci, "All Necessary Force," 37–38; http://scholarworks.uno.edu.

Chapter 7

1. "My Whiskey Is Good, Says McCoy," *Harrisburg Telegraph* (Harrisburg, PA), November 27, 1923.

2. Ling, *Run the Rum In*, 55; "Sea Rumrunner Held on Two Liquor Charges," *New York Times*, November 27, 1923.

3. "McCoy Brothers Everglade Line," *Miami Herald Record* (Miami, FL), April 15, 1918; "Everglades Line," *Miami Herald Record* (Miami, FL), December 8, 1920.

4. Van de Water, *Real McCoy*, 4–5, 217; "Sea Rumrunner Held on Two Liquor Charges," *New York Times*, November 27, 1923.

5. Van de Water, *Real McCoy*, 6; "Britain Bars Seizure of Rum Ship at Sea," *New York Times*, September 19, 1921.

6. "Miami-Bahama Shipping Firm Secures Additional Office Space at City Dock," *Miami Herald Record* (Miami, FL), November 25, 1921; "Albury Freed on Charge of N.J. Rum Conspiracy," *Miami Herald Record* (Miami, FL), February 11, 1922.

7. Van de Water, *Real McCoy*, 11; "The Real McCoy," *San Antonio Light* (San Antonio, TX), March 20, 1949.

8. Van de Water, *Real McCoy*, 17–19.

9. *Ibid.*, 6, 25, 26; "Capital Confident in *Tomoka* Seizure," *New York Times*, November 29, 1923.

10. "Sea Rumrunner Held on Two Liquor Charges," *New York Times*, November 27, 1923; "Arrests Sequel to Seizure of Liquor Ship," *Lowell Sun* (Lowell, MA), August 3, 1921; Van de Water, *Real McCoy*, 34; "Rum Runner Caught; See 'Startling' Plot," *New York Times*, August 3, 1921.

11. Willoughby, *Rum War at Sea*, 24; "Rum Runner Caught; See 'Startling' Plot," *New York Times*, August 3, 1921; "Schooner with Cargo of Liquor Seized off New Jersey Coast," *Lowell Sun* (Lowell, MA), August 2, 1921.

12. Van de Water, *Real McCoy*, 35; "Rum Runner Caught; See 'Startling' Plot," *New York Times*, August 3, 1921.

13. Van de Water, *Real McCoy*, 219.

14. "Crosland Gives Bond on Charge of Conspiracy," *Miami Herald Record* (Miami, FL), August 19, 1921.

15. "Wealthy Man Held by U.S. Officers," *Steubenville Herald Star* (Steubenville, OH), August 18, 1921; "Supreme Court," *Wall Street Journal*, October 24, 1922; Van de Water, *Real McCoy*, 171; "New Warehouse at Miami," *Wall Street Journal*, February 5, 1927.

16. "Rum Ship Seized under Act of 1799," *New York Times*, August 14, 1921; "Forfeit Rum Ship Taken Nine Miles Out," *New York Times*, June 20, 1923; Van de Water, *Real McCoy*, 189.

17. "Seized Rum 'King' Tangles Capital," *Boston Daily Globe*, November 27, 1923; "Sea Rumrunner Held on Two Liquor Charges," *New York Times*, November 27, 1923; Van de Water, *Real McCoy*, 34–35.

18. Ling 58; Van de Water, *Real McCoy*, 167; "Capital

Confident in *Tomoka* Seizure," *New York Times*, November 29, 1923.

19. "Skipper Defies Prohibitionists," *Boston Daily Globe*, August 11, 1921.

20. "Floating Saloon Does Big Business off Vineyard," *Boston Daily Globe*, August 12, 1921.

21. "Says *Arethusa* Sells Rum by Drink or Barrel," *New York Times*, August 13, 1921; "Skipper Defies Prohibitionists," *Boston Daily Globe*, August 11, 1921; "*Arethusa* Quits the Coast," *New York Times*, August 15, 1921.

22. "Skipper Defies Prohibitionists," *Boston Daily Globe*, August 11, 1921.

23. "Seize Whiskey off *Arethusa*," *Boston Daily Globe*, August 14, 1921.

24. *Ibid.*

25. "Revenue Cutter *Ossipee* Fails to Find *Arethusa*," *Boston Daily Globe*, August 14, 1921; "Officers Too Late to Catch *Arethusa*," *Boston Daily Globe*, August 16, 1921; "*Arethusa* Now off Thatcher's Island," *Boston Daily Globe*, August 18, 1921; "Baffled in Attempt to Board *Arethusa*," *Boston Evening Globe*, August 15, 1921.

26. "British Rum Ship Seized Seven Miles Out," *New York Times*, September 15, 1922.

27. "Three Foreign Vessels Seized by Dry Navy Ordered Released," *Brooklyn Daily Eagle*, November 10, 1922.

28. Van de Water, *Real McCoy*, 58, 90–91, 93–94.

29. *Ibid.*, 126.

30. *Ibid.*, 12, 132.

31. "West Indian Rum Runners Were Up for Questioning," *Lebanon Daily News* (Lebanon, PA), November 26, 1923.

32. "Subject: Seizure of Schooner *Tomoka*," November 25, 1923, "Records Relating to Seized Vessels 1926–1935," Records of the U.S. Coast Guard, RG 26, Box 7, National Archives, Washington, D.C.

33. *Ibid.*

34. *Ibid.*

35. "Rummy Bill Asks for His $68,000," *Dallas Morning News* (Dallas, TX), November 27, 1923.

36. "Sea Rumrunner Held on Two Liquor Charges," *New York Times*, November 27, 1923.

37. *Ibid.*; "Rummy Bill Asks for His $68,000," *Dallas Morning News* (Dallas, TX), November 27, 1923; "My Whisky Good Says M'Coy, of Rum Row Fame," *Harrisburg Telegraph* (Harrisburg, PA), November 27, 1923.

38. "My Whisky Good Says M'Coy, of Rum Row Fame," *Harrisburg Telegraph* (Harrisburg, PA), November 27, 1923; "Rummy Bill Asks for His $68,000," *Dallas Morning News* (Dallas, TX), November 27, 1923.

39. "Seized Rum 'King' Tangles Capital," *Boston Daily Globe*, November 27, 1923.

40. "Washington Doubts Ship's Registry," *New York Times*, January 5, 1924; "London Wants Crew of *Tomoka* Freed," *New York Times*, January 5, 1924.

41. Van de Water, *Real McCoy*, 189.

42. "Dry Agents Arrest Chicago Delegate," *New York Times*, June 27, 1924; Van de Water, *Real McCoy*, 200.

43. "The Real McCoy," *San Antonio Light* (San Antonio, TX), March 20, 1949.

44. Van de Water, *Real McCoy*, 187, 188, 219.

45. *Ibid.*, 189, 199, 219.

46. *Ibid.*, 199, 201, 220.

47. *Ibid.*, 201.

48. "$20,000 Boat for FDR Planned," *Montana Standard* (Butte, MT), January 1, 1938.

49. Ling, *Run the Rum In*, 62.

50. *Ibid.*; "The Real McCoy," *San Antonio Light* (San Antonio, TX), March 20, 1949.

51. "Hart Invents a New Kidney Blow," *Nevada State Journal* (Reno, NV), June 28, 1905.

Chapter 8

1. H. DeWinton Wigley, *With the Whiskey Smugglers* (London: Daily News Ltd., 1923), 25, 26; "The Pathos of Being a Rum Queen," *Canton Daily News* (Canton, OH), April 25, 1926.

2. Gertrude C. Lythgoe, *The Bahama Queen: The Autobiography of Gertrude "Cleo" Lythgoe* (Mystic, CT: Flat Hammock Press, 2007), 1–2.

3. *Ibid.*, 4–5, 7.

4. *Ibid.*, 6, 11, 14.

5. *Ibid.*, 27, 29, 34. "Liquor Queen Due in East," *Los Angeles Times*, December 26, 1923.

6. Lythgoe, *Bahama Queen*, 38, 40–41; "'Cleo' Going It Alone Won Respect of Bahama Men by Playing Rum Running Game Same as They Played It," *Winnipeg Free Press* (Winnipeg, Canada), May 10, 1924.

7. Lythgoe, *Bahama Queen*, 44–46, 66–67.

8. *Ibid.*, 47; "Rumrunners Hold Fire Dance to Celebrate Big Profits," *Sheboygan Press Telegram* (Sheboygan, WI), November 14, 1921.

9. Lythgoe, *Bahama Queen*, 71, 78.

10. *Ibid.*, 72–73, 76.

11. *Ibid.*, 76.

12. *Ibid.*

13. *Ibid.*, 81.

14. "Queen of the Rum Runners Faced Perils of Liquor Lane without Asking Any Odds," *Winnipeg Free Press* (Winnipeg, Canada), May 17, 1924.

15. Lythgoe, *Bahama Queen*, 82.

16. *Ibid.*, 83.

17. *Ibid.*, 83–84.

18. "Queen of the Rum Runners Faced Perils of Liquor Lane without Asking Any Odds," *Winnipeg Free Press* (Winnipeg, Canada), May 17, 1924.

19. *Ibid.*

20. *Ibid.*

21. Lythgoe, *Bahama Queen*, 96, 98. "Rum Runners Spurn Fortune Offered by Opium Traders, Says Woman Dealer," *Winnipeg Free Press* (Winnipeg, Canada), May 24, 1924.

22. Lythgoe, *Bahama Queen*, 126–130, 135.

23. "Bootleg Queen Caught in Miami on Rum Charges," *New Orleans Times-Picayune*, October 20, 1925; "Rum Queen Tells of Big Business, Liquor Dealings," *New Orleans Times-Picayune*, December 8, 1925; "Jury Gets Case of Two Accused in Liquor Plot," *New Orleans Times-Picayune*, December 9, 1925.

24. "Rum Queen in Dread of Mysterious 'Jinx,'" *Rhinelander Daily News* (Rhinelander, WI), May 25, 1926; Lythgoe, *Bahama Queen*, 164.

Chapter 9

1. "Queen of the Rum Runners," Part II, *Atlanta Constitution*, June 10, 1923.

2. "Queen of the Rum Runners," Part I, *Atlanta Constitution*, June 3, 1923.

3. *Ibid.*

4. "Home and Husband Beat Life of Thrills, Says Actress in Real Melodrama," *Evening Independent* (St. Petersburg, FL), August 31, 1922.

5. *Ibid.*; "Cassese to Face New Rum Charge on Own Volition," *Brooklyn Daily Eagle*, January 9, 1927.

6. "Home and Husband Beat Life of Thrills, Says

Actress in Real Melodrama," *Evening Independent* (St. Petersburg, FL), August 31, 1922.

7. "Queen of the Rum Runners," Part II, *Atlanta Constitution*, June 10, 1923.

8. "Queen of the Rum Runners," Part IV, *Atlanta Constitution*, June 24, 1923.

9. "Queen of the Rum Runners," Part I, *Atlanta Constitution*, June 3, 1923.

10. *Ibid.*

11. *Ibid.*

12. *Ibid.*

13. *Ibid.*

14. "Queen of the Rum Runners," Part III, *Atlanta Constitution*, June 17, 1923.

15. *Ibid.*

16. *Ibid.*

17. *Ibid.*

18. "Girl, Nineteen, Is Held," *Boston Daily Globe*, July 28, 1922.

19. *Ibid.*

20. "Queen of the Rum Runners," Part IV, *Atlanta Constitution*, June 24, 1923.

21. *Ibid.*

22. *Ibid.*

23. *Ibid.*

24. "Queen of the Rum Runners," Part V, *Atlanta Constitution*, July 1, 1923.

25. *Ibid.*; "Rum Ship Is Seized After Pistol Fight," *New York Times*, June 4, 1922.

26. "Queen of the Rum Runners," Part V, *Atlanta Constitution*, July 1, 1923.

27. "Rum Ship Is Seized after Pistol Fight," *New York Times*, June 4, 1922.

28. *Ibid.*

29. "Girl Denies She Is Bootlegger's Queen," *Los Angeles Times*, July 31, 1922; "Woman Ran a Still to Feed Her Babies," *New York Times*, July 27, 1922.

30. "Girl Denies She Is Bootlegger's Queen," *Los Angeles Times*, July 31, 1922.

31. "Catch Liquor Craft after Run in Dark," *New York Times*, August 8, 1922.

32. *Ibid.*; "Nearly Pinch Izzy Chasing Rum Truck," *New York Times*, August 9, 1922.

33. "Mrs. Stevens Freed of Liquor Charge," *New York Times*, August 10, 1922.

34. *Ibid.*

35. *Ibid.*; "Home and Husband Beat Life of Thrills, Says Actress in Real Melodrama," *Evening Independent* (St. Petersburg, FL), August 31, 1922.

36. "Queen of the Rum Runners," Part VI, *Atlanta Constitution*, July 8, 1923.

37. "Opposes Wife Remarrying," *New York Times*, August 19, 1922; "Husband Wins Big Alienation Verdict from Bootleg King," *Miami News* (Miami, OK), December 27, 1922.

38. "Queen of the Rum Runners," Part VI, *Atlanta Constitution*, July 8, 1923.

39. *Ibid.*; "King of Bootleggers' Caught in Savanah," *New York Times*, October 15, 1922.

40. "Visits Cassese Trial, Is Jailed as Witness," *New York Times*, November 3, 1922.

41. *Ibid.*

42. "Queen of the Rum Runners," Part VI, *Atlanta Constitution*, July 8, 1923.

43. "Rum Ship Skipper at Cassese Trial," *New York Times*, November 21, 1922.

44. "Two Years in Prison and $10,000 Fine for Bootlegger Mogul of Brooklyn," *New York Times*, November 22, 1922.

45. *Ibid.*

46. "Cassese Gives up Fight; Will Serve His Time in Prison," *Brooklyn Daily Eagle*, February 23, 1923.

47. "Queen of the Rum Runners," Part VI, *Atlanta Constitution*, July 8, 1923.

48. "Cassese to Face New Rum Charge on Own Volition," *Brooklyn Daily Eagle*, January 9, 1927.

Chapter 10

1. "L.I. Rum Smugglers Flood Market with Liquor for Holidays," *Brooklyn Daily Eagle*, November 7, 1924.

2. *Ibid.*

3. "Army of Baymen [*sic*] Now Rum Runners," *New York Times*, March 11, 1923.

4. "L.I. Rum Smugglers Flood Market with Liquor for Holidays," *Brooklyn Daily Eagle*, November 7, 1924.

5. Morrison, *Alcohol, Boat Chases, and Shootouts*, 44; "Army of Baymen [*sic*] Now Rum Runners," *New York Times*, March 11, 1923.

6. "L.I. Rum Smugglers Flood Market with Liquor for Holidays," *Brooklyn Daily Eagle*, November 7, 1924.

7. "Army of Baymen [*sic*] Now Rum Runners," *New York Times*, March 11, 1923.

8. "L.I. Rum Smugglers Flood Market with Liquor for Holidays," *Brooklyn Daily Eagle*, November 7, 1924.

9. "Christmas Rum Meets Stiffer Blockade," *New York Times*, December 14, 1924.

10. "L.I. Rum Smugglers Flood Market with Liquor for Holidays," *Brooklyn Daily Eagle*, November 7, 1924.

11. Morrison, *Alcohol, Boat Chases, and Shootouts*, 114; Bernie Bookbinder, *Long Island: People and Places, Past and Present* (New York: Henry N. Abrams, 1998), 190–191.

12. Lawson, *Smugglers, Bootleggers, and Scofflaws*, 25.

13. "Army of Baymen [*sic*] Now Rum Runners," *New York Times*, March 11, 1923.

14. "$11,200,000 in Liquor Waits Twelve Miles Out," *New York Times*, March 7, 1924.

15. "Five Rum Boats Captured with $183,000 Cargo," *Scranton Republican* (Scranton, PA), April 7, 1924; "Tiny Customs Ships Routed by Big Rum Yachts on Sound," *Brooklyn Daily Eagle*, June 2, 1924.

16. "Tiny Customs Ships Routed by Big Rum Yachts on Sound," *Brooklyn Daily Eagle*, June 2, 1924.

17. "Ask Nassau Sheriff to Aid Liquor Fight," *New York Times*, April 27, 1923; "Mystery in Strange Silence Following Rum Ship Seizure Puzzles Federal Prosecutor," *Brooklyn Daily Eagle*, April 30, 1925.

18. "Army of Baymen [*sic*] Now Rum Runners," *New York Times*, March 11, 1923.

19. *Ibid.*

20. *Ibid.*

21. *Ibid.*

22. "Smuggling Booze from Nassau Easy," *Dallas Morning News* (Dallas, TX), August 29, 1921.

23. *Ibid.*

24. *Ibid.*

25. *Ibid.*

26. "Judge Inch Ends Bank Fraud Case with $5,000 Fine," *Brooklyn Daily Eagle*, May 7, 1926; "Wylk, Indicted with Dooley, Asks for Dismissal," *Brooklyn Daily Eagle*, September 17, 1926; "Court Dismisses Wylk Indictment," *Brooklyn Daily Eagle*, September 21, 1926.

27. "Indictments Bare Huge Liquor Ring," *New York Times*, March 16, 1929.

28. *Ibid.*

29. "Clever Ruses of Rum Squad Are Revealed," *Springfield Leader* (Springfield, MO), March 17, 1929.

30. "Shipload of Rum Seized; Take Wylk, Seven Others in Raid," *Brooklyn Daily Eagle*, December 21, 1922.

31. "Rumrunner's Crew Released on Bail; $10,000 from Wylk," *Brooklyn Daily Eagle*, December 23, 1922.

32. "Wylk Brings Suit for Whiskey Seized in Raid at Baldwin," *Brooklyn Daily Eagle*, March 28, 1923; "Convict Arrives to Give Nassau Jury Bootleg Evidence," *Brooklyn Daily Eagle*, June 29, 1923.

33. "Four Shanghaied Seamen Found Starving Aboard Seized Rum Smuggler," *Brooklyn Daily Eagle*, October 31, 1924.

34. *Ibid.*

35. "Shanghaied," *Reading Times* (Reading, PA), May 12, 1925; "Shanghaied on Rum Row! A Sailor's Own Story," *Manitowoc Herald Times* (Manitowoc, WI), May 20, 1925.

36. "Shanghaied," *Reading Times* (Reading, PA), May 12, 1925.

37. *Ibid.*

38. "Quartet of Starving Sailors Picked Up; British Boat Held," *Escanaba Daily Press* (Escanaba, MI), November 1, 1924.

39. "Shanghaied," *Reading Times* (Reading, PA), May 12, 1925.

40. "Shanghaied on Rum Row! A Sailor's Own Story," *Manitowoc Herald Times* (Manitowoc, WI), May 20, 1925.

41. *Ibid.*

42. *Ibid.*

43. *Ibid.*

44. "Shanghaied on Rum Row, Final Chapter of Booze Pirates' Captive," *Olean Evening Times* (Olean, NY), May 13, 1925.

45. *Ibid.*

46. *Ibid.*

47. *Ibid.*

48. "Four Shanghaied Seamen Found Starving Aboard Seized Rum Smuggler," *Brooklyn Daily Eagle*, October 31, 1924.

49. "Shanghaied on Rum Row, Final Chapter of Booze Pirates' Captive," *Olean Evening Times* (Olean, NY), May 13, 1925; "Albert E. Burgomaster," *Manitowoc Times Herald* (Manitowoc, WI), May 11, 1925.

50. "Memo re *Amaranth, Vinces, Dorothy M. Smart,*" December 5, 1926, "Records Relating to Seized Vessels 1926–1935," Records of the U.S. Coast Guard, RG 26, Box 5, National Archives, Washington, D.C.

51. *Ibid.*

52. Gillam v. United States, 27 F.2d 296 [1928]; Willoughby, *Rum War at Sea*, 140; The *Vinces*, 20 F.2d 164, 172 [1927].

53. Willoughby, *Rum War at Sea*, 140.

54. *Ibid.*

55. *Ibid.*, 140–141; Gillam v. United States, 27 F.2d 296 [1928]; The *Vinces* 20 F 2d 164, 172 [1927].

56. The *Vinces*, 20 F 2d 164 [1927]; Gillam v. United States, 27 F.2d 296 [1928].

57. "Liquor Ring Witness Tells of Seizing Ship," *New York Times*, November 26, 1929.

58. Willoughby, *Rum War at Sea*, 93–94, 147, 170.

59. "Memorandum for the Acting Commandant," September 9, 1927, "Records Relating to Seized Vessels 1926–1935," Records of the U.S. Coast Guard, RG 26, Box 5, National Archives, Washington, D.C.

60. "Fugitive Is Found Aboard Liquor Ship," *New York Times*, December 11, 1929; "War on Rum Boats Told at Trial of Eight," *New York Times*, November 22, 1929.

61. "Indictments Bear [*sic*] Huge Liquor Ring," *New York Times*, March 16, 1929.

62. *Ibid.*; "Clever Ruses of Rum Squad Are Revealed," *Springfield Leader* (Springfield, MO), March 17, 1929.

63. "Indictments Bear [*sic*] Huge Liquor Ring," *New York Times*, March 16, 1929.

64. "Eight Go on Trial in Huge Liquor Ring," *New York Times*, November 21, 1929.

65. "War on Rum Boats Told at Trial of Eight," *New York Times*, November 22, 1929; "Liquor Ring Witness Tells of Seizing Ship," *New York Times*, November 26, 1929.

66. "Says He Put Radios on Rum Ring's Ships," *New York Times*, November 23, 1929.

67. *Ibid.*; "Liquor Ring Witness Tells of Seizing Ship," *New York Times*, November 26, 1929; "Rum Ring Used Radio in Business," *Danville Bee* (Danville, VA), November 25, 1929.

68. "Six Found Guilty of Liquor Ring Plot," *New York Times*, November 28, 1929; "Six in Liquor Ring Get Sentences to Prison," *New York Times*, December 5, 1929.

69. Lawson, *Smugglers, Bootleggers, and Scofflaws*, 123.

70. *Ibid.*, 132.

71. "State May Inquire into Big Rum Ship," *Binghamton Press* (Binghamton, NY), January 3, 1925.

72. Romano v. United States, 9 F.2d 522, 523 [1925].

73. *Ibid.*

74. "State May Inquire into Big Rum Ship," *Binghamton Press* (Binghamton, NY), January 3, 1925.

75. "Seized a Rum Boat Far off Its Course," *Brooklyn Daily Eagle*, March 30, 1925; "Mystery in Strange Silence Following Rum Ship Seizure Puzzles Federal Prosecutor," *Brooklyn Daily Eagle*, April 30, 1925; "Seize Italian Ship as Liquor Suspect," *New York Times*, January 2, 1925.

76. "Mystery in Strange Silence Following Rum Ship Seizure Puzzles Federal Prosecutor," *Brooklyn Daily Eagle*, April 30, 1925; "Fixes $26,000 Bail for Bootleggers Pending Appeal," *Brooklyn Daily Eagle*, April 3, 1925.

77. Romano v. United States, 9 F.2d 522, 523 [1925]; "Hot Fight Looms in Rum Ship Case," *Brooklyn Daily Eagle*, April 2, 1925.

78. Romano v. United States, 9 F.2d 522, 523 [1925].

Chapter 11

1. Jay Maeder, "The Sporting Life: Big Bill Dwyer," *New York Daily News*, October 5, 1999.

2. Trent Frayne, *The Mad Men of Hockey* (New York: Dodd, Mead and Company, 1974), 58, 60.

3. *Ibid.*, 60–61.

4. *Ibid.*, 57.

5. "Biggest Liquor Ring Smashed by Arrests of Twenty Accused Here," *New York Times*, December 4, 1925; "One Pleads Guilty at Trial of Dwyer," *New York Times*, July 10, 1926.

6. "Confession Proves Liquor Ring Bribery, Buckner Declares," *New York Times*, December 5, 1925.

7. *Ibid.*; "Biggest Liquor Ring Smashed by Arrests of Twenty Accused Here," *New York Times*, December 4, 1925.

8. "Eludes Rum Navy, Runs Foul [*sic*] of Police," *New York Times*, April 27, 1925.

9. "Commuters Watch Rum Craft Seized," *New York Times*, October 24, 1925; "Biggest Liquor Ring Smashed by Arrests of Twenty Accused Here," *New York Times*, December 4, 1925.

10. "Commuters Watch Rum Craft Seized," *New York Times*, October 24, 1925.

11. "Should a Man Tell?" *Zanesville Signal* (Zanesville, OH), October 10, 1926.

12. *Ibid.*; "Capture Rum Vessel but Cargo Delivered," *Bakersfield Californian* (Bakersfield, CA), July 28, 1925.

13. "Biggest Liquor Ring Smashed by Arrests of Twenty Accused Here," *New York Times*, December 4, 1925.

14. "Confession Proves Liquor Ring Bribery, Buckner Declares," *New York Times*, December 5, 1925.

15. *Ibid.*

16. "Biggest Liquor Ring Smashed by Arrests of Twenty Accused Here," *New York Times*, December 4, 1925.

17. *Ibid.*; "Confession Proves Liquor Ring Bribery, Buckner Declares," *New York Times*, December 5, 1925; Martin Mayer, *Emory Buckner: A Biography* (New York: Harper and Row, 1968), 204.

18. "Confession Proves Liquor Ring Bribery, Buckner Declares," *New York Times*, December 5, 1925.

19. "Biggest Liquor Ring Smashed by Arrests of Twenty Accused Here," *New York Times*, December 4, 1925; "Federal Dry Agent Taken in Round-up as Liquor Ring Aid [*sic*]," *New York Times*, December 6, 1925.

20. "Coast Guards Named in Rum Indictments," *Brooklyn Daily Eagle*, January 26, 1926.

21. "Biggest Liquor Ring Smashed by Arrests of Twenty Accused Here," *New York Times*, December 4, 1925; "Confession Proves Liquor Ring Bribery, Buckner Declares," *New York Times*, December 5, 1925.

22. "Federal Dry Agent Taken in Round-up as Liquor Ring Aid [*sic*]," *New York Times*, December 6, 1925.

23. *Ibid.*

24. "Biggest Liquor Ring Smashed by Arrests of Twenty Accused Here," *New York Times*, December 4, 1925.

25. Mayer, *Emory Buckner*, 204.

26. *Ibid.*

27. "One Pleads Guilty at Trial of Dwyer," *New York Times*, July 10, 1926.

28. "Swears Police Saw Dwyer Boats Land," *New York Times*, July 13, 1926.

29. "Catch Chief Witness Who Quit Rum Trial," *New York Times*, July 23, 1926; "Rum Trial Witness Held for Perjury," *New York Times*, July 24, 1926.

30. "Dwyer Found Guilty of Rum Conspiracy," *New York Times*, July 27, 1926.

31. "Fugitive Appears and Turns on Dwyer," *New York Times*, July 16, 1926.

32. *Ibid.*

33. "Testifies Dwyer Said He Had Pull," *New York Times*, July 17, 1926.

34. "Dwyer's Counsel Faced by Bielaski, Won't Question Him," *New York Times*, July 20, 1926.

35. Mayer, *Emory Buckner*, 205.

36. *Ibid.*

37. "Rum Trial Witness Held for Perjury," *New York Times*, July 24, 1926; "Dwyer Trial Near End," *New York Times*, July 26, 1926; "Dwyer Found Guilty of Rum Conspiracy," *New York Times*, July 27, 1926.

38. Mayer, *Emory Buckner*, 205.

39. "Dwyer Found Guilty of Rum Conspiracy," *New York Times*, July 27, 1926.

40. "Upholds Conviction of Dwyer and Cohron," *New York Times*, February 8, 1927; "No Dwyer-Cohron Review," *New York Times*, June 6, 1927; "Dwyer Leaves for Prison," *New York Times*, July 19, 1927; Frayne, *Mad Men*, 59.

41. "Dwyer Wins Parole from Atlanta Prison; 'Bootleg King,' Very Ill, Pays $10,000 Fine," *New York Times*, August 10, 1928; Frayne, *Mad Men*, 59.

42. "Bill Dwyer Dies, 'Bootlegger King,'" *New York Times*, December 11, 1946; Maeder, *New York Daily News*, October 5, 1999.

43. Frayne, *Mad Men*, 72–74.

44. "The Auctioneer's Hammer Smashed the Gamblers' Swanky Dream," *San Francisco Chronicle*, August 23, 1926.

45. *Ibid.*

46. "U.S. Wins $3,715,907 in Ten-Minute Trial," *New York Times*, May 26, 1939.

47. "Bill Dwyer Dies, 'Bootlegger King,'" *New York Times*, December 11, 1946; Frayne, *Mad Men*, 59.

48. "Thirty-three Men Are Indicted as Rum Import Ring," *New York Times*, November 19, 1926.

49. George Wolf and Joseph Dimona, *Frank Costello: Prime Minister of the Underworld* (New York: William Morrow and Co., 1974), 63.

50. "Thirty-three Men Are Indicted as Rum Import Ring," *New York Times*, November 19, 1926.

51. "Ex-Rum Runner Now Under-cover Man for Bielaski," *Brooklyn Daily Eagle*, January 5, 1927.

52. "Used Plane to Hunt Lost Liquor Ship," *New York Times*, January 5, 1927.

53. *Ibid.*

54. "Says Patrol Boats Guided Rum Ships," *New York Times*, January 7, 1927.

55. "How Navy Craft Ran Liquor for Rum Row Bared," *Brooklyn Daily Eagle*, January 6, 1927.

56. "Says Patrol Boats Guided Rum Ships," *New York Times*, January 7, 1927.

57. "Admits Rum Trade of Coast Guard," *New York Times*, January 8, 1927.

58. *Ibid.*

59. *Ibid.*

60. *Ibid.*

61. "Former Captain Dry Navy Tells How He Captured, Robbed, Scuttled Rummer," *Decatur Evening Herald* (Decatur, IL), January 11, 1927; "Sank Rum Runner and Sold the Cargo," *Ottawa Journal* (Ottawa, Canada), January 11, 1927.

62. "Former Captain Dry Navy Tells How He Captured, Robbed, Scuttled Rummer," *Decatur Evening Herald* (Decatur, IL), January 11, 1927; "Sank Rum Runner and Sold the Cargo," *Ottawa Journal* (Ottawa, Canada), January 11, 1927.

63. "Says Patrol Boats Guided Rum Ships," *New York Times*, January 7, 1927.

64. "Rum Case Principal Says He Was Beaten," *New York Times*, January 19, 1927.

65. "Liquor Ring Case in Hands of Jury," *New York Times*, January 20, 1927.

66. "Costello Jurors Clear Eight, Split on Six in Liquor Ring Trial," *New York Times*, January 21, 1927.

67. *Ibid.*; Wolf and Dimona, *Frank Costello*, 72.

68. Wolf and Dimona, *Frank Costello*, 72.

69. *Ibid.*

Chapter 12

1. "F.F. Redfern of Commerce Department Decoded Rum Ring Messages," *New York Times*, October 18, 1929.

2. "130 Dry Raiders Sweep along Coast; Get Arsenal and Rum Ring's Wireless," *New York Times*, October 17, 1929; "Liquor Syndicate Paid $30,000 Graft Weekly to Police," *Clearfield Progress* (Clearfield, PA), October 18, 1929.

3. "130 Dry Raiders Sweep Along Coast; Get Arsenal and Rum Ring's Wireless," *New York Times*, October 17, 1929.

4. "Rum Ring Paid Big Bribes, Seized Records Reveal; Six Months' Profit $2,000,000," *New York Times*, October 18, 1929.

5. "130 Dry Raiders Sweep along Coast; Get Arsenal and Rum Ring's Wireless," *New York Times*, October 17, 1929.

6. "Rum Ring Paid Big Bribes, Seized Records Reveal; Six Months' Profit $2,000,000," *New York Times*, October 18, 1929; "130 Dry Raiders Sweep along Coast; Get Arsenal and Rum Ring's Wireless," *New York Times*, October 17, 1929; "Liquor Syndicate Paid $30,000 Graft Weekly to Police," *Clearfield Progress* (Clearfield, PA), October 18, 1929.

7. "Rum Ring Paid Big Bribes, Seized Records Reveal; Six Months' Profit $2,000,000," *New York Times*, October 18, 1929.

8. "Rum Rings Got Hint of Raids in Advance," *New York Times*, October 21, 1929.

9. *Ibid.*

10. "130 Dry Raiders Sweep along Coast; Get Arsenal and Rum Ring's Wireless," *New York Times*, October 17, 1929.

11. *Ibid.*; "Rum Ring Paid Big Bribes, Seized Records Reveal; Six Months' Profit $2,000,000," *New York Times*, October 18, 1929.

12. "Rum Ring Paid Big Bribes, Seized Records Reveal; Six Months' Profit $2,000,000," *New York Times*, October 18, 1929.

13. "Town Seething in Liquor," *New York Times*, January 12, 1923.

14. *Ibid.*

15. "Rum Rings Got Hint of Raids in Advance," *New York Times*, October 21, 1929.

16. *Ibid.*

17. "$15,000,000 Rum Ring Bared by Radio Raid," *New York Times*, September 28, 1930.

18. *Ibid.*

19. *Ibid.*; "Guilty in Rum Radio Case," *New York Times*, April 15, 1931; "Cleared in Radio Case," *New York Times*, February 9, 1932; United States v Molyneaux, 55 F.2d 912, 913 [1932].

20. "Fourth Radio Plant of Rum Ring Seized," *New York Times*, October 8, 1930.

21. "Rum Boat Shelled; Linked to Radio Ring," *New York Times*, November 16, 1930.

22. "Justice for Liquor Smugglers' King," *Atlanta Constitution*, June 11, 1933.

23. *Ibid.*

24. *Ibid.*

25. *Ibid.*; Neville Williams, *Contraband Cargo: Seven Centuries of Smuggling* (London: Longmans Green and Co., 1959), 249.

26. Williams, *Contraband Cargo*, 249, 250.

27. "Fifty Are Indicted as Huge Liquor Ring," *New York Times*, April 15, 1930; "Say Liquor Ring Put $1,000,000 in Banks," *New York Times*, April 16, 1930.

28. "Rum Ring Trial On; Police Implicated," *New York Times*, June 23, 1931.

29. *Ibid.*; "Life on Rum Row Depicted at Trial," *New York Times*, June 25, 1931.

30. "Upholds Rum Search in Atlantic Highlands," *New York Times*, June 30, 1931.

31. "Radio Expert Bares Rum Ring Messages," *New York Times*, June 24, 1931.

32. "Life on Rum Row Depicted at Trial," *New York Times*, June 25, 1931.

33. *Ibid.*

34. "Radio Expert Bares Rum Ring Messages," *New York Times*, June 24, 1931.

35. "Coast Guards Tell of Rum Row Chases," *New York Times*, June 26, 1931.

36. *Ibid.*

37. "Rum Jury Hears Bankers," *New York Times*, July 3, 1931; "Links Drafts to Rum Ring," *New York Times*, July 9, 1931; "Rum Ring Charges Go to Newark Jury," *New York Times*, July 11, 1931.

38. "Say Liquor Ring Put $1,000,000 in Banks," *New York Times*, April 16, 1930; "Rum Jury Hears Bankers," *New York Times*, July 3, 1931.

39. "Rum Ring Trial On; Police Implicated," *New York Times*, June 23, 1931.

40. "'Rum Ring' Charges Go to Newark Jury," *New York Times*, July 11, 1931; "Testify to Whisky Orders," *New York Times*, July 8, 1931.

41. "Rum Ring Charges Go to Newark Jury," *New York Times*, July 11, 1931.

42. "Jury Acquits Seventeen in 'Rum Ring' Trial," *New York Times*, July 12, 1931.

43. "Rum Radio Ring Head Slain in New Jersey," *New York Times*, March 24, 1933.

44. "Spade King Clue in Lillien Slaying," *New York Times*, March 25, 1933.

Chapter 13

1. "Coast Guard Lays Siege to Runners," *Boston Daily Globe*, September 26, 1927.

2. "The Rum Patrol," *New York Times*, May 11, 1924.

3. Morrison, *Alcohol, Boat Chases, and Shootouts*, 244, 245.

4. Willoughby, *Rum War at Sea*, 35; "Pirates Board Ship, Get $400,000 in Rum," *New York Times*, February 15, 1923.

5. Willoughby, *Rum War at Sea*, 35.

6. "Find Eight Dead in Sea and Barrels of Ale," *New York Times*, April 8, 1923.

7. Willoughby, *Rum War at Sea*, 35.

8. "Naval Divers Used in Dwight Mystery," *New York Times*, June 27, 1923; "Diver Explores Wreck of Rum Runner *John Dwight*," *Lewiston Daily Sun* (Lewiston, ME), May 5, 1923.

9. "Crew Say [*sic*] Pirates Got Liquor Cargo," *New York Times*, March 12, 1923; Geoff Robinson and Dorothy Robinson, *Duty-Free: A Prohibition Special* (Summerside, Canada: Alfa-Graphics, 1992), 36.

10. "Charge of Piracy," *Sydney Morning Herald* (Sydney, Australia), September 19, 1924.

11. Morrison, *Alcohol, Boat Chases, and Shootouts*, 245.

12. *Ibid.*, 248, 253.

13. "Treasury Men Visit Liquor Smugglers," *New York Times*, April 26, 1923.

14. *Ibid.*; Willoughby, *Rum War at Sea*, 36–37; Morrison, *Alcohol, Boat Chases, and Shootouts*, 124–125.

15. Parker and Tyrell, *Rumrunner*, 66, 86–87; Robinson and Robinson, *Duty-Free*, 39–40.

16. "Nab Two Men on Piracy Charges," *Santa Ana Register* (Santa Ana, CA), November 10, 1924; "Canadians Will Fight Extradition," *Santa Ana Register* (Santa Ana, CA), December 4, 1924; "Deputy Kills Acid Thrower," *Santa Cruz Evening News* (Santa Cruz, CA), January 28, 1925.

17. "One Rum Pirate Killed Another Is Latest Version," *Santa Cruz Evening News* (Santa Cruz, CA), January 29, 1925.

18. "Milo and Theodore Eggers Fleeing to Mexico Is the Belief," *Santa Cruz Evening News* (Santa Cruz, CA), January 29, 1925.

19. "Arraigned on Charges of Trying to Murder Officer," *Santa Cruz Evening News* (Santa Cruz, CA), May 20, 1925; "Admits Helping Brother to Flee; Given Six Months," *Santa Cruz Evening News* (Santa Cruz. CA), October 6, 1925.

20. "Up-to-the-Minute News," *San Mateo Times* (San Mateo, CA), March 8, 1926; "Hijacker Granted Partial Rehearing," *Modesto News Herald* (Modesto, CA), May

19, 1926; "Eggers to Be Deported," *Oregon Statesman* (Salem, OR), May 10, 1927; "Spirited from Jail," *Santa Cruz Evening News* (Santa Cruz, CA), May 12, 1927; "May Be Compelled to Release Eggers," *Modesto News Herald* (Modesto, CA), May 27, 1927.

21. Rich Mole, *Rum-runners and Renegades: Whisky Wars of the Pacific Northwest, 1917–2012* (Victoria, Canada: Heritage House Publishing Company, 2013), 102.

22. Mole, *Rum-runners and Renegades*, 92.

23. *Ibid.*, 95–100.

24. *Ibid.*; Greene, *Personality Ships*, 258.

25. Mole, *Rum-runners and Renegades*, 95–100.

26. Van de Water, *Real McCoy*, 167; Ling, *Run the Rum In*, 55.

27. "Used Plane to Hunt Lost Liquor Ship," *New York Times*, January 5, 1927; "Rum Fleet Paralyzed," *New York Times*, May 9, 1925.

28. "New Dry and Wet Fleets Mobilize for War," *New York Times*, March 29, 1925.

29. *Ibid.*

Chapter 14

1. "Whiskey Smugglers Outwit Uncle Sam, Play Tag with Boat," *Sheboygan Press Telegram* (Sheboygan, WI), October 22, 1921.

2. "Florida Dry Fleet Seizes Five Craft," *New York Times*, January 13, 1928.

3. "Coast Guard Tells of a Sea Battle," *New York Times*, February 28, 1927.

4. Paul S. George, "Bootleggers, Prohibitionists, and Police: The Temperance Movement in Miami, 1896–1920," *Tequesta* 1, no. 39 (1979): 34–41.

5. *Ibid.*, 35.

6. *Ibid.*, 36–37.

7. *Ibid.* 38.

8. Buchanan, "Miami's Bootleg Boom," 13.

9. "'Wet' New York Disappointing to One Who Knows His Florida," *New York Times*, November 26, 1922.

10. *Ibid.*

11. Buchanan, "Miami's Bootleg Boom," 13–15.

12. "Seek to Dam Flood of Rum into South," *New York Times*, March 5, 1922.

13. Ron Chepesiuk, *Gangsters of Miami: True Tales of Mobsters, Gamblers, Hit Men, Con Men, and Gang Bangers from the Magic City* (Fort Lee, NJ: Barricade Books, 2010), 21.

14. Carter, "Florida and Rumrunning during National Prohibition," 54.

15. *Ibid.*

16. "Federal Rum War Begins in Florida," *New York Times*, March 21, 1922.

17. *Ibid.*

18. *Ibid.*

19. *Ibid.*; "Liquor Raids Are Started in South," *Dallas Morning News* (Dallas, TX), March 21, 1922.

20. "Dry Agents Arrest a Miami Banker," *New York Times*, March 22, 1922.

21. "Federal Rum War Begins in Florida," *New York Times*, March 21, 1922.

22. Buchanan, "Miami's Bootleg Boom," 17; "A Writer Tells of Bootlegging," *Hutchinson News* (Hutchinson, KS), July 10, 1923.

23. Buchanan, "Miami's Bootleg Boom," 17; "'Wet' New York Disappointing to One Who Knows His Florida," *New York Times*, November 26, 1922.

24. "Coast Patrol in Florida Has Real Hazards," *Rhinelander Daily News* (Rhinelander, WI), September

10, 1927; "Shannon Prank Costs His Life," *Ogden Standard Examiner* (Ogden, UT), March 7, 1926.

25. Willoughby, *Rum War at Sea*, 1; Buchanan, "Miami's Bootleg Boom," 20, 21.

26. Willoughby, *Rum War at Sea*, 1.

27. *Ibid.*

28. Willoughby, *Rum War at Sea*, 1–2; Buchanan, "Miami's Bootleg Boom," 21.

29. Willoughby, *Rum War at Sea*, 2.

30. *Ibid.*

31. *Ibid.*

32. *Ibid.*

33. "Bullet Ends Life of King [*sic*] Rumrunners," *Sioux City Journal* (Sioux City, IA), March 7, 1926.

34. *Ibid.*

35. Buchanan, "Miami's Bootleg Boom," 21, 22.

36. "Shannon Prank Costs His Life," *Ogden Standard Examiner* (Ogden, UT), March 7, 1926.

37. Buchanan, "Miami's Bootleg Boom," 21.

38. *Ibid.*, 24.

39. *Ibid.*

40. "Coast Guards Not Guilty on Murder Charge," *Billings Gazette* (Billings, MT), February 25, 1928.

41. Buchanan, "Miami's Bootleg Boom," 21–22.

42. *Ibid.*, 22.

43. *Ibid.*

44. *Ibid.*, 22–23.

45. *Ibid.*

46. *Ibid.*

47. "Coast Guard Bullets Hit Miami House Boat," *New York Times*, April 15, 1929.

48. Buchanan, "Miami's Bootleg Boom," 23.

49. *Ibid.*; "Coast Guard Bullets Hit Miami House Boat," *New York Times*, April 15, 1929.

50. "Coast Guardsman Dropped," *New York Times*, April 24, 1929.

51. Buchanan, "Miami's Bootleg Boom," 23.

Chapter 15

1. Carter, "Florida and Rumrunning During National Prohibition," 53.

2. James Kaserman and Sarah Kaserman, *Florida Pirates: From the Southern Gulf Coast to the Keys and Beyond* (Charleston, SC: The History Press, 2011), 99–100.

3. Buchanan, "Miami's Bootleg Boom," 25.

4. Willoughby, *Rum War at Sea*, 126; Alderman v. United States, 31 F.2d 499 [1929].

5. Willoughby, *Rum War at Sea*, 126.

6. *Ibid.*; Alderman v. United States, 31 F.2d 499 [1929].

7. "Coast Guard Tells of a Sea Battle," *New York Times*, August 28, 1927; Alderman v. United States, 31 F.2d 499 [1929].

8. "Coast Guard Tells of a Sea Battle," *New York Times*, August 28, 1927; Alderman v. United States, 31F.2d 499 [1929].

9. "Coast Guard Tells of a Sea Battle," *New York Times*, August 28, 1927; Alderman v. United States, 31 F.2d 499 [1929].

10. Alderman v. United States, 31 F.2d 499 [1929].

11. *Ibid.*

12. *Ibid.*; "Coast Guard Tells of a Sea Battle," *New York Times*, August 28, 1927.

13. "Coast Guard Tells of a Sea Battle," *New York Times*, August 28, 1927.

14. *Ibid.*; Willoughby, *Rum War at Sea*, 127.

15. Buchanan, "Miami's Bootleg Boom," 27–28.

16. Willoughby, *Rum War at Sea*, 127.

17. Buchanan, "Miami's Bootleg Boom," 27–28; Alderman v. United States, 31 F.2d 499 [1929].

18. "The Gallows and the Deep," *Broward Palm Beach New Times* (Hollywood, FL), 4 December 1997; Alderman v. United States, 31 F.2d 499 [1929].

19. Buchanan, "Miami's Bootleg Boom," 28; "Rum Pirate Hanged for Double Killing," *New York Times*, August 18, 1929.

20. "Judge Refused to Halt Execution," *Morning Herald* (Hagerstown, MD), August 15, 1929; Alderman v. United States, 31 F.2d 499 [1929].

21. Buchanan, "Miami's Bootleg Boom," 28.

22. "Hoover Refuses Clemency to Slayer of Coast Guards," *New York Times*, August 4, 1929.

23. Buchanan, "Miami's Bootleg Boom," 29.

24. *Ibid.*; "Preparations Complete for Hanging of James Alderman," *Kingsport Times* (Kingsport, TN), August 16, 1929.

25. "Wanted Sociable Hanging," *New York Times*, August 8, 1929; Buchanan, "Miami's Bootleg Boom," 30.

26. "Rum Pirate Executed in Plane Hangar," *Danville Bee* (Danville, VA), August 17, 1929; "The Gallows and the Deep," *Broward Palm Beach New Times* (Hollywood, FL), December 4, 1997.

27. Ling, *Run the Rum In*, 137; "Rum Pirate Hanged for Double Killing," *New York Times*, August 18, 1929.

28. Ling, *Run the Rum In*, 134, 136–138.

29. "Rum Pirate Hanged for Double Killing," *New York Times*, August 18, 1929; Buchanan, "Miami's Bootleg Boom," 30–31.

30. Ling, *Run the Rum In*, 138; "The Gallows and the Deep," *Broward Palm Beach New Times* (Hollywood, FL), December 4, 1997.

31. Buchanan, "Miami's Bootleg Boom," 31.

Chapter 16

1. "Liquor Runners Beyond Rule, Say U.S. Agents," *San Francisco Chronicle*, September 17, 1921.

2. Greene, *Personality Ships*, 238.

3. Rosemary Neering, *Smugglers of the West: Tales of Contraband and Criminals* (Victoria, Canada: Heritage House Publishing, 2011), 112.

4. Schneider, *Iced*, 192; Kenneth D. Rose, "Wettest in the West: San Francisco and Prohibition in 1924," *California History* 65, no. 4 (1986): 291.

5. "Coast Rum Ring Landing Field Found by Dry Aids [*sic*]," *San Francisco Chronicle*, November 17, 1926.

6. Schneider, *Iced*, 192.

7. "Rum Supply for July 4 Reported Lying Off Coast," *Oakland Tribune*, June 15, 1926.

8. "Consul Aids British Rum Ship Crew," *Oakland Tribune*, October 13, 1924.

9. "Liquor Boat Is Blamed for S.F. Cable Rupture," *Oakland Tribune*, October 17, 1924; Miles, *Slow Boat*, 245.

10. Philip Metcalfe, *Whispering Wires: The Tragic Tale of an American Bootlegger* (Portland, OR: Ink Water Press, 2007), 56, 59.

11. "Coast Rum Ships Found to Run Stills," *Oakland Tribune*, December 2, 1927.

12. "Two Swift Revenue Cutters to Block S.F. Rum Runners," *San Francisco Chronicle*, June 23, 1922; Miles, *Slow Boat*, 222; "S.F. Dry Navy Moves on Rum Fleet," *San Francisco Chronicle*, May 13, 1925.

13. "Half-million Cargo Is Taken," *Reno Evening Gazette* (Reno, NV), October 13, 1924.

14. "Two Swift Revenue Cutters to Block S.F. Rum Runners," *San Francisco Chronicle*, June 23, 1922.

15. Rose, "Wettest in the West," 290.

16. "S.F. Dry Navy Moves on Rum Fleet," *San Francisco Chronicle*, May 13, 1925; "National Rum War Ordered by Coolidge," *San Francisco Chronicle*, May 14, 1925; "U.S. Surrounded by Rum Smugglers, Guard Helpless," *San Bernardino County Sun* (San Bernardino, CA), May 17, 1925.

17. "Four Rum-chasers for Pacific Coast," *New York Times*, June 18, 1925; "Southern California to Be New Rum Base," *San Bernardino County Sun* (San Bernardino, CA), August 3, 1925.

18. Rose, "Wettest in the West," 290.

19. *Ibid.*, 291.

20. Greene, *Personality Ships*, 147; 273 U.S. 593.

21. 273 U.S. 593.

22. "Consul Aids British Rum Ship Crew," *Oakland Tribune*, October 13, 1924.

23. "Half-million Cargo Is Taken," *Reno Evening Gazette* (Reno, NV), October 13, 1924; "Liquor Ship's Crew Held in $175,000 Bail," *San Francisco Chronicle*, October 14, 1924.

24. "Plot to Scuttle $500,000 Booze Ship Suspected," *Oakland Tribune*, October 14, 1924; "Ten Million Rum-running Outfit Hunted," *San Francisco Chronicle*, October 15, 1924.

25. "Consul Aids British Rum Ship Crew," *Oakland Tribune*, October 13, 1924; "Plot to Scuttle $500,000 Booze Ship Suspected," *Oakland Tribune*, October 14, 1924.

26. 273 U.S. 593.

27. "Booze Chief Suspect to Surrender," *Oakland Tribune*, November 15, 1924; "Rum Runner Methods to Be Revealed," *Oakland Tribune*, November 20, 1924.

28. "*Quadra* Rum Fight Will Open Today," *San Francisco Chronicle*, November 22, 1924; "Prominent Vancouver Men Are Indicted," *Manitoba Free Press* (Winnipeg, Canada), November 13, 1924.

29. "Canada Stirred by U.S. Arrest of Millionaire," *Oakland Tribune*, November 15, 1924.

30. "Booze Chief Suspect to Surrender," *Oakland Tribune*, November 15, 1924.

31. Rose, "Wettest in the West," 291; "S.F. Rum Row Stirs Canada," *San Francisco Chronicle*, December 1, 1924.

32. "Finance Chief in Rum Net," *San Francisco Chronicle*, November 15, 1924; "Handwriting May Convict Broker," *Bakersfield Californian* (Bakersfield CA), March 14, 1925; "Booze Chief Suspect to Surrender," *Oakland Tribune*, November 15, 1924; 273 U.S. 593.

33. "*Quadra*'s Seizure Upheld by U.S.," *San Francisco Chronicle*, January 6, 1925.

34. 273 U.S. 593; "*Quadra* Trial Opens; Thirty Are Fugitives," *San Francisco Chronicle*, March 11, 1925.

35. "*Quadra*'s Rum Cargo Lugged into Court," *San Francisco Chronicle*, March 12, 1925.

36. *Ibid.*

37. "*Quadra* Owned by S.F. Capitalists," *Oakland Tribune*, October 15, 1924; 273 U.S. 593.

38. "Navy Officer Attacked in Booze Trial," *Oakland Tribune*, March 11, 1925; "Two Witnesses in *Quadra* Rum Trial Disappear," *Oakland Tribune*, April 18, 1925.

39. "Rum Runners Turn against Mother Ship," *San Francisco Chronicle*, March 13, 1925.

40. "Handwriting May Convict Broker," *Bakersfield Californian* (Bakersfield, CA), March 14, 1925.

41. "*Quadra*'s Men Stick to Tale," *San Francisco Chronicle*, March 19, 1925.

42. "*Quadra* Trial Surprise Move," *San Francisco Chronicle*, March 21, 1925; "*Quadra* Case Nears Finish," *San Francisco Chronicle*, March 25, 1925.

43. "*Quadra* Case Nearing End," *San Francisco Chronicle*, April 3, 1925.

44. 273 U.S. 593.

45. *Ibid.*; "Prison Term Given Ten in *Quadra* Case," *Oakland Tribune*, April 4, 1925.

46. "Trial of Britons Taken at Sea Is Not Against Treaty," *Reno Evening Gazette* (Reno, NV), October 27, 1926; 273 U.S. 593.

47. "Rum Treaties Score Victory," *Dallas Morning News* (Dallas, TX), April 12, 1927; "*Quadra* Ruling to Guide U.S. on Ship Seizures," *Oakland Tribune*, April 12, 1927; 273 U.S. 593.

48. "Rum Runner with Her Ten Thousand Cases Is Prize of the *Cahokia*," *Santa Cruz Evening News* (Santa Cruz, CA), February 18, 1925.

49. "Rum Chaser Captain Faces Call to Stand," *Oakland Tribune*, February 24, 1928.

50. "Captain in Boat Arrest Faces Charge," *Oakland Tribune*, March 6, 1928; Willoughby, *Rum War at Sea*, 82; "Coast Guard Officer Put on Probation," *Oakland Tribune*, December 7, 1930.

51. "Government Loses *Coal Harbor* Case," *Berkeley Daily Gazette* (Berkeley, CA), March 8, 1928; "U.S. Loses Rum Ship Case on Issue of Time," *Oakland Tribune*, March 8, 1928; "Captain in Boat Arrest Faces Charge," *Oakland Tribune*, March 6, 1928.

52. "Clemency Is Expected for Ship Witness," *San Mateo Times* (San Mateo, CA), April 4, 1928; "Rum Chaser Begins Term for Perjury," *Oakland Tribune*, May 2, 1928; "Coast Guard Skipper Gets Prison Term for Perjury," *Modesto News Herald* (Modesto, CA), April 25, 1929; "Coast Guard Officer Put on Probation," *Oakland Tribune*, December 7, 1930; "Probation Denied Coast Guardsman," *Berkeley Daily Gazette* (Berkeley, CA), April 25, 1929.

53. "Liquor Ship Case Compromised," *New York Times*, May 26, 1928.

54. "Vessel Sold," *San Francisco Chronicle*, March 16, 1929; "*Quadra*'s $500,000 Rum Treasure Smashed by U.S. as Crowd Sniffs Rare Bouquets," *San Francisco Chronicle*, September 20, 1929.

55. Stone, *My Dad*, 43; "Rich Fugitive Taken at Sea," *Los Angeles Times*, March 3, 1927.

56. "Guns Roar in Seizure," *Los Angeles Times*, March 4, 1927; "S.F. Cutter Takes Giant Rum Runner," *Oakland Tribune*, March 2, 1927; "Captured Rum Ship Crew Will Fight Seizure Made by U.S. upon High Seas," *Oakland Tribune*, March 4, 1927.

57. "Brought in by Cutters," *Montreal Gazette* (Montreal, Canada), March 4, 1927.

58. "Guns Roar in Seizure," *Los Angeles Times*, March 4, 1927.

59. Willoughby, *Rum War at Sea*, 84.

60. *Ibid.*; "Guns Roar in Seizure," *Los Angeles Times*, March 4, 1927.

61. Willoughby, *Rum War at Sea*, 85; "Sixty-one Are Indicted as Rum-Runners," *New York Times*, March 6, 1927.

62. Stone, *My Dad*, 47; "Sixty-one Are Indicted as Rum-Runners," *New York Times*, March 6, 1927.

63. Willoughby, *Rum War at Sea*, 85; "Question Legality of Rum-Ship Seizure," *New York Times*, March 20, 1927; Stone, *My Dad*, 45.

64. "Question Legality of Rum-Ship Seizure," *New York Times*, March 20, 1927; Willoughby, *Rum War at Sea*, 85.

65. "Court Upsets Seizure of Canadian Rum Ship," *New York Times*, April 21, 1927.

66. "Asks Release of Ship," *New York Times*, April 28, 1927; "Orders *Federalship* Freed," *New York Times*, May 4, 1927.

67. Untitled Article, *New York Times*, May 5, 1927.

68. "Gurgles Out with Chasers," *San Francisco Examiner*, May 5, 1927.

69. "*Federalship* in Vancouver," *New York Times*, May 12, 1927; "A Ship without a Country," *San Jose News* (San Jose, CA), December 3, 1927.

70. "Mystery Shrouds British Rum Ship," *Oakland Tribune*, November 10, 1928.

71. *Ibid.*; "Seized Rum Runner Ordered Released," *Modesto News Herald* (Modesto, CA), November 8, 1928; "Hunt Started by U.S. Ships after Release," *Press Courier* (Oxnard, CA), November 10, 1928; "Rum Vessels Revert to Original Owners," *Tyrone Daily Herald* (Tyrone, PA), March 7, 1930.

Chapter 17

1. Stone, *My Dad*, 63; Greene, *Personality Ships*, 219.

2. Stone, *My Dad*, 95–96.

3. *Ibid.*, 63; "Booze Worth $2,000,000 Is Landed in California," *Charleston Daily Mail* (Charleston, WV), July 19, 1923; "Official Has Chance to Join Bootleggers," *Winnipeg Free Press* (Winnipeg, Canada), December 8, 1926.

4. Schneider, *Iced*, 191; "Booze Worth $2,000,000 Is Landed in California," *Charleston Daily Mail* (Charleston, WV), July 19, 1923.

5. Mole, *Rum-runners and Renegades*, 79.

6. Miles, *Slow Boat*, 248.

7. Greene, *Personality Ships*, 222.

8. *Ibid.*

9. 273 U.S. 593; "Canadian Distillery Mulcted on Exports," *San Antonio Express* (San Antonio, TX), March 15, 1931.

10. "$2,500,000 Load Liquor for South America," *Oakland Tribune*, November 23, 1924; "Scarcity of Booze Sends Prices High," *Oakland Tribune*, December 19, 1924.

11. "California Yule Liquor Supply Is Lowest in Years, Declares Rutter," *Oakland Tribune*, December 20, 1924.

12. *Ibid.*

13. "Schooner with Cargo of Booze Still Missing," *Oakland Tribune*, December 23, 1924; "Twenty-seven of Crew Perish when Rum Ships Sink in Gale," *Bakersfield Californian* (Bakersfield, CA), January 2, 1925.

14. "Rum Ship Lurks off San Simeon, Monterey Hears," *Oakland Tribune*, December 30, 1924; "Twenty-seven of Crew Perish when Rum Ships Sink in Gale," *Bakersfield Californian* (Bakersfield, CA), January 2, 1925.

15. "Rum Runners Baffle Search," *San Francisco Chronicle*, January 10, 1925; "Ocean Hunt for Rum Ships in Dense Fog," *Danville Bee* (Danville, VA), January 13, 1925.

16. "Goff Defied by Canadian Rum Runners," *San Francisco Chronicle*, January 25, 1925.

17. "Cutter Watches Rum Runner to Stop Smuggling," *Oakland Tribune*, February 14, 1925; "Rum Runner *Malahat* Arrives Off 'Gate,'" *San Francisco Chronicle*, February 17, 1925.

18. "$2,000,000 Armed Rum Ship Seized," *Oakland Tribune*, February 18, 1925; "Cutter Watches Rum Runner to Stop Smuggling," *Oakland Tribune*, February 14, 1925.

19. "$2,000,000 Armed Rum Ship Seized," *Oakland Tribune*, February 18, 1925.

20. "Rum Ship Crew Held in Jail in Default of Bail," *Oakland Tribune*, February 19, 1925.

21. "Drys Triple Guard in Rum Runner Fight," *San Francisco Chronicle*, February 20, 1925; "Rum Ships Land Cargoes in South," *Oakland Tribune*, March 9, 1925.

22. "Canadian Liquor Schooner Missing," *Oakland Tribune*, April 24, 1925.

23. "Foreign Ports," *Oakland Tribune*, August 19, 1925; "Millions in Rum Reported on Way Here," *San Francisco*

Chronicle, November 7, 1925; "Last Minute News," *Bakersfield Californian* (Bakersfield, CA), November 17, 1925.

24. "Booze Reported Landed on Coast for City Trade," *San Mateo Times and Daily News Leader* (San Mateo, CA), February 3, 1926; "Seas Rock Rumrunners," *Oakland Tribune*, April 9, 1926.

25. "Rum Supply for July 4 Reported Lying off Coast," *Oakland Tribune*, June 15, 1926.

26. "Two Wounded in Hijacker Fight," *Oakland Tribune*, June 29, 1926.

27. "Ghost Vessels Sell Liquor to Small Runners," *Oakland Tribune*, August 6, 1925.

28. "Canada Told Arrest Reason," *Reno Evening Gazette* (Reno, NV), April 26, 1927; "Keep Eye on *Malahat*," *Lethbridge Herald* (Lethbridge, Canada), June 13, 1927; "Coast Guard on Lookout for Ship from South Seas," *Los Angeles Times*, June 13, 1927.

29. "Keep Eye on *Malahat*," *Lethbridge Herald* (Lethbridge, Canada), June 13, 1927; "Cutter Has Rum Craft Cornered," *Bakersfield Californian* (Bakersfield, CA), June 23, 1927; "Joe Parente Taken in Raid; Again Freed," *Oakland Tribune*, June 11, 1927.

30. "Liquor Craft Believed in S.B. Channel," *Oxnard Daily Courier* (Oxnard, CA), June 15, 1927.

31. "Cutter to Cease *Malahat* Vigil," *Santa Cruz Evening News* (Santa Cruz, CA), June 24, 1927.

32. "Cutter Has Rum Craft Cornered," *Bakersfield Californian* (Bakersfield, CA), June 23, 1927.

33. *Ibid.*

34. "Canada Patrol Hunt Rum Ships," *Oakland Tribune*, July 8, 1927; "Rum Runner Wins Game against Coast Guard," *Twin Falls Daily News* (Twin Falls, ID), July 9, 1927.

35. "Phantom of Pacific Is out of Trade," *Oakland Tribune*, June 22, 1928; Stone, *My Dad*, 50, 61.

36. "Suspected Rum Ship Watched," *Oakland Tribune*, June 5, 1929; "Drys Reduce Xmas Liquor by Vigilance," *San Francisco Chronicle*, December 20, 1929.

37. Stone, *My Dad*, 97, 100.

38. *Ibid.*, 99–100.

39. *Ibid.*, 103, 105.

40. *Ibid.*, 101.

41. *Ibid.*

42. "Rum Chaser Saves Smugglers, Puts Nine on Liquor Vessel," *Woodland Daily Democrat* (Woodland, CA), December 11, 1930.

43. Stone, *My Dad*, 87, 91, 93.

44. *Ibid.*, 93.

45. *Ibid.*, 96–97; Miles, *Slow Boat*, 132, 134.

46. "Four Coast Ships Loaded with Holiday Liquor," *Oakland Tribune*, December 18, 1932.

47. Miles, *Slow Boat*, 132, 134, 158.

48. "Four Coast Ships Loaded with Holiday Liquor," *Oakland Tribune*, December 18, 1932.

49. Stone, *My Dad*, 121, 122.

50. Miles, *Slow Boat*, 224.

Chapter 18

1. Marion Elizabeth Rodgers, *Mencken: The American Iconoclast* (New York: Oxford University Press, 2005), 222.

2. Walker, *One Eye Closed*, 378.

3. *Ibid.*

4. Rose, "Wettest in the West," 286; "San Francisco," *New York Times*, March 22, 1926; Walker, *One Eye Closed*, 375.

5. Walker, *One Eye Closed*, 381.

6. Walker, *One Eye Closed*, 380.

7. *Ibid.*

8. Merritt Barnes, "'Fountainhead of Corruption': Peter P. McDonough, Boss of San Francisco's Underworld," *California History* 58, no. 2 (1979): 144.

9. Kevin J. Mullen, *Dangerous Strangers: Minority Newcomers and Criminal Violence in the Urban West, 1850–2000* (New York: Palgrave MacMillan, 2005), 99.

10. "Chicago's Hot Shots Fail in S.F. Invasion," *San Francisco Chronicle*, November 17, 1931.

11. Mullen, *Dangerous Strangers*, 99.

12. *Ibid.*, 100.

13. "Chicago's Hot Shots Fail in S.F. Invasion," *San Francisco Chronicle*, November 17, 1931.

14. "Madden's Boat Plant Destroyed by Fire," *Sausalito News* (Sausalito, CA), August 21, 1920; "Work at Madden's Yards," *Sausalito News* (Sausalito, CA), June 17, 1922.

15. "Five Surrendered in Bay City Liquor Case," *Los Angeles Times*, August 13, 1927; "California Yule Liquor Supply Is Lowest in Years, Declares Rutter," *Oakland Tribune*, December 20, 1924.

16. "Monterey Rum Smugglers Are Racing up Coast," *Oakland Tribune*, July 8, 1925.

17. "Shots Rout Bogus 'U.S.' Rum Vessel," *Oakland Tribune*, June 22, 1925.

18. *Ibid.*

19. *Ibid.*

20. *Ibid.*

21. "Rum Runner Describes Fight to Death on Landing," *Oakland Tribune*, November 25, 1925.

22. "Three Bootleg Suspects Jailed after Battle; One Officer Slain, Two Wounded," *Oakland Tribune*, July 7, 1925; "Rum Pirates Shoot Three in California," *Ogden Standard Examiner* (Ogden, UT), July 7, 1925.

23. "Three Bootleg Suspects Jailed after Battle; One Officer Slain, Two Wounded," *Oakland Tribune*, July 7, 1925; Lisa Eisemann, *The First Policewoman: A History of the Salinas Police Department* (Victoria, Canada: Trafford Publishing, 2005), 42; "Mayor Named in Rum Affray," *Los Angeles Times*, July 10, 1925.

24. "Three Bootleg Suspects Jailed after Battle; One Officer Slain, Two Wounded," *Oakland Tribune*, July 7, 1925; Eisemann, *First Policewoman*, 42, 43.

25. "Three Bootleg Suspects Jailed after Battle; One Officer Slain, Two Wounded," *Oakland Tribune*, July 7, 1925.

26. *Ibid.*; "State Troops Aid Manhunt," *Los Angeles Times*, July 8, 1925.

27. "Three Bootleg Suspects Jailed after Battle; One Officer Slain, Two Wounded," *Oakland Tribune*, July 7, 1925; Eisemann, *First Policewoman*, 42, 43.

28. "State Troops Aid Manhunt," *Los Angeles Times*, July 8, 1925; "Monterey Rum Smugglers Are Racing Up Coast," *Oakland Tribune*, July 8, 1925.

29. "Three Bootleg Suspects Jailed after Battle; One Officer Slain, Two Wounded," *Oakland Tribune*, July 7, 1925.

30. "Rum Captive Bares Plot to Kill Drys," *Oakland Tribune*, July 10, 1925; "Rum Runner Describes Fight to Death on Landing," *Oakland Tribune*, November 25, 1925; "Rum Battler Confesses," *San Mateo Times* (San Mateo, CA), November 10, 1925; "Suspected Rum Ring Head Held," *Berkeley Daily Gazette* (Berkeley, CA), October 1, 1925.

31. "Three Surrender for Smuggling," *Nevada State Journal* (Reno, NV), July 11, 1925; "Rum Captive Bares Plot to Kill Drys," *Oakland Tribune*, July 10, 1925; "Suspected Rum Ring Head Held," *Berkeley Daily Gazette* (Berkeley, CA), October 1, 1925; "Rum Battler Confesses," *San Mateo Times* (San Mateo, CA), November 10, 1925.

32. "Moss Landing Rum Battle Quiz Shifts to Bay Cities," *Oakland Tribune*, November 11, 1925.

33. "Rum Battler Confesses," *San Mateo Times* (San Mateo, CA), November 10, 1925.

34. "Fatal Liquor Fight Related," *Los Angeles Times*, November 25, 1925; "Rum Runner Describes Fight to Death on Landing," *Oakland Tribune*, November 25, 1925.

35. Eisemann, *First Policewoman*, 43.

36. *Ibid.*; "Must Stand Trial," *Berkeley Daily Gazette* (Berkeley, CA), December 23, 1925.

37. "Up-to-the-Minute News," *San Mateo Times* (San Mateo, CA), March 6, 1926; "Rummer Is State Witness at Trial," *Nevada State Journal* (Reno, NV), March 7, 1926.

38. "New Testimony in Booze Trial," *Bakersfield Californian* (Bakersfield, CA), March 10, 1926.

39. "State Rests in Moss Landing Booze Trial," *Bakersfield Californian* (Bakersfield, CA), March 17, 1926.

40. "Booze Slaying Case Undecided," *Nevada State Journal* (Reno, NV), March 24, 1926; "Bube Statement Read in Court," *Nevada State Journal* (Reno, NV), March 13, 1926.

41. Eisemann, *First Policewoman*, 44.

42. "Ed Ferris, Notorious as Hi-jacker, Held Following Capture," *San Mateo Times* (San Mateo, CA), September 10, 1926.

43. "Bube Freed by Judge in Rum Murder Trial," *Oakland Tribune*, June 30, 1926; Eisemann, *First Policewoman*, 44.

44. "Simon Bube to Serve Term for Liquor Running," *San Mateo Times* (San Mateo, CA), September 16, 1926; "Eight Defendants Sentenced in Moss Landing Liquor Case," *San Francisco Chronicle*, November 4, 1926.

45. "Booze Jury Indicts Twenty and Mayor," *Oakland Tribune*, December 2, 1925; "Indict Twenty-one for Liquor Battle," *San Bernardino County Sun* (San Bernardino, CA), December 2, 1925; "Madden Rum Smugglers Indicted," *San Francisco Chronicle*, December 2, 1925.

46. "Two Linked in Booze Traffic at S.F. Trial," *Oakland Tribune*, October 19, 1926; "Rum Smuggling Case Is Lively," *Reno Evening Gazette* (Reno, NV), October 20, 1926; "Hearing Turns toward Humor," *San Bernardino County Sun* (San Bernardino, CA), October 20, 1926.

47. "He Matches Wits with Lawyers and Battle Is Draw," *Reno Evening Gazette*, October 21, 1926; "Student Witness Commits Error," *Bakersfield Californian* (Bakersfield, CA), October 22, 1926.

48. "Phone Bills Moss Landing Evidence," *Oakland Tribune*, October 25, 1926.

49. "Moss Landing Battle Echoes in Rum Trial," *Nevada State Journal* (Reno, NV), October 19, 1926; "Confession Barred at Booze Trial," *Oakland Tribune*, October 23, 1926.

50. "Two Linked in Booze Traffic at S.F. Trial," *Oakland Tribune*, October 19, 1926.

51. "Up-to-the-Minute News," *San Mateo Times* (San Mateo, CA), October 28, 1926; "Seven Sentenced in Moss Landing Rum Fight Case," *Oakland Tribune*, November 3, 1926; "Two in Parente Rum Trial Sent to Jail," *Oakland Tribune*, March 3, 1926; "Brokaw, Madden, Four Others Convicted as Rum Plotters," *San Francisco Chronicle*, October 29, 1926.

52. "Mayor Named in Rum Affray," *Los Angeles Times*, July 10, 1925.

53. "First German Steamer Since Before War Reaches S.F.," *San Francisco Chronicle*, November 27, 1922.

54. "Bay Mayor Surrenders in Rum Plot," *Oakland Tribune*, July 8, 1925; "Up-to-the-Minute News," *San Mateo Times* (San Mateo, CA), July 8, 1925.

55. "Sausalito Election Returns Officers," *Santa Cruz Evening News* (Santa Cruz, CA), September 12, 1925; "Recall Candidates Are Defeated by a Narrow Margin,"

Sausalito News (Sausalito, CA), September 12, 1925; "San Rafael Mayor Asked to Resign," *Oakland Tribune*, November 27, 1925; "Mayor Madden Refuses to Quit," *Oakland Tribune*, December 2, 1925.

56. "Arraignment of Mayor on Rum Charge Is Set," *Oakland Tribune*, September 23, 1925.

57. "Santa Cruzan Gets Big Post," *Santa Cruz Evening News* (Santa Cruz, CA), November 11, 1925; "Santa Cruzan Prosecuting Big Rum Case," *Santa Cruz Evening News* (Santa Cruz, CA), February 19, 1926; "Sausalito Mayor Tries to Prove Rum Ship Not His," *Oakland Tribune*, February 11, 1926.

58. "$1,000 Needed as Grease Money to Land Booze Here," *Oakland Tribune*, February 18, 1926.

59. "Government Closes Case against Two," *Modesto News Herald* (Modesto, CA), February 24, 1926; "Mayor Madden Jibes Evidence," *Oakland Tribune*, February 24, 1926.

60. "Lawyer Accused of Intimidation Demands Trial," *Oakland Tribune*, February 19, 1926; "Mayor Facing Tamper Charge," *Nevada State Journal* (Reno, NV), February 19, 1926; "Madden Scores Heavily in Big S.F. Rum Trial," *Sausalito News* (Sausalito, CA), February 20, 1926.

61. "Sausalito Mayor Tries to Prove Rum Ship Not His," *Oakland Tribune*, February 11, 1926.

62. "Mayor Madden Jibes Evidence," *Oakland Tribune*, February 24, 1926; "Sausalito Mayor Gets Prison Term," *Oakland Tribune*, February 28, 1926; "Madden Loses Office," *Santa Cruz Evening News* (Santa Cruz, CA), March 2, 1926.

63. "Jury Verdict Is Surprise in Booze Cases," *Santa Cruz Evening News* (Santa Cruz, CA), March 1, 1926; "Madden and Parente Lose Appeal Case," *Sausalito News* (Sausalito, CA), June 18, 1927; "Sausalito Ex-mayor Asks Probation," *Oakland Tribune*, July 26, 1927; "Must Serve Term," *San Mateo Times* (San Mateo, CA), August 8, 1927.

64. "Former Mayor Will Not Appeal Verdict," *Sausalito News* (Sausalito, CA), July 16, 1927; "Jail Looms as Parente Loses Appeal," *San Mateo Times* (San Mateo, CA), November 21, 1927.

65. "Rum King Fades out of Picture," *Altoona Mirror* (Altoona, PA), December 9, 1927; Walker, *One Eye Closed*, 350.

66. "Arrest Bootleg King, Vancouver," *Bakersfield Californian* (Bakersfield, CA), December 21, 1927.

67. "Parente Hearing Is Continued by Court," *Modesto News Herald* (Modesto, CA), January 24, 1928; "Chase for Parente on in Canada," *Oakland Tribune*, January 26, 1928; "Court Refuses Bail Forfeiture," *Los Angeles Times*, December 18, 1927; "$70,000 Value Is Put on Head of Joe Parente," *Oakland Tribune*, April 11, 1928.

68. "Fugitive Liquor Baron Captured," *Centralia Daily Chronicle* (Centralia, WA), November 15, 1928; "Parente Back from Canada," *Los Angeles Times*, November 18, 1928; "Joe Parente Back in Federal Prison," *Bakersfield Californian* (Bakersfield, CA), December 3, 1928; "Parente Gets Four Years," *Woodland Daily Democrat* (Woodland, CA), February 22, 1929.

69. "J.H. Madden Is Back Home, 'All Square with the World,'" *Sausalito News* (Sausalito, CA), November 16, 1928.

70. "Hoover Pardons Herbert Madden," *San Mateo Times* (San Mateo, CA), July 20, 1932; "Madden Citizenship Restored," *Sausalito News* (Sausalito, CA), July 22, 1932; "San Anselmo's $90,000 Bond Issue Carries," *San Francisco Chronicle*, April 15, 1936.

71. "Rites for Ex-Sausalito Mayor James Madden," *San Francisco Chronicle*, November 11, 1975.

Chapter 19

1. "Ask 'Tax for Prosperity,'" *New York Times*, May 15, 1932; "Beer Parade Broadcast to the Nation," *New York Times*, May 15, 1932.

2. "Repeal Rejected, 681–472," *New York Times*, June 16, 1932; "The Prohibition Plank Which Was Adopted," *New York Times*, June 16, 1932.

3. "The Democrats Adopt Wet Plank," *Sikeston Standard* (Sikeston, MO), July 1, 1932.

4. "Reports out Measure to Repeal Law," *Daily Mail* (Hagerstown, MD), January 9, 1933; "Dry Repeal Resolution Is Passed by Congress," *North Adams Transcript* (North Adams, MA), February 20, 1933.

5. "Beer Bill Ready to Be Signed," *Moberly Monitor Index* (Moberly, MO), March 21, 1933; "Roosevelt Gets First Cases of Capital's 3.2 Beer," *New York Times*, April 7, 1933.

6. "Utah Vote Ends Prohibition Era," *Salt Lake City Tribune* (Salt Lake City, UT), December 6, 1933.

7. "Text of Roosevelt's Repeal Proclamation," *Salt Lake City Tribune* (Salt Lake City, UT), December 6, 1933.

8. "Prohibition's Failure Explained by Silloway," *Sheboygan Press* (Sheboygan, WI), March 14, 1929.

9. Miles, *Slow Boat*, 221.

10. *Ibid.*, 226.

Bibliography

Adams, Phelps Haviland. "Right off the Boat." *North American Review* 230, no. 3 (1930): 285–290.

Andrieux, J.P. *Prohibition and St. Pierre*. Lincoln, Canada: W.F. Rannie, 1983.

Babcock, Judith A. "The Night the Coast Guard Opened Fire." *Yankee* 63, no. 12 (1999). www.ebscohost.com/c/articles/2562298.

Barnes, Merritt. "'Fountainhead of Corruption': Peter P. McDonough, Boss of San Francisco's Underworld." *California History* 58, no. 2 (1979): 142–153.

Bookbinder, Bernie. *Long Island: People and Places, Past and Present*. New York: Henry N. Abrams, 1998.

Buchanan, Patricia. "Miami's Bootleg Boom." *Tequesta* 1, no. 30 (1970): 13–31.

Canney, Donald L. *Rum War: The U.S. Coast Guard and Prohibition*. Washington, D.C.: The U.S. Coast Guard, 1989.

_____. *U.S. Coast Guard and Revenue Cutters, 1790–1935*. Annapolis, MD: U.S. Naval Institute Press, 1995.

Carter, James A., III. "Florida and Rumrunning during National Prohibition." *The Florida Historical Quarterly* 48, no. 1 (1969): 47–56.

Chepesiuk, Ron. *Gangsters of Miami: True Tales of Mobsters, Gamblers, Hit Men, Con Men, and Gang Bangers from the Magic City*. Fort Lee, NJ: Barricade Books, 2010.

Clifford, Harold B. *The Boothbay Region, 1906 to 1960*. Freeport, ME: Bond Wheelwright Company, 1961.

Eisemann, Lisa. *The First Policewoman: A History of the Salinas Police Department*. Victoria, Canada: Trafford Publishing, 2005.

Ensign, Eric S. *Intelligence in the Rum War at Sea, 1920–1933*. Washington, D.C.: Joint Military Intelligence College, 2001.

Frayne, Trent. *The Mad Men of Hockey*. New York: Dodd, Mead and Company, 1974.

George, Paul S. "Bootleggers, Prohibitionists, and Police: The Temperance Movement in Miami, 1896–1920," *Tequesta* 1, no. 39 (1979): 34–41.

Grant, Barry J. *When Rum Was King: The Story of the Prohibition Era in New Brunswick*. Frederickton, Canada: Fiddlehead Poetry Books, 2007.

Greene, Ruth. *Personality Ships of British Columbia*. West Vancouver, Canada: Marine Tapestry Publications, 1969.

Hart, Steven. *American Dictators: Frank Hague, Nucky Johnson, and the Perfection of the Urban Political Machine*. New Brunswick: Rutgers University Press, 2013.

Hunt, C.W. *Booze, Boats and Billions: Smuggling Liquid Gold*. Toronto: McClelland and Stewart, 1988.

_____. *Whiskey and Ice: The Saga of Ben Kerr, Canada's Most Daring Rumrunner*. Toronto: Dundurn Press, Ltd., 1995.

Kaserman, James, and Sarah Kaserman. *Florida Pirates: From the Southern Gulf Coast to the Keys and Beyond*. Charleston, SC: The History Press, 2011.

Lawson, Ellen NicKenzie. *Smugglers, Bootleggers, and Scofflaws: Prohibition and New York City*. Albany, NY: State University of New York Press, 2013.

Ling, Sally J. *Run the Rum In: South Florida during Prohibition*. Charleston, SC: The History Press, 2007.

Lythgoe, Gertrude C. *The Bahama Queen: The Autobiography of Gertrude "Cleo" Lythgoe*. Mystic, CT: Flat Hammock Press, 2007.

Mayer, Martin. *Emory Buckner: A Biography*. New York: Harper and Row, 1968.

Mencken, H.L., and George Jean Nathan. "Clinical Notes." *American Mercury* 1, no. 4 (January-April 1924): 451.

Merritt, Jim. "New York's Rum Row: Bootlegging on Long Island." *New York Archives* 2, no. 3 (2003). www.nysarchivestrust.org/apt/magazine.

Metcalfe, Philip. *Whispering Wires: The Tragic Tale of an American Bootlegger*. Portland, OR: Ink Water Press, 2007.

Miles, Fraser. *Slow Boat on Rum Row*. Madeira Park, Canada: Harbour Publishing, 1992.

Mills, Eric. *Chesapeake Rumrunners of the Roaring Twenties*. Centreville, MD: Tidewater Publishers, 2000.

Mole, Rich. *Rum-runners and Renegades: Whisky Wars of the Pacific Northwest, 1917–2012*. Victoria, Canada: Heritage House Publishing Company, 2013.

Morrison, James. *Alcohol, Boat Chases, and Shootouts!*

Part 1: 1919–1924. Charleston, SC: Royal Exchange Publications, 2008.

Mowry, David P. *Listening to the Rumrunners.* Fort George G. Meade, MD: Center for Cryptologic History, National Security Agency, 1996.

Mullen, Kevin J. *Dangerous Strangers: Minority Newcomers and Criminal Violence in the Urban West, 1850–2000.* New York: Palgrave MacMillan, 2005.

Neering, Rosemary. *Smugglers of the West: Tales of Contraband and Criminals.* Victoria, Canada: Heritage House Publishing, 2011.

Ogle, Maureen. *Key West: History of an Island of Dreams.* Gainesville: University Press of Florida, 2003.

Okrent, Daniel. *Last Call: The Rise and Fall of Prohibition.* New York: Scribner, 2010.

Parker, Marion, and Robert Tyrell. *Rumrunner: The Life and Times of Johnny Schnarr.* Victoria, Canada: Orca Book Publishers, 1992.

Reeves, Ira L. *Ol' Rum River: Revelations of a Prohibition Administrator.* Chicago: Thomas S. Rockwell Co., 1931.

Ricci, Joseph Anthony. "'All Necessary Force': The Coast Guard and the Sinking of the Rum Runner *I'm Alone.*" University of New Orleans Theses and Dissertations, Paper 1342. http://scholarworks.uno.edu.

Robinson, Geoff, and Dorothy Robinson. *Duty-Free: A Prohibition Special.* Summerside, Canada: Alfa-Graphics, 1992.

Rodgers, Marion Elizabeth. *Mencken: The American Iconoclast.* New York: Oxford University Press, 2005.

Rose, Kenneth D. "Wettest in the West: San Francisco and Prohibition in 1924." *California History* 65, no. 4 (1986): 284–295.

Schneider, Stephen. *Iced: The Story of Organized Crime in Canada.* Mississauga, Canada: John Wiley and Sons, 2009.

Seibold, David J., and Charles J. Adams III. *Shipwrecks and Legends 'round Cape May.* Reading, PA: Exeter House Books, 1987.

Skoglund, Nancy Galey. "The *I'm Alone* Case: A Tale from the Days of Prohibition." *University of Rochester Library Bulletin* 23 no. 3 (1968). rbscp.lib.rochester.edu/1004

Stone, Jim. *My Dad, the Rum Runner.* Waterloo, Canada: North Waterloo Academic Press, 2002.

U.S. State Department. *I'm Alone Case.* Arbitration Series Two. Washington, D.C.: Government Printing Office, 1935.

Van de Water, Frederic F. *The Real McCoy.* New York: Doubleday, Doran, and Company, 1931.

Walker, Clifford James. *One Eye Closed, the Other Red: The California Bootlegging Years.* Barstow, CA: Back Door Publishing, 1999.

Waters, Harold. *Smugglers of Spirits: Prohibition and the Coast Guard Patrol.* New York: Hastings House, Publishers, 1971.

Wigley, H. DeWinton. *With the Whiskey Smugglers.* London: Daily News Ltd., 1923.

Williams, Neville. *Contraband Cargo: Seven Centuries of Smuggling.* London: Longmans Green and Co., 1959.

Willoughby, Malcolm F. *Rum War at Sea.* Washington, D.C.: United States Printing Office, 1964.

Wolf, George, and Joseph Dimona. *Frank Costello: Prime Minister of the Underworld.* New York: William Morrow and Co., 1974.

Index

199